HIGH TECH, LOW PAY

A MARXIST ANALYSIS OF THE CHANGING CHARACTER OF THE WORKING CLASS

SAM MARCY

WORLD VIEW FORUM • NEW YORK

High Tech, Low Pay

A Marxist Analysis of the
Changing Character of the Working Class

by Sam Marcy
with introduction
by Fred Goldstein

© Copyright 2009

ISBN 9780895671523

Published by
World View Forum
55 West 17th Street, 5C
New York, NY 10011

www.workers.org

First published 1986 on the 100th anniversary of May Day
Edited by Deirdre Griswold and Gary Wilson

Original cover design by Janet Miller
Produced by Lallan Stein, Naomi Cohen, Kathy Durkin, Sue Davis

Cataloging Data

High Tech, Low Pay: A Marxist analysis of the changing character of the working class/
by Sam Marcy with introduction by Fred Goldstein.—2 ed. rev.

p.   cm.   Includes bibliographic references and index.
ISBN 9780895671523 (pbk.: alk. paper)

1. High technology industries. 2. Working class.
HC 79.H53 M37 2009
331.25   2009932307

CONTENTS

Introduction by Fred Goldstein   v

Foreword   xxxiii

PART 1
The Scientific-Technological Revolution and the Changing Character of the Working Class

CHAPTER 1

The Crisis in the Trade Unions   1
AFL-CIO report on "changing situation of workers"   1
Destructive social impact of revolutions in technology   3
Labor organization in different stages of capitalist production   4
The current scientific-technological revolution   6
Turning point for labor movement   7

CHAPTER 2

The Scientific-Technological Revolution   11
Technology and trade union tactics   11
Plant closings and high-tech obsolescence   12
The end of the AT&T myth   14
Mass layoffs at Caterpillar   16
The GE-RCA merger   17
Saturnization   19
View of UAW militants   19
Another 'Ford revolution'?   20
The GM-Hughes merger and military technology   22
Military reorganization of the economy   26
The crisis in agriculture   29

CHAPTER 3

The Ups and Downs of the Capitalist Economy   35

How cyclical crises affect trade unions   35

Capitalist recessions have lengthened   36

Campaigns for prenotification   38

Pentagon plant closings   39

CHAPTER 4

The Changing Character of the Working Class   41

The new social composition of labor   42

The "feminization" of labor   45

Changing composition of capital   48

Decline in trade union strength   49

Prospects for a classwide movement   52

PART 2
Technology and National Oppression

CHAPTER 5

Black Labor from Chattel Slavery to Wage Slavery   55

The compass and the slave trade   55

The banks and the drug trade   57

The invention of the cotton gin   58

The Haitian Revolution and U.S. slave revolts   61

Slavery vs. capitalist production   63

Black scientists and inventors   64

The Third World brain drain   69

Black labor today   70

The Black freedom struggle   71

The impact of high tech on Black postal workers   74

CHAPTER 6

Latin Workers and Latin American Underdevelopment 81

The Latin struggle in the U.S. 81

U.S. economic hold over Latin America 82

Keeping high tech under lock and key 83

Loans for debt, not for development 85

CHAPTER 7

Native People under the Gun 87

Gunpowder and mass production of firearms 87

Expansion of slave plantations onto Native land 88

Mass migrations from Europe and the Utopians 90

Leninist stand on national oppression 92

PART 3
Strategies for a Working Class Fightback

CHAPTER 8

Defensive Trade Union Strategies 97

Difference between a workers' party and a trade union 97

Limits of trade union approach 99

Problems of the strike weapon 100

CHAPTER 9

Offensive Strategies: Workers' Control 103

New forms of struggle necessary 103

Seizure and occupation of the plants 104

Bankruptcy and workers' control 106

The Wheeling-Pittsburgh bankruptcy 108

Question of legality 110

Struggle engenders new laws 111

CHAPTER 10

A Mixed Bag of Other Tactics   113
The Youngstown case: what went wrong   113
Eminent domain   115
ESOPs   118
What workers can do about existing ESOPs   121
ESOPs and the Great Crash   122
Vigilance committees   124
Hormel strike and the AFL-CIO leadership   126
Inner struggles in the ruling class   130

CHAPTER 11

Conclusion   131
Two bourgeois theories on the scientific-technological revolution   131
Capitalist concentration and the middle class   133

APPENDIX A

137

APPENDIX B

141

BIBLIOGRAPHY

147

INDEX

149

Introduction

Sam Marcy, the author of *High Tech, Low Pay: A Marxist Analysis of the Changing Character of the Working Class,* was a Marxist theoretician and working-class strategist.[1] He wrote this book in 1986, more than halfway through the Reagan administration, when the working class and oppressed people in the United States were under siege from all directions. The book had a very practical goal at the time: to give advanced workers and trade unionists strategic and tactical ammunition with which to resist the developing assaults on the labor movement and the entire working class.

The presentation is characterized by a seamless transition from Marxist theory and sociological analysis to working-class strategy and tactics. Several dominant themes are reiterated throughout the book.

- The growing pauperization of the working class under the impact of the scientific-technological revolution.

- The leveling down of the white, male, labor aristocracy and the growing social weight in the labor movement of African-American, Latina/o, Asian, Native and women workers—that is, of the lower-paid and the oppressed—thus raising the historic potential of a left-wing, more militant movement.

- The need for labor, if it is to overcome the relentless drive for concessions and plant closings, to break out of the narrow, restrictive "capital-labor framework" that subordinates the rights of workers to the sanctity of profits, the capitalist market and private property.

- The urgent necessity for the labor movement to abandon the "guerrilla warfare" strategy of isolated strikes, to transcend its narrow role of only bargaining over wages and conditions, and to open up a class-wide offensive against capital in alliance with the communities suffering under the weight of capitalist restructuring.

- Identifying the laws of capitalist development that drive the introduction of new technology in order to shed labor, reduce skills, intensify exploitation and expand the mass of profit—what Karl Marx meant in the *Communist Manifesto* when he declared that "the bourgeoisie must constantly revolutionize the means of production."

- Expanding the concept of workers' rights to include the workers' claim to their jobs as a property right; the corollary right to occupy and operate workplaces; the right to intervene in bankruptcy proceedings as primary creditors; the use of the right of eminent domain on behalf of communities and workers to take over abandoned factories, and many other tactics.

These themes and prescriptions discussed by Marcy were an attempt to provide the legal, practical and ideological bases to fight back against the attacks of the Reagan period.

The anti-labor offensive had actually begun during the Carter administration and was in full force at the time Marcy was writing this book. In the summer of 1981 a strike of the Professional Air Traffic Controllers Organization had been brutally crushed by Reagan. He summarily fired 18,000 controllers within 48 hours of their having walked out to demand relief from extremely stressful working conditions. Reagan then brought in strikebreakers—who had been secretly mobilized in advance—and barred the air traffic controllers from federal employment for life.

This was a signal to capital that Washington would not only support but was encouraging the use of permanent strikebreakers. The bosses got the message. Union after union, confronted with demands for concessions, was forced out on strike. Once out of the workplace, the workers were then faced with invasions of permanent strikebreakers escorted by police or National Guard troops—with the full support of the courts.

The attacks were leveled at the strongholds of industrial unionism. Autoworkers, steelworkers, rubber workers, copper miners, electrical workers, meatpackers and others came under fierce assault. The National Labor Relations Board closed its eyes to this wholesale violation of the right to collective bargaining. A dangerous shift to the right in labor relations was underway.

It soon became clear that the bosses were aiming to reverse the historic gains of the working class that dated back to the tempestuous class struggles of the Roosevelt New Deal era and the advances made in the period soon after World War II.

But the strength of organized labor was being sapped by more than just union busting and concessions bargaining. The greatest leverage capital enjoyed in its struggle to reverse the historic gains of the working class was the scientific-technological revolution percolating in corporate and university laboratories, often supported by the Pentagon.

The anti-labor campaign was launched simultaneously and in conjunction with a technological assault on jobs and wages. The industrial working class and a growing number of service workers were living under the constant and expanding threat of seeing their jobs destroyed by robots, computers, communications satellites and the like. In fact, millions of high-wage union jobs were being destroyed and replaced by lower-paying service jobs, almost always non-union.

Giant transnational corporations were "downsizing." General Motors was becoming the largest consumer of robots in the world. The steel industry was abandoning large, integrated factories for mini-mills and replacing blast furnaces with basic oxygen and electric arc furnaces. AT&T was spinning off local phone companies to free up capital so it could enter into the realm of space-age satellite communications. General Electric and RCA merged to combine technologies. Auto barons were visiting Toyota City in Japan to study "just-in-time" production methods and rapid advances in die changeovers.

All these developments were accompanied by massive layoffs—at first tens of thousands and eventually millions of workers were "downsized." Marcy showed that between 1979 and 1985 some 11.5 million U.S. workers lost their jobs.

Marcy brought to light the salient facts summarizing this development and illustrated the dire situation with the latest statistics and numerous concrete examples. As such, the book is of great historical interest.

However, since 1986, when the book was first published, technology and the organization of production, commerce and finance have been transformed on a global scale. Production has been broken up into segments and parceled out across the globe by the giant transnational corporations.

Trillions of dollars in financial transactions fly around the world at the speed of light. In place of capitalist recovery, there is capitalist crisis. When Marcy wrote, union membership was somewhat less than 19 percent of the workforce, compared to 12.4 percent today. Tens of millions of workers have lost what once were long-term jobs. Millions of homes have been lost to foreclosure and millions more are destined for the auction block. On the surface, the world is a far cry from what it was some 25 years ago.

Lessons for today

The reader may well ask: Is *High Tech, Low Pay*, written about a bygone period, of contemporary value? Does this book about the past inform the present?

The answer is a resounding yes. Although written a generation ago, the analysis, strategies and tactical approaches developed by Marcy are needed even more urgently today.

The problems of the workers and the unions that Marcy addressed in 1986 have not diminished. On the contrary, they have grown to crisis proportions during the present world economic downturn—the worst since the Great

Depression. Stopping plant closings, layoffs, downsizing and concessions are among the most urgent tasks facing the workers.

Considering the present-day role of the banks, the auto companies, and the entire galaxy of corporations, large and small, that are laying off millions of workers and extracting concessions from those still working, Marcy's theme of opening up a class-wide offensive to defend the working class is more relevant today than ever.

The strategies and tactics he designed to combat the Reagan-era restructuring were not taken up by the labor movement in the U.S. Such bold, aggressive assertions of the rights of workers as against the rights of capital are now even more urgently needed.

Marcy's words sound completely current. Writing in Chapter 1 (The Crisis in the Trade Unions) about the destructive social impact that revolutions in technology have had under capitalism, he warned that the scientific-technological revolution was having as significant an effect on the labor movement as the Industrial Revolution had on the earliest labor organizations.

In Chapter 2 (The Scientific-Technological Revolution) in a section about the merger of General Electric and RCA, he said of the transnational giants: "By virtue of their vast facilities, often in other countries and not unionized, these corporate monsters have gained broad social, political and diplomatic leverage against single unions. These concentrations of capital are class-wide organizations to which the workers in the unions have to develop a class-wide perspective, nationally as well as internationally, in order to be able to get a firm handle on how to fight the companies."

Marcy considered the labor unions potentially the most formidable organizations of the working class in capitalist society. Yet, because of their class-collaborationist leadership, they stood in danger of being absorbed into the capitalist system and turned into a cog in the wheel of big business.

He urged the labor movement and the leaders of the workers in general to think out of the box so that they could fight their way out of the stranglehold that capitalism placed them in, especially during an economic crisis.

In Chapter 3 (The Ups and Downs of the Capitalist Economy), in a section on how capitalist recessions had lengthened, he argued that this imposed on the workers and the trade unions the need to develop a defensive strategy, but one that could be transformed into an offensive if the leaders made the effort to break out of the "accepted bourgeois conception of the capital-labor relationship."

He picked up on the same theme again in Chapter 8 (Defensive Trade Union Strategies). Marcy wrote, "Once the workers are frozen into the capital-labor relationship, once that is dogmatically accepted as the permanent condition of the workers ... it inevitably follows that the workers must make concessions regardless of whether the union is strong or weak. The issue becomes saving the company or industry."

These words are eerily prophetic of what has happened, especially since the current economic crisis began.

The leaders of the once mighty United Auto Workers are collaborating with the auto makers and the capitalist government, through the bankruptcy process, to impose unprecedented, draconian sacrifices on the workers. They argue this is necessary **in order to save the companies and the industry**.

The UAW leaders accept the fundamental proposition that the only basis on which the auto industry can run is for profit and exploiting labor; that the workers and the union must be slaves to the capitalist market. In a word, they have already agreed that there is no alternative to abject surrender.

As of June 2009, two dozen plants are slated to be shut down, 3,000 auto dealerships are to be closed, untold thousands of direct layoffs of autoworkers are to take place and ten times that number or more will be indirectly hurt through the ripple effect. A six-year no-strike pledge and wage freeze has been conceded to both GM and Chrysler. The union has accepted stock ownership (non-voting) in both companies in place of cash for its retirement fund. This places the union in the contradictory position of having to keep the stock price up, which inevitably means intensifying the exploitation of the workers.

The mindset of the UAW leadership is to bring so-called "leaner" auto companies back to profitability—i.e., to remain locked in the traditional capital-labor relationship. Profit and exploitation is the only basis on which this form of production can take place. If the company cannot find profits in the markets, the workers must pay the price.

In this regard, the outlook of the UAW leadership is not fundamentally different from that which has characterized most of the rest of the top labor leadership in the United States over the last three decades of concession bargaining. The only difference is that the UAW leaders have been thrust into the spotlight because of the centrality of the auto industry to U.S. capitalism and the magnitude of the crisis of GM and Chrysler. Industry after industry has been downsized and suffered drastic layoffs in the latest crisis.

A job is a right

Marcy based his analysis on the proposition that workers, as the creators of the wealth upon which the workplaces were constructed, have a right to their jobs. Furthermore, he drew the radical conclusion in Chapter 9 (Offensive Strategies: Workers' Control) that from this flowed the right to take over the workplaces. This was the principal method proposed by Marcy for breaking out of the capital-labor relationship.

Marcy was dealing with a period in which workers were losing strike after strike. He stressed the need "to recognize that the conventional, traditional weapons—including the indispensable strike weapon—have to be refined and supplemented by new methods which include the right to seize, occupy, take over and operate plants, equipment and industry."

As a prime example of breaking out of the capital-labor relationship, he cited the great sit-down strikes of the 1930s, in which the right to occupy the plants was won on the ground. Such a right was crucial to the victory of the CIO and industrial unionism.

While not putting it forward as a blueprint, Marcy stated that workers must "extend their rights to seize and occupy the plants. It is a logical outcome and inevitable phase in the struggle of the labor movement, as imperative a necessity and as vital to the existence of the trade union movement as any of the preceding phases in its history." To seize the plants would not solve the problem, but it would put the workers on more favorable ground in the struggle and "force a new and different type of crisis on the ruling class."

In the present crisis, it is clear that restricting the workers to basic bargaining—where the capitalists retain the advantage of being able to shut down the plants or wait out a strike—is a losing strategy. Only by asserting their right to occupy plants—before they can be dismantled and expensive machinery removed—can the workers protect their interests and put themselves in a much stronger bargaining position.

Furthermore, with the capitalist government having just handed over trillions of dollars to the banks and tens of billions to the auto industry, it is a totally justified and practical demand that these funds be diverted in order to keep workplaces open under the operation of the workers.

Using the strike weapon during a period of depression and mass unemployment is highly risky. Clearly only bold and dramatic measures that put workers' rights ahead of the rights of capital can reverse the steadily declining situation of the workers.

Marcy offered a number of other tactics. He promoted the legal concept of the workers intervening in bankruptcy proceedings and pressing their claim as the primary creditors of the company. He was an early advocate of the concept that a labor-community alliance could use the right of eminent domain to take over plants already closed and get government appropriations to open them up again.

The changing social character of the working class

During the 1980s many economists, representing both business and labor, took note of the effect technology was having in destroying manufacturing jobs and expanding the service sector. They noted that the transformation from manufacturing to services was also creating a shift from high-wage to low-wage jobs.

Marcy examined this trend and drew sociological and political conclusions from it. He saw the increasing social weight of the low-paid as against the higher-paid in the workforce. This included a growing proportion of Black, Latina/o, Asian, Native, undocumented, women and lesbian and gay workers. (These are, of course, overlapping categories. Some of the most militant workers in the recent period have been women of color.) While this could be interpreted as a mere numerical change, it "goes beyond that," he wrote. "It involves a relative reduction in the percentage of skilled workers and a tremendous increase in the number of semi-skilled. Also, on an overall scale, it means the creation of lower-paying jobs as against higher-paying ones. It means the decline of the traditionally more privileged workers and industries with higher wages and the creation of a vast pool of lower-paid workers. This trend is still surfacing and has yet to be given any kind of independent political expression," he wrote. "From a class point of view, it is truly one of the most profound, socially significant trends to emerge. The number of lower-paid workers is bound to increase at the expense of the more privileged workers."

Marcy showed that while the technological revolution was ravaging the living standards of the workers, it also laid the objective basis for their politicization, for moving in a more leftward direction and for organization on a broad scale, but that this would lag behind the changed material conditions.

The continued decline in the standard of living of the workers since the book was written has confirmed the trend highlighted by Marcy. In fact, there is no such thing in the U.S. any more as a secure job. More than 30 million workers lost "safe" jobs between 1984 and 2004.[2] Out of every 100 workers who had been laid off during this period, 73 percent were either making less money or were not working at all.[3] Workers have been pushed out of higher-paying manufacturing jobs en masse into lower-paying service jobs.

The political expression of this new trend has been long delayed—because of historical conditions discussed later in this introduction.

Marcy's work includes brilliant and very important sections on national oppression and technology in which he applies historical materialism in a penetrating way. For example, he shows the connection between the invention of the compass, advances in navigation and ship building, and the development of the trans-Atlantic slave trade. He further shows how the invention of the cotton gin in 1793 at first strengthened slavery but then helped the development of capitalism—which ultimately destroyed chattel slavery and replaced it with wage slavery.

He discusses the manner in which technology has been kept from the Latin American colonies and neo-colonies of the U.S. in order to keep them dependent on imperialism. Weapons technology played the decisive role in the conquest of the Native nations and their expulsion from their lands. Thus the development of technology has shaped relations between oppressor and oppressed as well as between the working class and the bosses.

The falling rate of profit

Finally, Marcy reintroduced into the sphere of radical economic analysis a long-neglected but crucial Marxist concept: the tendency of the rate of profit to fall. This law, inherent in capitalism, was discovered and elaborated by Marx. It explains scientifically how the ceaseless struggle of the bosses against the falling rate of profit inexorably drives the present-day technological revolution, as it has from the very dawn of capitalism.

Marcy gave an excellent and easily understandable explanation of this law in Chapter 4 (The Changing Character of the Working Class), in the section on "Changing composition of capital." Marx called this law "in every respect the most important law of modern political economy."[4]

Marx explained that profit is generated not by machines but by the living labor that operates the machines. Machines—and today software, robots, etc.—are like any other item consumed in the production process, from the plant and equipment used to the raw materials. They have value, but it comes from the past labor incorporated in them when they were created. As they are gradually used up in the process of production, this value is transferred to the new products. The capitalist makes sure that the cost of replacing these items is part of the total price of what is being produced. What the bosses paid out to acquire these items and what they get back to replace them eventually evens out. No profit is generated in this process.

What the capitalists spend for all these items Marx called constant capital, or dead labor. He called wages living labor, or variable capital—variable because how much the bosses must spend on wages depends on how intensely they can exploit the workers.

Profits come from unpaid living labor, or surplus value. The value represented by the wages the workers receive is less than the new value they produce. The more unpaid labor the bosses can extract from the workers and the lower they can push wages, the more profit. Only living labor creates new value.

High Tech, Low Pay

Under capitalism, all technological innovation is aimed at getting more profit, which is derived from surplus value. Each employer seeks wherever possible to replace workers with machines, as GM has been doing with its robotization. A company which brings in new technology costing less in the long run than the labor it will replace gets an immediate competitive advantage over rival capitalists operating with the old technology.

Prices are based on generalized costs. The boss whose plant produces items at a lower unit cost because of a technological advantage can lower prices and outsell the competition—but only until everyone else adopts the same technology. Then prices fall all around. Now everyone is operating with less labor and more expensive technology. The ratio of variable capital (living labor) to constant capital (dead labor) falls. Since profit comes from living labor and not from technology, the rate of profit falls.

In order to make up for the fall in the rate of profit, production must be expanded. It takes greater sales, i.e., expanded markets, to get the same mass of profit because the rate of profit on each unit sold has declined. Once the acquisition of new technology by all has evened the playing field, each capitalist inevitably looks for even newer technology to regain the advantage.

This process goes on inexorably under capitalism. It intensifies the capitalist competitive struggle for market share and inevitably results in overproduction and crisis.

In fact, the revolutionary socialist perspective hinges upon the operation of this law. The application of this crucial law in the present book is one of the more important contributions made by Marcy to the revival of Marxist theory.

This law is what drove GM, the largest industrial corporation in the U.S., to become the largest single user of robots in the world, beginning in the 1980s. It explains the development and use of management software by Oracle, IBM, Boeing and an array of giant monopolies so they could send everything from engineering to back-office jobs around the globe seeking the lowest wages and salaries.

Marcy traced the different stages of capitalist production, beginning with handicraft and simple cooperation through manufacturing, the industrial revolution and the age of mass production introduced by Ford, all the way up to the scientific-technological revolution in electronics, computers, robots, automated production and so on. He illustrated how the present-day revolution in technology is racing ahead at breakneck speed.

The increasing cost of more sophisticated, high-tech means of production and the simultaneous shedding of workers makes the struggle for profitability a greater and greater burden for capital—and profit is the lifeblood of the system.

After discussing the pauperization of the working class under the impact of the scientific-technological revolution, Marcy concluded his Foreword to the book with the prediction that a crisis of capitalism was coming and that it would heighten the class struggle: "The devastating effects of monopoly capitalism's latest assault will, after trials and errors, inevitably give birth to an upsurge in the movement of the working class and oppressed peoples—and one which has incalculable potential for progressive and revolutionary working-class solidarity."

This prognosis, while still completely valid, was delayed by momentous historical developments that necessarily postponed the crisis and the anticipated surge in the class struggle.

As history turned out, Marcy was writing during the early stages of an entirely new configuration of the world capitalist economy. Capitalist imperialism, as a world economic system, was about to take a dramatic turn as a result of two profound developments: the catastrophic demise of the Soviet Union and the East European bloc and the quantum leap forward in the application of the scientific-technological revolution by the capitalist ruling class.

What transpired between *High Tech, Low Pay* and *Low-Wage Capitalism*

In 2008 this author wrote a follow-up to Marcy's work entitled *Low-Wage Capitalism—Colossus with Feet of Clay.*[5] The book traces the drastic global restructuring that has taken place in the quarter of a century since the publication of *High Tech, Low Pay.* This transformation of world capitalism developed prior to the present economic crisis and, in many ways, laid the basis for its global character and its severity. Much of what follows here is based on material presented in that work.

Marcy wrote three years before the counter-revolution in the USSR and Eastern Europe of 1989-1991. These developments drastically changed the relationship of world forces in favor of imperialism. The greatest setback for socialism since the collapse of the Second International at the outset of World War I, it opened up vast new spheres for super-exploitation.

For more than 70 years, beginning with the 1917 Bolshevik Revolution, the territorial domain of imperialism had been contracting. Socialist revolutions swept China, Korea, Vietnam, Laos, Cambodia, Cuba, Angola, Mozambique, Guinea-Bissau, Ethiopia and South Yemen. National liberation movements resisted imperialist domination, from Algeria to Egypt, Palestine, Iraq, Iran, the Philippines, Nicaragua, El Salvador, Namibia, Zimbabwe and many other countries.

This situation was reversed with the collapse of the USSR and Eastern Europe. It offered the first major territorial expansion for world capitalism since the "scramble for Africa" in the 1880s. Western and Japanese corporations poured investments into the new-found spheres of influence.

In addition, the fall of the USSR, the material center of the socialist camp, strengthened the "open door" orientation of China toward allowing imperialist corporations to invest there. It pushed India to further open up its economy to foreign capitalist investment. And it removed any protective force—economic, military or political—that could give the former colonial countries some modicum of balance against the influence of imperialism.

It is estimated that between the years 1984 and 2000, another 3 billion people were deeply absorbed into the world capitalist market and that the global workforce available for exploitation doubled, from 1.46 billion to 2.93 billion.[6] Such a development could not but have profound effects on the working class and the class struggle, not only in the U.S. but around the world.

Technology and imperialist globalization

When Marcy wrote about high tech, it was even before the full development of the Internet and the World Wide Web, before work-flow software allowed the bosses to have real-time oversight around the globe, before a trillion dollars had been invested in fiber-optic cable, before advances in satellite communication, supertankers with powerful and high-speed turbine engines, high-capacity jumbo jet transports, vast computerized ports which became giant distribution hubs, and many other technological innovations.

These technological advances permitted the transnational capitalist monopolies, with huge treasuries and links to the giant banks, to create a new division of labor around the world—what Marx called the social division of labor, as distinct from the division of labor in the workplace.

The new technology opened up to the capitalist class the ability to reorganize and relocate production processes around the globe, using both new and old methods. This process accelerated a worldwide corporate race to find the cheapest labor in the less-developed countries (and in low-wage areas at home) and incorporate them into the networks of the most modern productive processes, as well as to import low-wage labor from abroad.

The process of imperialist super-exploitation was freed from all geographical limits by the scientific-technological revolution. It could now be carried out wherever workers could be rounded up on the globe.

This restructuring was attested to by Ben Bernanke, who in February 2006 replaced Alan Greenspan as chairperson of the Federal Reserve System, making him the principal manager of U.S. finance capital. Bernanke has tried to rescue U.S. capitalism from collapse by handing over trillions of dollars to the banks and other corporate institutions. In more stable times than the present, Bernanke spoke in August 2006 on the subject of global restructuring to a gathering of central bankers at a retreat in Jackson Hole, Wyoming.

Bernanke gave a quick survey of globalization, beginning with the Roman Empire and continuing through Christopher Columbus to the post-Napoleonic era and up until today. After going over what he considered to be similar threads running through the ages, he zeroed in on the new elements.

Among the factors he cited were the "emergence" of China, India and the former socialist-bloc countries, which indicated that "the greater part of the earth's population is now engaged, at least potentially, in the global economy. There are no historical antecedents for this development." While Columbus's voyage led to vast economic changes, they took centuries. By contrast, the imperialists got an opening to China in a few decades.

Furthermore, Bernanke noted, "the traditional distinction between core and periphery is becoming increasingly less relevant, as mature industrial economies and emerging-market economies become more integrated and interdependent. Notably, the nineteenth-century pattern, in which the core exported manufactures to the periphery in exchange for commodities, no longer holds, as an increasing share of world manufacturing capacity is now found in emerging markets."

Bernanke also stressed how "production processes are becoming geographically fragmented to an unprecedented degree. Rather than producing goods in a single process in a single location, firms are increasingly breaking the production process into discrete steps and performing each step in whatever location allows them to minimize costs. For example, the U.S. chip producer AMD locates most of its research and development in California; produces in Texas, Germany and Japan; does final processing and testing in Thailand, Singapore, Malaysia and China; and then sells in markets around the globe."[7]

World-wide wage competition, race to the bottom

The principal feature of the post-Soviet stage of globalization is wage competition among the workers of the world, organized by giant corporations that are orchestrating the depression of wages in a race to the bottom.

For the first time in the history of capitalism, technology has advanced to the point at which transnational corporations are able to pit workers in the rich, developed imperialist countries in a direct job-for-job wage competition with workers in poor, underdeveloped, low-wage countries. They are doing so on an ever-widening scale.

Autoworkers in Detroit are set in competition with autoworkers in Mexico. Customer service workers in Phoenix are set against customer service workers in Mumbai. The wages of legal secretaries in New York City are measured by law firms against those of legal secretaries in the Philippines. Computer programmers and engineers are set against their counterparts in Moscow or Bangalore.

The other side of off-shoring for low wages abroad is the presence of millions of low-wage immigrant workers in the United States. Millions have been forced to flee the poverty and unemployment imposed on their countries by corporate neo-liberalism and settle for meager wages in the U.S. Thus, the corporations have an expanded army of vulnerable workers. The threat of deportation hangs over them as a bludgeon, enabling employers to impose low wages and miserable working conditions. This is an integral part of the era of globalization.

This is not a temporary phase that world capitalism and the working classes are passing through. It is the result of changes that are as profound as the Industrial Revolution and the age of colonization.

In fact, the revolution in technology and the globalization of capitalist production and services are eroding the national determination of wages.

The wage level of the working class in the imperialist countries, under pressure of the global competition set up by the giant monopolies, is being **increasingly determined internationally under the downward pressure** of the wage level in the low-wage countries. From the point of view of the bosses, a worker in Detroit with health care, a pension, vacation and a living wage is overpriced, given the world labor market. Stating it from a Marxist point of view, the boss views wages paid that worker to be above the socially necessary value of labor power. The value of labor power, as far as General Motors, IBM or General Electric is concerned, should be closer to the wages in China, Mexico or the Philippines than to the wages hitherto existing in Detroit, New York or Chicago.

During the quarter of a century since Marcy wrote, there has been further devastating harm inflicted on the working class by the capitalist development of technology. Workers now face an era of permanent layoffs. In addition, real wages have been declining since 1973.

The new technology requires fewer skills, so millions of workers who mastered earlier skills find that those skills no longer qualify them for jobs. When jobs require lower skills, workers are more easily replaceable, require less training and consequently get lower wages. Students graduate college into a job market below their skills level and must accept lower wages. Again, this negative development took effect even before the current economic crisis.

Families that used to survive on a single income can no longer do so. It takes two, three or more wage earners just to keep a family afloat. This is, in effect, a wage cut for the entire working class. The number of poverty-level and low-income (defined as no more than twice the poverty level) wage workers rose dramatically even before the crisis.

In other words, prior to the current economic crisis, the working class in the United States, and especially African-American, Latina/o, Middle Eastern, Asian and Native workers, as well as women, lesbian, gay, bi and trans workers, were already suffering from the new regime of low-wage capitalism.

Most of the labor leaders, as Marcy warned, have been absorbed more and more deeply into the capitalist system. They have become enmeshed in the process of transferring the capitalist crisis onto the workers.

With 30 years of concession bargaining, they have taken on the role of saving the "competitive" position of the bosses. Some have called for a "partnership" between labor, business and the government. But government is the representative of big business. There can be no partnership between the exploited and the exploiters. Their interests are irreconcilable.

Now that a full-fledged capitalist crisis has arrived, the labor leaders have led an even further and more ignominious retreat. They have been paralyzed in the face of the crisis and have not summoned the workers to struggle.

The labor leaders repeat the line of the propagandists of capital in calling the present situation an economic crisis—a classless characterization—when, in fact, it is a **capitalist** economic crisis. It is a crisis of the system of exploitation in which the bosses are trying to pass their crisis of profitability onto the backs of the workers.

The first step in dealing with the crisis is to clearly define it and give the workers a class understanding of what is taking place. This is the only basis on which one can rally resistance to capital. The rank-and-file must take control of the unions and form alliances with communities, as Marcy advocated, based upon a class understanding of their position as an exploited class.

This is not a crisis brought about by greed alone. It is not a crisis brought about by speculation alone. It has not been caused by deregulation alone. There have been greed and reckless gambling by millionaires and billionaires. There has been complicity by all the regulatory agencies in allowing the bankers and financiers of all types to evade every restraint on their machinations and schemes, including subprime mortgages, mortgage-backed securities, derivatives, and other deceptive and secretive measures meant to defraud the people and each other.

But the causes of this crisis are far more fundamental.

The workers and the business cycle

One of Marcy's concerns was to show how the capitalist business cycle put limits upon what the workers could get and what they would have to give up, so long as they accepted the traditional capital-labor relationship. This problem becomes extremely aggravated during the downturn part of the cycle or the "bust" part of the boom-and-bust, which he took up in Chapter 3.

When Marcy wrote this book, the working class had recently lived through the sharp recession of 1980-1982. Official unemployment reached a post-World War II high of 11 percent. The bosses used the recession to demand concessions and carry out restructuring. The unions were thrust onto the defensive.

During a downturn, the bosses shrink production and there is high unemployment. Marcy showed that, at such times, if the labor leadership simply confines itself to bargaining for wages and conditions, concessions must necessarily follow. He wanted to signal to the more advanced workers in the labor movement that, the next time the cycle turned down again, new strategies would be required to combat the bosses' offensive.

Marcy's concern has an urgent relevance in the midst of the current global capitalist crisis, when workers are on the defensive because of the severe rise in unemployment. But it is also timely in a deeper sense because, since he wrote, the capitalist business cycle has changed in general, making the situation even worse as far as the workers are concerned. The "boom" has weakened and the "bust" has dragged on and deepened.

Traditionally, during a capitalist boom the workers can regain some of the positions they lost during the previous bust phase. The bosses, in the race to take advantage of new profit opportunities presented by the capitalist revival, are in great need of expanding their workforce. The reserve army of unemployed contracts sharply. This reduces the competition among the workers, puts them in a stronger bargaining position, and leads to higher wages. At the same time it also leads to much higher profits for the bosses.

The era of 'jobless recoveries'

As the scientific-technological revolution was progressing "at breakneck speed," as Marcy put it, there occurred a change in the historic pattern of the business cycle. After the recession of 1990-1991, U.S. capitalism entered the era of "jobless recoveries." For the first time, employment either continued to decline or remained flat long after the economy began to recover. Jobs were either being lost or remained flat for 18 months after the start of the economic upturn. Prior to that time, there had been a typical lag of one quarter, or three months, between the start of economic expansion and job recovery.

The divergence between economic growth and joblessness caused concern among bourgeois economists for a while. However, after the 1990-1991 recession came the collapse of the USSR and Eastern Europe. There followed a surge in investment abroad, a technology boom at home, and the longest period of economic expansion in U.S. history.

The economists promptly forgot about the jobless recovery of 1991-92. They declared the arrival of the "new economy" and the "end of history," speculating about the end of the business cycle.

The hopes were that, after 75 years of being constrained by socialist revolution and national liberation struggles, the collapse of the material center of the socialist camp would somehow allow infinite expansion and enable the capitalists to overcome the inner contradictions of their system. But as Marx wrote: "The **real barrier** of capitalist production is **capital itself**."[8]

The hopes of the bourgeoisie came crashing down in 2000 with the collapse of the technology bubble and the loss of jobs along with $5 trillion in paper wealth. The vast expansion of capital to every corner of the globe could not eradicate the contradictions inherent in the profit system. It took a speculative boom in technology, with hundreds of companies being created every week, to pump up the economy even with the overseas expansion. The capitalist downturn followed the boom, just as it had since 1825 when the first global downturn took place.

More important than the downturn itself was the nature of the second "jobless recovery" that followed. It turned out that the jobless recovery of 1991-1992 had not been an anomaly but an ominous harbinger of things to come.

During the first 27 months of the next recovery, from November 2001 to March 2004, there was **a net loss of 594,000 jobs**. It took more than five years for the job level to reach the point at which it had been before the downturn began. According to Stephen Roach, the chief economist of Morgan Stanley at the time, job growth by 2004 was 8 million less than growth in a "normal" recovery.[9]

It is no accident that Marcy focused on the business cycle and its consequences for the workers. The question of the business cycle has been of great concern to the working class since Marx first subjected it to scientific analysis.

The boom-and-bust cycle is an essential expression of the fundamental contradiction of the capitalist system. Historically, it has brought both opportunity for struggle as well as shock and disaster to the workers. Understanding it is key to preparing for the class struggle. Studying changes in the boom-and-bust cycle can reveal important underlying features of the evolution of capitalism that the workers need to be aware of.

Marx and Engels on the business cycle

As far back as 1847, in *Wage Labor and Capital,* Marx discussed the question of the workers and the business cycle. Referring to the upside or boom part of the cycle, the period of rapid growth in profits and capitalist accumulation, Marx wrote:

"Even the **most favorable situation** for the working class, the **most rapid possible growth of capital**, however much it may improve the material existence of the worker, does not remove the antagonism between his interests and the interests of the bourgeoisie, the interests of the capitalists. **Profit and wages** remain as before in **inverse proportion**.

"If capital is growing rapidly, wages may rise; the profit of capital rises incomparably more rapidly. The material position of the worker has improved, but at the cost of his social position. The social gulf that divides him from the capitalist has widened.

"Finally:

"To say that the most favorable condition for wage labor is the most rapid possible growth of productive capital is only to say that the more rapidly the working class increases and enlarges the power that is hostile to it, the more favorable will be the conditions under which it is allowed to labor anew at increasing bourgeois wealth, at enlarging the power of capital, content with **forging for itself the golden chains by which the bourgeoisie drags it in its train**."[10] [Emphasis added—Goldstein.]

Engels gave the classic description of the capitalist boom-and-bust cycle in his work *Socialism, Utopian and Scientific,* published in 1880.

"As a matter of fact, since 1825, when the first general crisis broke out, the whole industrial and commercial world ... [is] thrown out of joint once every ten years. Commerce is at a standstill, the markets are glutted, products accumulate, as multitudinous as they are unsalable, hard cash disappears, credit vanishes, factories are closed, the mass of the workers are in want of the means of subsistence, because they have produced too much of the means of subsistence; bankruptcy follows upon bankruptcy.... The stagnation lasts for years; productive forces and products are wasted and destroyed wholesale, until the accumulated mass of commodities finally filters off ... until production and exchange gradually begin to move again. Little by little the pace quickens. It becomes a trot. The industrial trot breaks into a canter, the canter in turn grows into the headlong gallop of a perfect steeplechase of industry, commercial credit, and speculation which finally, after breakneck leaps, ends up where it began—in the ditch of crisis. And over and over again."[11]

Thus it was Marx who gave a description of the situation of the workers as regards the capitalist business cycle of the time. The period of "rapid accumulation," that is, the period of the vigorous boom of business following a downturn, has been the most favorable historically for the working class. And it was Engels who described how capitalism goes from crisis to boom to crisis, continuing in that cycle "over and over."

Even before the 1990s the capitalist business cycle, described a century earlier by Engels, had changed in favor of capital. Marcy, in Chapter 3, focuses on the fact that capitalist recession lengthened in the post-World War II period and that "this is very important in relation to strike strategy, which had a lot to do with the duration of the capitalist economic crisis." It raises the question of what workers can do if a recession turns out to be protracted and the bosses can hold out for a long time.

Workers, 'boom-and-bust' and low-wage capitalism

The new era of low-wage capitalism, worldwide wage competition and slowing capitalist economic growth has put workers under pressure even during times of capitalist upturn. The booms have weakened and have benefited only the bosses, with not even relative gain for the workers.

The era of rapid accumulation, that is, rapid and tempestuous growth of capital investment, has been undercut by the growing productivity of labor and the speed with which markets become saturated. The relative labor shortage during the upturn is a thing of the past. Instead, there are jobless recoveries and the consequent eradication of the opportunity for the workers to make up lost wages by forcing increases on the bosses.

The "golden chains" Marx referred to are not so golden anymore. Marx spoke of workers getting higher wages during a boom while the capitalist got even higher profits. This meant that workers' real wages went up, although their wages declined relative to the larger profit gains of the bosses. In the present era, these conditions no longer obtain.

For the last several decades, with a slight exception in the mid 1990s, workers' real wages have gone down or stagnated even during the periods of expanded capitalist accumulation—during upturns. Because of off-shoring, outsourcing and wage competition with workers in low-wage areas, workers in the United States went into massive personal debt and worked extra jobs; whole families worked just to compensate for the wage decline. Not only did the relative wages of the workers decline, but their **absolute** standard of living plummeted—and this was **before the crisis**.

This makes Marcy's work, his admonitions to the labor movement to develop new strategies to deal with protracted crisis, to engage in class-wide struggle, to break out of the traditional capital-labor relationship, more pressing than ever before.

Engels spoke of the continuous cycle of boom and bust. Certainly the cycle continues, but under conditions of structural changes to capitalism. Booms have become weaker and weaker over time. The classic booms that reemploy most of the workers laid off during the bust are a thing of the past. That is the meaning of the increasingly protracted jobless recoveries.

Solving a crisis by creating a bigger one

In fact, the immediate roots of the latest global capitalist crisis, which began in December 2007, can be traced back to the attempt by the financial authorities to overcome the jobless recovery of 2001-2004, referred to earlier, and the weakness of the capitalist upturn.

The Federal Reserve System pumped hundreds of billions of dollars into the economy by lowering interest rates from 5.5 percent to 1 percent. Alan

Greenspan directed much of this credit toward creating an artificial housing boom. He publicly urged home buyers to take out adjustable-rate mortgages. The housing market regulators gave a pass to the most egregious, often racist, subprime mortgage-lending practices. The Securities and Exchange Commission synchronized its efforts with the Fed by deliberately closing its eyes to the burgeoning market in mortgage-backed securities, derivatives and other shady practices. The rating agencies Moody's and Standard & Poor's played their part by giving potentially toxic assets triple-A ratings.

Much of the credit made available went straight to stock market speculation and banking operations. Huge sums of fictitious capital, paper wealth with no underlying value, found their way through an unregulated conduit known as the shadow banking system—hedge funds, private equity funds and insurance companies—backed by the big Wall Street banks. This shadow system was used to evade even the minimal constraints on finance capital.

In the end, a crisis emerged in the overproduction of housing. The bubble burst, housing prices plummeted and masses of people lost their homes. Throughout the economy, production had outstripped consumption. Auto sales and construction collapsed. Record credit-card debt could not bridge the gap. Debts based on housing sales, credit cards, student loans and auto loans became bad debts. Banks were insolvent.

As Engels had predicted, hard cash disappeared, credit vanished, goods piled up, means of production were destroyed. And in the end the attempt to stem the original crisis by artificially creating a housing boom led to an even greater crisis that enveloped the globe at the speed of light.

Analyzing the present crisis

The meaning of the crisis and its ultimate direction are questions for the ruling class and for the working class, from diametrically opposed points of view. The bourgeoisie has no theoretical framework within which to begin to approach the question. Their system is anarchic. Even government intervention and some limited planning cannot eradicate the anarchy imposed on a system based on private profit.

The bosses operate in competition and in secrecy. Their economists can really only look backward over time at what has happened and hope to divine some pattern that can be used for the future. But they cannot, dare not, analyze the system; they can only describe its behavior in a pragmatic, strictly empirical fashion.

Marxists have a broad theoretical framework combined with powerful, scientific analytical tools at their disposal. These tools must be wielded on behalf of the struggle of the workers and therefore cannot be based upon wishful thinking or pure speculation.

The broad theoretical framework within which to analyze the present situation was laid out by Marx in 1857, in his Preface to *A Contribution to the Critique of Political Economy*:

"In the social production of their life, men enter into definite relations that are indispensable and independent of their will, relations of production which correspond to a definite stage of development of their material productive forces. The sum total of these relations of production constitutes the economic structure of society, the real foundation, on which rises a legal and political superstructure and to which correspond definite forms of social consciousness. ... At a certain stage of their development, the material productive forces of society come in conflict with existing relations of production, or—what is but a legal expression for the same thing—with the property relations within which they have been at work hitherto. From forms of development of the productive forces these relations turn into their fetters. Then begins an epoch of social revolution. With the change in the economic foundation the entire immense superstructure is more or less rapidly transformed."[12]

This is Marx's most general statement about the basis for the revolutionary transformation of society. In numerous places throughout his writings he applies this theory to the capitalist system. He describes how capitalism concentrates the proletariat into factories and workplaces, creating an increasingly complex division of labor in the productive process that involves more and varied types of labor from geographically diverse regions.

Marx showed how capitalism, by constantly revolutionizing the means of production under the internal compulsion of the system, socializes the productive forces—bringing workers everywhere into objective cooperation in the production of commodities. He scientifically demonstrated how this socialized production comes into conflict with private property, resulting in repetitive crises for the workers and, ultimately, for society in general.

The fundamental assertion implied by the paragraph quoted above is that sooner or later, capitalist property relations become a "fetter," a brake on further development of the productive forces. Society cannot move forward any longer because of the stranglehold of private property. Revolution then ensues. The clash between socialized production and private ownership can only be resolved by socializing the ownership—that is, by bringing socialized ownership into harmony with socialized production and setting society on a new course of planned production for human need.

Marx was referring not just to the periodic crises and suffering brought about by capitalism. Nor does his point refer to capitalism holding back development that would be of great benefit to society—such as environmentally safe methods of production and green products. Nor is it a question of the enormous waste and gross inefficiency produced by capitalism. These are relative brakes on development.

Marx posits that at some point, capitalism inevitably becomes an absolute brake on the development of the productive forces, with a consequent crisis for the masses. Society is stymied by capitalist private property and cannot go on in the old way.

It is always helpful for clarity and educational purposes to discuss this fundamental premise put forward by Marx. It is the starting point of understanding Marxism. But it is only at rare historical moments that the discussion goes beyond making a general historical point and is raised in relation to imminent developments.

This question arose at the end of World War I when the economies of Europe had collapsed in the face of military devastation. There was revolutionary ferment in Germany, Hungary and other countries in the wake of the Bolshevik Revolution. Capitalism seemed to be on the ropes.

World War I had signified the beginning of the historic crisis of the capitalist system. The development of imperialism soon resulted in the complete division of the globe among the imperialist powers, as described by Lenin in 1916 in his book *Imperialism, the Highest Stage of Capitalism*. It meant that capitalism had outgrown the national state as a framework for development. Soon it came to pass that even imperialist expansion could not give capitalism sufficient room to grow by ordinary economic means. It had reached such an impasse that it could only resolve its contradictions through a devastating imperialist war.

The ruling classes in Europe survived these post-war revolutionary crises, only to soon be plunged into the Great Depression. It was during the world depression of the 1930s that the question of the absolute decline of capitalism was widely discussed in concrete terms pertaining to the immediate perspective of proletarian revolution.

For the entire decade, save for a brief period in the mid 1930s, capitalist society appeared to be in a downward spiral with no end in sight. Capitalism had reached a dead end. It seemed to fulfill Marx's general prognosis that social revolution was on the agenda.

Capitalist property, private property in the means of production, the profit system itself, had become a "fetter" on the further development of the productive forces. Capitalism had brought about the socialization of the productive process on a world scale. Yet a small group of property owners, monopolists, owned and operated this global system for the narrow purposes of enriching themselves through exploitation and profit.

The Great Depression seemed to be the end of the line. Capitalism was unable to revive itself by economic means. In the mid thirties there was a slight upturn, but then world production continued to decline. Massive unemployment remained. The colonial countries staggered under the weight of the world depression, which struck them even more drastically than the imperialist countries.

In the present period it is once again helpful from a working-class point of view to revive this discussion in order to get an accurate estimate of the period, clarify a perspective and prepare for struggle.

From the Civil War to the Great Depression

Many comparisons are made between the present crisis and the Great Depression. But while the depression of the 1930s is fully known, the present crisis is in its early stages and has yet to be played out. Many specifics cannot be known at this point. It is best from a Marxist point of view, i.e., from a materialist standpoint, to focus on what can be studied right now.

What can be compared are the historic periods leading up to the depression of the 1930s and later to the present crisis, which began with the collapse of the housing bubble in 2007. These periods can be effectively compared.

In the first crisis, the economic forces that drove U.S. capitalism forward in the 70 years from the U.S. Civil War to the world depression of the 1930s had exhausted themselves. They were no longer able to stimulate any significant capitalist revival during the entire decade from 1929 to 1939. No economic means could bring back capitalist prosperity.

What were those forces? The Indigenous nations had finally been driven from all their lands. The so-called "frontier" had been occupied, including the half of Mexico that was annexed to become the Southwest of the United States. After the Civil War the African-American population of the South had again been subjugated, this time into a state of semi-slavery through the sharecropping system. The railroad boom had run its course. Imperialist expansion in the so-called Spanish-American War of 1898 had brought Cuba, Puerto Rico and the Philippines into the U.S. empire, along with Samoa and Hawaii. U.S. businesses had pushed deeper into China and Latin America.

Profits rolled in from World War I and helped sustain the system for a period. There was rapid expansion of the auto industry, the electrification of the country and mass production of appliances. But by the late 1920s the expansion had led to overproduction. Massive credit and land speculation led to a crash in real estate and the stock market crash in 1929.

These were the forces that drove capitalism for 70 years after the Civil War. Once they were exhausted, the system went into a state of absolute decline and could only be revived by war preparations and, finally, World War II itself.

High Tech, Low Pay

It took 15 million U.S. soldiers under arms and an emergency regime of total war production to alleviate mass unemployment in the U.S. It took the deaths of 50 million people or more and the destruction of factories, mines, ports, railroads, bridges and residential buildings throughout Europe and Asia to overcome the pre-war economic crisis and put capitalism back on its feet.

From World War II to 2007

A review of the situation leading up to the present crisis bears an ominous resemblance to that which preceded the Great Depression. Namely, the forces that have propelled U.S. capitalism and the development of the means of production to higher and higher levels throughout the last 70 years, since the beginning of World War II, have exhausted themselves. Artificial means employed to keep the system going are no longer sufficient to revive it in any significant way. This has led to a period of profound stagnation and perhaps to absolute decline.

In the period since World War II, U.S. capitalism has relied on various artificial methods to keep the system from collapsing. War and war preparation were a basic stimulant for decades during the post-war period. The Korean War, the Vietnam War, the military buildup during the Cold War—all served to generate capitalist production and profits, as the system could not rely on the civilian economy to automatically keep it going. But by the end of the 1980s, even the $2 trillion Reagan military buildup in a "full-court press" to undermine the Soviet Union and the socialist camp was insufficient to sustain capitalist prosperity. The monstrous growth of the military-industrial complex has it limits as an economic stimulant.

Marcy dealt with the role of the military in bolstering the capitalist economy in Chapter 2. He showed how it fostered the scientific-technological revolution and shaped crucial sectors of the corporate economic structure to aid its design for world empire. At the same time, he showed how dependent even the largest corporations had become on the military.

The continuous development of the scientific-technological revolution, the restructuring of capitalist industry, the relentless anti-labor campaign of union-busting, the extraction of concessions, the destruction of benefits, the driving down of manufacturing wages and the steady expansion of the low-wage service economy—all enormously increased inequality in the national income in favor of capital and at the expense of the workers. All this served to bolster the profitability of the bosses and bankers. It gave the bosses a great infusion of surplus value, stolen from the workers, to ease the crisis of capital.

The collapse of the USSR and Eastern Europe in the 1990s and the opening up of China to capitalist investment gave imperialism a brief period of unprecedented global expansion. The monopolies seized this opportunity to create global networks of exploitation and vast super-profits as they engineered a worldwide wage competition among the international working class and promoted the vicious race to the bottom previously referred to. Driving down the value of labor is the time-tested method of capital for combating the declining rate of profit brought about by the growing cost allocated to constant capital (plant, equipment and raw materials) and the reduction in variable capital (wages).

Globalized production has now brought a worldwide epidemic of layoffs and mass unemployment.

Militarism, technological development and anti-labor attacks were not enough to save the banks and corporations. Huge injections of credit were required. The ruling class resorted to speculation, credit bubbles, mortgage schemes, exotic financial instruments and all manner of fraud to make profits based on trading in fictitious capital. To overcome the limitations on the profitability of industry, unlimited paper profits were conjured up.

Means of capitalist revival exhausted

In the present crisis, none of these measures is available to restart the system in any significant way.

The two wars now underway in Iraq and Afghanistan are draining the coffers of U.S. imperialism. Overall militarization has largely been accomplished. New rounds of military development are technology intensive, such as laser-guided bombs, satellite-guided missiles, Predator drones, high-tech missile ships and fighter planes. Current imperialist wars are limited and heavily dependent on air power. The hundreds of billions of dollars spent annually on militarism are essential to the system, but, at best, military spending can only help to slow down the economic crisis. It cannot restart the capitalist economy and generate prosperity.

The long period of creating a regime of low-wage capitalism, with a working class in debt and living closer and closer to the poverty level, has intensified. As this trend deepens it only aggravates the crisis of overproduction by further reducing the buying power of the masses. Driving down wages any more will only intensify the contradictions of the system.

Further use of credit on a major scale is a vanishing option. Credit has been stretched to its limit as a mechanism for reviving capitalist accumulation. The government's handout of trillions of dollars in financial bailouts to the banks and other financial institutions has stretched the credit option even beyond the limit.

Capitalism has reached a point where, even if the trillions of dollars that the ruling class is spending in an attempt to mitigate the crisis were to result in a revival, it would be weak and short-lived, leaving many millions unemployed as jobs continue to be lost even as capital accumulation expands. Capitalism is entering a period of permanent and deepening crisis for the masses.

In the present crisis the historic methods of reviving the profitability of capitalism, of restoring capitalist accumulation and prosperity, appear to have run their course, as they did leading up to the Great Depression. This is what has the ruling class running scared.

Marx's proposition about the inevitability of social revolution, already quoted, bears repeating here. It was phrased in the most general way:

"At a certain stage of their development, the material productive forces of society come in conflict with existing relations of production or—what is but a legal expression for the same thing—with the property relations within which they have been at work hitherto. From forms of development of the productive forces these relations turn into their fetters. Then begins an epoch of social revolution."

This is a summary of the broad contours of history. The specifics can only be filled in by analyzing the concrete development of the productive forces of capitalism at each stage.

Sam Marcy in his Foreword to this book gave an economic characterization of the period that pointed clearly in the direction of the present profound crisis of capitalism.

"The justification for each new social system as against its predecessor is that it raises society to a higher level. It has done so in each succeeding social order by raising the productivity of labor. The great achievement of capitalism was that it not only promoted a tempestuous development of the productive forces, of science and invention on an unheard of scale, but it raised the productivity of labor. Over a period of centuries it laid the basis for raising the material standards of society and the wage levels of the working class as a whole.

"The distinctive feature of this particular phase of capitalist development, the scientific-technological phase, is that while it enormously raises the productivity of labor, it for the first time simultaneously lowers the general wage patterns and demolishes the more high-skilled, high-paid workers. It enhances the general pauperization of the population."

But Marcy looked beyond the crisis to the future of the struggle. He discussed the changing character of the working class from a revolutionary, optimistic point of view that was firmly rooted in a materialist analysis.

He spoke at that time of the fundamental trend arising out of the objective changes in the capitalist economy: the vast expansion of lower-paid workers and the decline of the higher-paid, which he regarded as one of the most significant and profound developments to emerge in the history of capitalism.

Its significance is ultimately political. It means that the lower-paid workers, the downtrodden and oppressed who can ill afford to be held down by a conservative labor leadership, will ultimately become the predominant voice in the labor movement and provide it with the militant and ultimately revolutionary energy to challenge capital. He showed that this transformation of the working class must ultimately have a political expression.

The consciousness of the workers is forced to catch up to their condition. A delay in this process is inevitable, but overcoming this lag is equally inevitable. Being ultimately determines consciousness.

Historical circumstances have delayed this radical development among the workers. But Marcy's projection of the pauperization of the working class has developed more fully since he wrote.

The days when the conservative labor leadership can hold the working class in check are numbered. Its base is shrinking with each round of concessions it makes to the bosses, with each sweetheart contract it signs. As Marcy noted, at the beginning of each crisis the workers are thrown back onto the defensive. But sooner or later they will cry "Enough is enough!" Then the tide will turn.

There is no bourgeois economist who can see ahead past one quarter. Yet Marcy's analysis of 25 years ago, proceeding from Marxist theory, put a sharp focus on trends deep within the organism of capitalism and outlined the forces that have shaped the present.

The inevitable imbalance between production and consumption has finally led to a protracted and profound crisis of overproduction. This is certainly the worst crisis in the post-World War II era. As of June 2009, it has lasted the longest—19 months. The measures taken by the world capitalist class to overcome it are by far the greatest. It follows two previous jobless recoveries, the second far more pronounced than the first, which were only overcome by extraordinary, non-reproducible measures (expansion in the wake of the collapse of the USSR, massive bubble-creating measures in the dot.com and housing markets).

Even the most optimistic bourgeois economists concede that a recovery of capitalist production would still leave massive unemployment, as the system will be unable to reabsorb a large proportion of the workers laid off in the present crisis.

Furthermore, in the era of imperialism and the scientific-technological revolution, each round of new technological innovation by the ruling class makes it more and more difficult to start the capitalist system up again after a bust. The two most important reasons are that technology reduces the skills and buying power of the workers, while at the same time increasing productivity, thus insuring that production saturates the markets at a faster and faster rate.

The question that remains for the working class is whether or not quantity has turned into quality in the matter of the capitalist recovery—that is, whether or not the scientific-technological revolution and its effects, so profoundly analyzed by Marcy, have brought capitalism to the point where society will not be able to go forward. Has the profit system reached an impasse?

Because of the previous period of expansive globalization of capital, this crisis is the most far-reaching in terms of the numbers of workers affected. The world socialization of the production process has been brought to an extraordinarily high level. Private property is becoming a more and more intolerable brake internationally.

The ruling class is trying to shift this crisis entirely onto the backs of the workers and the oppressed, just as it did during the Great Depression.

Many are promoting the notion that crisis automatically leads to uprisings and the collapse of capitalism. This is sterile, abstract thinking, far removed from the reality of the working class. It fails to take into account the disintegrating forces exerted upon the workers by a capitalist crisis of unemployment. The workers become atomized and lose the sense of strength derived from being together on the job. Their sense of confidence and of their potential power is undermined by a crisis.

It takes great efforts by working-class leaders to find strategies and tactics to counteract the effects of the downturn, develop methods of resistance to every attack, and take advantage of every upturn in the economic situation to push the struggle forward onto the offensive.

This was the principal purpose of *High Tech, Low Pay* and of much of Marcy's life work, for that matter.

Marxism has no crystal ball. It does not dole out prescriptive formulas for how a major, global capitalist crisis of profound dimensions will play itself out.

Capitalism experienced a global economic collapse during the Great Depression. A decade of mass unemployment ensued that could not be overcome except by rearmament in the U.S. and Europe and ultimately war. Thus the manifestation of the absolute, general crisis of capitalism has been economic collapse. This variant must be taken seriously. But the possibility of a protracted period of weak and short-lived recoveries alongside growing and irreversible mass unemployment must also be considered. There could be a temporary delay in a sharp crisis as a result of massive financial manipulation and capitalist state intervention. However, that it could end either in collapse or war or both must also be considered.

The precise, immediate future cannot be known. What is known is that genuine working-class leaders must prepare for struggle and adapt to any eventuality to assist the workers in dealing with the crisis, whatever form it takes. Above all, the working class must rise to assume its historic destiny as the subject of history and lead the way out of the state of permanent crisis, into which capitalism has led humanity, towards a socialist future.

—*Fred Goldstein, June 2009*

Notes

1. The late Sam Marcy (1911-1998) was a Marxist theoretician, a working-class strategist and a life-long communist organizer. His articles, pamphlets and books range over a wide variety of subjects, from analysis of the Soviet Union and the Chinese Revolution to the nature of imperialism, anti-war strategy, the Pentagon, militarism and the capitalist economy. He has also written on the struggle against racism and the right of oppressed peoples to self-determination, the politics and inner struggles of the capitalist ruling class, aspects of the class struggle of the workers, both at home and around the world, and much more. Many of his books and writings can be found at www.workers.org.

2. Nayan Chandra, Yale Center for the Study of Globalization, interview with Louis Uchitelle, www.YaleGlobal.com, May 11, 2006.

3. Michel, Lawrence, Jared Bernstein and Sylvia Allegretto, *State of Working America 2006/2007,* Cornell University Press (Ithaca, New York, 2007), p. 169, cited in Goldstein, below.

4. Marx, Karl, *Grundrisse,* Penguin Books (London, 1973).

5. Goldstein, Fred, *Low-Wage Capitalism—Colossus with Feet of Clay: What the new globalized, high-tech imperialism means for the class struggle in the U.S.*, World View Forum (New York, 2008).

6. Richard B. Freeman, "Doubling the Global Workforce: Presentation to Center for Global Development," Nov. 8, 2004, www.iie.com/publications/papers/freeman1104.pdf.

7. Ben S. Bernanke, "Global Economic Integration: What's New and What's Not?" Remarks at the Federal Reserve Bank of Kansas City's Thirtieth Annual Economic Symposium, Jackson Hole, Wyoming, Aug. 25, 2006.

8. Marx, Karl, *Capital,* Vol. III, International Publishers (New York, 1967), p. 250.

9. Goldstein, *op. cit.,* p. 69.

10. Marx, Karl, *Wage Labor and Capital,* Progress Publishers (Moscow, 1976), p. 37. Also, for the writings of Marx, Engels and Lenin online, see www.marxists.org.

11. Engels, Frederick, *Socialism, Utopian and Scientific,* in *Marx/Engels Selected Works,* Progress Publishers (Moscow, 1970), vol. 3, p. 143.

12. Marx, Karl, *A Contribution to the Critique of Political Economy, in Marx, Engels, Lenin on Historical Materialism,* Progress Publishers (Moscow, 1972), pp. 137-38.

Foreword

This study is an elaboration of a thesis developed in a memorandum on "The Changed Character of the Working Class" written in the summer of 1984 and submitted for publication to *Workers World* newspaper in October 1984. [1] At that time we said that high technology, that is, the scientific-technological revolution, had become such an enormous economic factor that it had changed the social composition of the U.S. working class.

The basic content of the change has been a massive general shift of the workers away from relatively high-skilled, high-paid jobs into lower-skilled, lower-paid service jobs. Because of this shift, the social weight of the lower-skilled, lower-paid workers, made up mostly of Black and Latin people and women, has become preponderant in the general workforce of the U.S.

At the time of that writing there was already abundant data to confirm our general analysis. It may have appeared, however, that the data was still of only a tentative and conditional character and therefore inconclusive.

However, a new flood of statistics based on studies of not only the 1980 U.S. census but updated reports since then has lent further support to our thesis. One of these valuable studies to which we refer later is by Ward Morehouse and David Dembo of the Council on International and Public Affairs and includes a series of special reports, the first written in October 1984 under the title "The Underbelly of the U.S. Economy: Joblessness and Pauperization of Work in America." [2] These studies were also bolstered by a United Auto Workers (UAW) Research Bulletin of May-June 1985. [3]

Finally, an official report issued February 6, 1986, by the U.S. Congressional Office of Technology Assessment fully confirms our analysis. While the full study containing some 450 pages of data was not available at the time of the writing of this book, abundant excerpts were published in many newspapers throughout the country. [4]

A principal finding of this report was that in the five years from 1979 to 1984 as many as 11.5 million workers either lost their jobs or shifted to lower-paying service jobs. "Nearly half of all workers displaced from 1979 to 1984 worked in manufacturing industries such as steel, auto, industrial equipment, textiles and apparel. [As many as] 45% have taken a pay cut and two-thirds of those were earning less than 80% of their former income." The report went on to state, "Given the pace of technological and structural economic change, [many more workers] may be left behind."

With regard to the nature of the shift away from the heavy industries, the report said that 95% of the new jobs created in the period studied were lower-paid service jobs. In 1984, the report said, the average hourly wage in manufacturing was $9.18. However, the average hourly wage for production and non-supervisory workers in all service-producing sectors was $7.52. It would be correct to assume that the gap between the higher wage scale and the lower ones has since widened and not narrowed.

This is a social trend wholly unanticipated by those who had expected the great advances and discoveries in science and technology to have brought about "upward mobility." This is what was looked for from the scientific and technological revolution. Instead, all of the studies disclose a clear trend in the opposite direction.

Instead of raising the level of Black, Latin, women and other oppressed workers in capitalist society to that of the higher paid, more privileged, so-called aristocratic sector of workers, the scientific-technological revolution is mercilessly and ruthlessly leveling down and demolishing the higher social stratum in the working class and reducing it to the level of the lower paid.

While the apologists for the ruling class are celebrating this new condition of the working class, they stop short at drawing the deeper social and political significance it has for the process of the newly emerging social composition of the working class. The growing demolition of vast sections of highly paid workers and their sinking to the level of the more oppressed sections spells out a new constellation of internal forces in the working class. It will, for one thing, fundamentally alter the relationship between Black and white workers.

This developing relationship bodes ill for capitalist apologists because it discloses a new material basis for classwide solidarity and even a revolutionary potential for the working class. The new composition of the working class will give it a more homogeneous character and limit greatly the racist, hierarchical stratification upon which the ruling class has been able to thrive and which it has cultivated and promoted all these years.

It will inevitably shift the political balance away from the more privileged layers of the working class in favor of the hitherto underprivileged, unrepresented and more scattered oppressed workers. The internal political relations between the different strata of the working class will become more harmonized on the level of working class politics. This new trend in the working class goes contrary to the historical tendency of capitalist development in the past.

The scientific-technological revolution is a truly global phenomenon and should not be assessed solely on the basis of its national manifestation in the

U.S. Its influence stretches from one end of the globe to the other. Its effects can be felt in Tokyo and Sweden, in France and Mexico, all over the globe. (Its development in the socialist countries is not the object of our study here.)

It is a phenomenon that cannot be reversed. Those who bemoan its existence today must look to the future, not to a return to the past, which in any case is impossible.

Of course, it is possible for the growth of the productive forces, of science and technology, to slow down and possibly stagnate, as happened in the period immediately after the great economic crisis of the early 1930s. Even then, however, research and development continued, if at a slower pace. But what was developed slowly in the laboratories at that time took on a feverish momentum once the buildup began for the Second World War.

It is wrong to underestimate high technology by viewing it as only a narrow sector of the economy. This was the conclusion of the study by the United Auto Workers (UAW) research department printed in the May-June 1985 Research Bulletin and referred to earlier: "High-tech firms represent only a small portion of our economy and with high projected growth fewer than a million jobs are likely to be created in the next decade in high-tech firms."

That may be true enough. The Congressional Office of Technology Assessment report confirmed it: "Jobs in computer and semiconductor manufacturing are unlikely to rescue many workers from traditional manufacturing jobs because employment in these industries is small." And of course, the total number of jobs in computer and semiconductor industries is small by comparison with the overall workforce, which counts in the tens of millions.

But this is an evasion of the fundamental issue involved in the scientific-technological revolution. While it is a very narrow sector, its influence is decisive for all sectors of the economy.

These technological changes alter fundamental social trends and bring to the fore new political forces. It is therefore wholly inadequate to point to the mere number of workers directly involved in this particular narrow sector without showing its overwhelming influence in all phases of the capitalist economy. Moreover, high technology has fueled the enormous growth of the military-industrial complex.

It need only be recalled that in July 1985 the heretofore leading civilian corporation, General Motors, acquired Electronic Data Systems (EDS) and its computer services. The whole purpose was to acquire high technology and move this civilian sector of the economy closer to the military-industrial complex. Even such a homespun company as Singer Sewing Machine, a household name for decades, as of February 1986 abandoned the business of manufacturing sewing machines by announcing that it would dismantle its plants (at who knows what cost to the workers) and move completely into the aerospace industry. Now its only connection to sewing machines will be the marketing of "Singer" machines made by other companies.

The justification for each new social system as against its predecessor is that it raises society to a higher level. It has done so in each succeeding social order by raising the productivity of labor. The great achievement of capitalism was that it not only promoted a tempestuous development of the productive forces, of science and invention on an unheard-of scale, but it raised the productivity of labor. Over a period of centuries it laid the basis for raising the material standards of society and the wage levels of the working class as a whole.

The distinctive feature of this particular phase of capitalist development, the scientific-technological phase, is that while it enormously raises the productivity of labor, it for the first time simultaneously lowers the general wage patterns and demolishes the more high-skilled, high-paid workers. It enhances the general pauperization of the population.

At a time when the ruling class is boasting of capitalist prosperity, the two independent studies already cited, one by the UAW Research Department and the other by the Council on International and Public Affairs, have confirmed that halfway through the 1980s there were more than 15.6 million unemployed and underemployed (unemployed, discouraged and part-time workers). How is it possible for there to be so-called capitalist prosperity and the addition of millions of workers to the workforce, as the Reagan administration boasts, and at the same time an expanding pool of unprecedented numbers of unemployed?

The reason lies deep in the objective process of capitalist production. The latter even in its most prosperous phase of the capitalist economic cycle continually expels more and more workers from the productive apparatus. The difference introduced by the scientific-technological revolution is simply that it has vastly accelerated this continuous expulsion of more and more workers from the process of production, even in a period of so-called growth.

No one knows what the economic situation will be once the economic cycle of development progresses, as it eventually will, from the so-called prosperous phase to crisis to economic collapse. This explains why the ruling class, which has been so lyrical about the huge profits it is garnering, is at the same time so worried about future developments.

This latest phase in the development of capitalism has to be seen in the light of its evolution of more than a half century and the role of the U.S. in the global economy at the end of the Second World War. At that time this country held a predominant position in both science and technology. It controlled the fundamental levers of capitalist development in the West and had gained political and diplomatic predominance over Japan.

High Tech, Low Pay

Over the years, however, the fortunes of U.S. monopoly capitalism began to change. From shortly after the Second World War until the early 1950s, the U.S. had accounted for 50% of gross world production (that is, of the global bourgeois economy), which gave it enormous political, diplomatic and military leverage. However, as capitalist Europe recovered and Washington began to become very deeply involved in the Viet Nam adventure, the U.S. share of the capitalist world's gross production sank to what is variously estimated at 25% to 30%. It somewhat recovered for a short time after the war, but has since been steadily shrinking, so that estimates today run between 20% and 25%.

While the U.S. share of the capitalist world's gross production has declined, its military aspect has continually increased. This has imparted a debilitating aspect to the nature of capitalist development in this period. The figures show that the military expansion of the U.S. has been contemporaneous with a contracting share of world capitalist production. This is an enormous factor in imparting economic instability and promoting military adventurism.

It is thus impossible to discuss the effects of the scientific-technological revolution solely in terms of a national phenomenon. In the following pages we examine the havoc wrought by this technological transformation on the labor movement and the oppressed people. However, it is the international implications which often prove of decisive significance, especially in terms of the relationship of military production to the world capitalist economy and the relations of U.S. imperialism to the oppressed peoples and socialist countries of the world. All this has to be borne in mind as we discuss strategy and tactics in the labor movement.

While it would be incorrect to try and draw an analogy between the fall of the ancient empires based on chattel slavery and the declining position today of U.S. imperialism, nevertheless certain similarities are worthy of comment. You just have to look at the rebellions going on in the Philippines, South Africa, Haiti, south Korea and elsewhere to be reminded of those ancient uprisings of the colonized peoples against the empire.

As in those days, there are loud voices in the ruling class today calling for strong leadership, for imposing order on the world. They were most vociferous during the Carter administration, which they viewed as well-nigh traitorous for not being able to prevent the downfall of the Shah of Iran. But in truth, the Reaganites, who were behind so much of that ultra-rightwing agitation, found once they got in that they were forced by the rebellions to carry out pretty much the same policy as Carter. Reagan had to get rid of Duvalier of Haiti and to cut loose the dictator of the Philippines, Marcos.

For all the tough talk of the Reagan administration, the only place they dared carry out an open military intervention was against Grenada. That would have been an easy victory 150 years ago.

The cost of militarism is rising. The trend in imperialism today is that the cost of maintaining the empire is beginning to overwhelm the loot that is brought in. When imperialism was stronger it brought in many more profits than losses. This allowed for the development of a relatively aristocratic top layer of the working class, mostly white, who gained something from imperialist expansionism. But today it is becoming ever more costly to maintain such a far-flung empire against increasingly conscious and determined liberation struggles. It takes enormous expenditures not only on the most sophisticated weapons and on maneuvers involving huge numbers of troops but even on endless diplomatic and political efforts. All this must ultimately come out of the hides of the workers here.

Seen in another sense, the imperialist system is becoming too costly to be able to reproduce itself. This stands out when capitalism is compared to both ancient slavery and feudalism, societies that remained relatively stable for centuries. Under these systems, the surplus produced by the laboring classes went directly into consumption. Very little was used to expand the means of production, unlike the present economic system, where the driving force of production is to generate capital.

Under modern-day monopoly capitalism, with its enormous and costly military superstructure and its irreversible drive to revolutionize the means of production, the cost of production has become excessive. The capitalists must make an ever greater effort to unload these excessive costs on the working class; hence, high tech and low wages. Their anti-labor offensive is not the product of an aberration on the part of individual capitalists but comes from deep historical roots. It is a symptom showing that the system is economically out of date and bound to decline.

At present the anti-labor offensive of the capitalist class shows no signs of receding. But it is instructive to look back to a hundred years ago, when the struggle of the working class in the U.S. was remarkable for its militancy. The international working class of that period viewed the struggles of the U.S. workers as exemplary. The struggle of U.S. workers for the eight-hour day in 1886 led to the proclamation of May Day as an international working class holiday. That historic period of upsurge also saw the rise of the organization of Black labor.

However, it should be noted that it was preceded by a period of a severe anti-labor offensive unleashed by the capitalist class that had its origins in the capitalist crisis of 1873. Labor historian Mary Beard, in her *A Short History of American Labor,* described the period: "With the paralysis of industry employers began to reduce wages and these reductions were followed by prolonged and desperate strikes. Within seven years, between 1873 and 1880, wages in the textile districts were cut to almost one-half the former standard. Similar action was taken in other industries. Unemployment became so widespread that strikes to maintain wages were perilous; where they were attempted, lockouts usually followed. Blacklists and prosecutions intimidated labor leaders. . . ." [5] The number of effective national craft unions fell to less than a third, and membership in unions declined drastically.

Is this really different, except perhaps for form and severity, from the current attack on the labor movement, the oppressed people, women, gay men and lesbians and the homeless? That period led to a great resurgence. The devastating effects of monopoly capitalism's latest assault will, after trials and errors, inevitably give birth to an upsurge in the movement of the working class and oppressed peoples—and one which has incalculable potential for progressive and revolutionary working class solidarity.

Notes

1. Marcy, Sam, "The Changed Character of the Working Class," *Workers World* (New York), Oct. 25, 1984.

2. Morehouse, Ward and David Dembo, "The Underbelly of the U.S. Economy: Joblessness and Pauperization of Work in America," a series of special reports prepared by the Council on International and Public Affairs (New York, 1984-85).

3. UAW Research Bulletin, May-June 1985 (Detroit).

4. See excerpts from report of U.S. Congressional Office of Technology Assessment, *New York Times,* Feb. 7, 1986, p. 1.

5. Beard, Mary, *A Short History of American Labor*, Arno Press (New York, 1969), pp. 80-81.

The Scientific-Technological Revolution and the Changing Character of the Working Class

Chapter 1

The Crisis in the Trade Unions

Beginning in the late 1970s, U.S. big business and the government launched a coordinated assault on the wages and living conditions of the working class which, at the time this is being written, has lasted nearly six years. The magnitude of this drive, judged by previous historical standards, makes it the longest and most severe ever.

This anti-labor attack did not fall from the sky. It is the product of a cumulative process over years. It has spanned successive U.S. administrations of both Republicans and Democrats, surfacing especially during the last two years of the Carter administration. That period saw the onerous double-barreled effects of stagflation—a large increase in unemployment accompanied by rising inflation—which gripped huge sections of the population, particularly the working class and the oppressed.

Nor should it be forgotten that even in the early 1970s, presumably a prosperous period, the administration of Richard Nixon imposed so-called voluntary wage and price controls. This was meant to not merely control but to in some cases actually reduce real wages while prices of basic commodities for everyday living were already soaring.

Some in the labor officialdom would like to ignore all this and confine themselves to a study of the Reagan years. This, however, would do violence to a clear understanding of the inseparable connection between the different phases in the struggle of the working class. It would put completely out of focus the sequence of events and their interconnections.

AFL-CIO report on "changing situation of workers"

On the 50th anniversary of the founding of the Committee for Industrial Organization (CIO), the Executive Council of the now merged AFL-CIO issued a study dealing with "the changing situation of workers and their unions."[1]

"The AFL-CIO Executive Council," the study said, "created the Committee on the Evolution of Work as part of its effort to assess the significance of the changes in the work environment for the federation and its affiliates." The committee was assisted by a group of luminaries that included Professor

James Medoff of Harvard University, Louis Harris & Associates, and Professor Thomas Kochan of MIT, who in fact prepared the study.

The study purported to review numerous complex factors which had created the situation confronting the workers and their unions. It discussed the "evolution of work" and arrived at the conclusion that "the United States—indeed every industrialized nation—is undergoing a scientific, technological, economic revolution every bit as significant as the Industrial Revolution of the 19th century."

The study, however, did not live up to its promise. While it presented a mass of statistical data, most of which had already been published in the capitalist press, it was altogether superficial and concentrated on presenting the external features of the profound changes taking place in the working class.

The study purported to give an analysis of the "evolution of work." But it evaded the crux of the matter. There is work and work. There has been work over the ages, if one seeks to go to the roots of its evolution. There's work today both at home and in the mines, mills, factories and offices.

If one prepares one's meals at home, repairs an appliance or a broken door or paints the apartment or house, that is work. But work in the plants, in mines and mills, has to be especially differentiated, even though the scientific-technological revolution may have affected both. What differentiates this work from that at home is not so much the physical differences, important as they are, but that the labor process in the mines, mills, factories and offices takes on a special character—that of the **exploitation of wage labor by capital.**

The study used the term "work" but disregarded the special social characteristic which distinguishes the labor process in the workplace of the employer from that at home. It attempted to analyze work independent of social relationships, which are based on class antagonisms.

The study mostly confined itself to the last two decades. This period, it said, has undergone a scientific-technological revolution every bit as significant as the Industrial Revolution. If it is that deep and profound, and we agree that it is, it certainly deserves greater scrutiny.

The phrase scientific-technological revolution has been used so frequently in and out of context by bourgeois sociologists that it has become a cliche. Furthermore, trade unionists should note that those who have cheered loudest for the technological revolution have also jeered the most at the labor movement over these last years.

To examine the relationship between the technological revolution and the Industrial Revolution, one must go beyond the framework set by bourgeois sociologists. For trade unions in particular it is necessary to view it from the perspective of the working class as against that of the bourgeoisie and its cheerleaders.

In fact, no one better described the revolutionary achievements of the bourgeoisie in the Industrial Revolution which brought it to power than Karl Marx. Conversely, almost all bourgeois historians will point out this or that aspect of the devastating effects the Industrial Revolution had on the workers. But then, of course, they will praise to the skies its achievements for the bourgeoisie.

Aside from all the cruelties and inhuman treatment of the workers, however, there is an instructive aspect of the Industrial Revolution which is particularly relevant to the effects the technological revolution today is having on the contemporary working class.

Destructive social impact of revolutions in technology

In *Capital*, Marx fully described how the basis for the Industrial Revolution was the expropriation of the land from the peasants and their concentration into factories. That was part of the process that undermined the feudal system, which stood in the way of the bourgeoisie.

The Industrial Revolution destroyed the feudal labor guilds, the first known labor organizations. These guilds had contained both masters and craftsmen or journeymen. It was these independent craftsmen of the feudal period, members of the guilds, who were then drawn or herded into the plants and factories, lost their status as independent producers and were reduced along with the peasants to the status of wage workers, of proletarians.

The current scientific-technological revolution, viewed from a trade union point of view (which is often completely ignored), is having every bit as significant an impact on the labor movement as the Industrial Revolution had on the first known labor organizations. Its tendency is not to demolish the unions per se but to swallow them up, bring them into the fold of so-called labor-management cooperation.

Therefore the destructive effect of the scientific-technological revolution upon the working class and particularly upon the unions has to be seen in the light of historical evolution.

It was the historic mission of the Industrial Revolution to bring together the scattered handicrafts, formerly the work of independent craftsmen and apprentice workers, and develop large-scale industry. It was a bloody process, but this large-scale production laid the basis for the creation of the modern working class, the modern proletariat. It was by such ruthless measures (the "evolution of work") that it came into existence.

This process was not without sporadic struggles of the workers. To the extent that these very early forms of workers' struggle are given any attention at all by the bourgeoisie, they do so in a derogatory manner, leaving out the essential lesson.

Luddites is a name frequently given to English workers who staged a series of uprisings between 1811 and 1816. These struggles began in Nottinghamshire, where groups of textile workers began to destroy knitting machines. They spread later to Lancashire, Cheshire and the West Riding of Yorkshire. Workers began to wreck cotton power looms and shearing machines. They had no coherent plan, no general aims and no political orientation.

This movement was of a thoroughly spontaneous character and was an expression of frustration. It was not ignorance as such which led to these wrecking and sabotage tactics. What it demonstrated was the organizational immaturity of the workers at that time, but also the character the class struggle can assume in the absence of a trade union that can respond to the needs and aspirations of the workers.

Marx said about the Luddites: "It took both time and experience before the workpeople learnt to distinguish between machinery and its employment by capital, and to direct their attacks, not against the material instruments of production, but against the mode in which they are used."[2]

It is very interesting that this form of struggle should be cropping up again today, and in a country which is supposed to be in the advance guard of the technological revolution, with all its highly touted "benefits" for the workers.

We are referring to the situation of the Japanese railroad workers. Few labor movements are more affected by the scientific-technological revolution. The Japanese government wants to split up the national railway and return the railroads to private industry, with the projected loss of 100,000 jobs, or one-third of the total number of railway workers. (Isn't this what the U.S. government wants to do with Conrail and Amtrak?) When on November 29, 1985, the workers went on strike, organized bands of radicals dismantled railroad facilities in Tokyo, Osaka and other cities in an effort, however fruitless, to aid the striking workers.

Labor organization in different stages of capitalist production

MANUFACTURING OR HANDICRAFTS

The first stage in the development of the working class movement took place in the period of manufacturing or simple cooperation, which brought the handicrafts under one roof for the purpose of exploitation. It led to some technological development and a further division of labor.

Manufacturing brought into one workplace the mechanical fitting together of partial products made independently. The final product owed its shape to a series of connected processes or manipulations. The manufacture of a watch illustrated this type of division of labor. The handicraft period of development left as a legacy such great inventions as the compass, gun powder, type printing and the watch. In that period machinery played a smaller, subordinate part.

It was the manufacturing period that in fact produced the skill of the detail laborer. This was done by reproducing and even driving to a great extreme within the workshop what Marx called the "naturally developed differentiation of trades" which had already existed in society.

While it developed great skill, it had its reactionary side. As Marx put it, "The conversion of fractional work into the life-calling of one man, corresponds to the tendency shown by earlier societies, to make trades hereditary; either to petrify them into castes, or . . . to ossify them into guilds."[3] This is in very sharp contrast to the later period of the rise of capitalist development proper, which did not at all try to preserve and enrich the skills of the workers but relentlessly and mercilessly reduced them.

The manufacturing period simplified, improved and multiplied the implements of labor by adapting them exclusively to special functions of each detail worker. (In the current stage of industrial development and technology, the detail laborer is reduced to the most minute, repetitive, monotonous operations requiring less and less adaptability and skill. The aim in fact is to abolish the worker altogether.)

It was in the period of manufacture that the separation of the workers from their means of production and the conversion of their property, their means of production, into capital began.

THE INDUSTRIAL REVOLUTION

The division of labor led eventually to the Industrial Revolution, or production based on the use of machinery. In the machine, wrote Marx, "we find . . . as a general rule, though often no doubt under very altered forms, the apparatus and tools used by the handicraftsmen or the manufacturing workmen, with this difference: that instead of being human implements they are the implements of a mechanism or a mechanical influence."[4]

The expansion of capitalist production by means of machinery was directly proportional to the number of workers whose independent means of livelihood gradually became destroyed by their inability to compete with the machinery.

However, the use and development of machinery allowed the organization of large-scale production. Each step was accompanied by a rise in the productivity of labor, either through greater intensity in the use of labor power or through the introduction of labor-saving devices.

All this laid the basis for the progressive development of the modern trade union movement. It is this second stage of capitalist production which gave a stimulus to the early development of the giant modern unions of today.

MASS PRODUCTION

Mass production, which began with what has been called the Ford Revolution, is the third stage. It further undermined the crafts and the skilled workers and created a new form, the so-called semi-skilled workers. Its merit was that it expanded the work force. The assembly line, which entailed the employment of more workers than ever, was considered the great accomplishment of Henry Ford.

The difference between mass production and the earlier forms of large-scale production is that it brought about a greater simplification and division of labor into ever smaller tasks, finely delimited methods and more detailed specification and further reduced the variability of jobs. This is the significance of the assembly line, of mass production.

The current scientific-technological revolution

This stage has now given way to another phase of technological development. The mass production period which began with Ford and continued for a period of time after the Second World War was characterized by expansion. But the current stage, the scientific-technological stage, while continuing some of the earlier tendencies of development, contracts the workforce.

Like all the previous stages of capitalist development, the current phase is based on the utilization of workers as labor power. But its whole tendency is to diminish the labor force while attempting to increase production. The technological revolution is therefore a quantum jump whose devastating effects require a revolutionary strategy to overcome.

The division of labor in the early manufacturing stage built up and developed the skills of the workers to the point where they became hereditary. The process of true capitalist production, however, with the introduction of machinery, began to reduce the skills of that early division of labor, until in the current period they have introduced a micro-division of labor where the workers are more and more an appendage of the machine, instead of the machine being an instrument to develop the aptitude of the worker.

Isn't this what Saturnization (the procedures to be introduced in GM's planned Saturn auto assembly plant in Tennessee, about which we'll have more to say later) is all about? It is hailed as ushering in a new period in labor relations where the workers, because of the further micro-division of labor and the introduction of computers and robotization, will have "less monotony" and "more variability" because they'll be doing more jobs. But in truth it means the wiping out of whole classifications of skills, the elimination of more workers and a greater rate of exploitation.

The problem with the AFL-CIO study on the "evolution of work" is that it presents a mere description of the technological revolution. It alludes to what are in effect mechanical processes as though in a void, without showing the different stages in the evolution of the class struggle. It is as though one had nothing to do with the other, as though the technological revolution were not in essence a social process.

The uninterrupted revolutions in science and technology which generally have gone by leaps and bounds in the modern era have now taken a quantum jump, producing a qualitative change. The technological revolution in relationship to the labor process, to the process of extracting profits from the workers, boils down to this: reducing their skills, displacing millions of workers and throwing them on the unemployment rolls.

When bourgeois sociologists refer to the scientific-technological revolution as a structural change, they are not including but are really excluding the social changes, the changes in class relations which are the result of the technological revolution. The latter is the cause of the former, not vice versa.

It is these so-called structural changes, these very deep and abiding technological revolutions, which have caused havoc and disorientation in the perspective of millions of workers and their unions. Clearly the trade unions, indeed the whole labor movement, have reached an historic turning point.

Turning point for labor movement

Some of the bourgeois ideologists are beginning to view the industrial infrastructure of the U.S., built over decades and decades of capitalist development, as a dinosaur. They are giving voice to the thinking in ruling class circles which likens the industrial infrastructure of the U.S. to huge ocean liners which should perhaps be broken up into the small ships and frigates of long ago—but based on the introduction of Saturn-type technology and above all Saturn-type labor relations.

What we are witnessing, therefore, is the wholesale dismantling of plants which began much longer than a decade ago and is now in full swing. All this propaganda about eliminating the "dinosaurs" and breaking the "ocean liners" into small vessels is meant to facilitate the abandonment of the huge steel mills, textile plants and other complexes for "mini-mills" which can reap "maxi-profits." It's a line of development which threatens the very existence of the unions.

It has also upset and undermined the traditional labor relations approach of the unions. The attempt of the bosses to introduce a "new type of labor relations," a "nonconfrontational" kind of "friendly cooperation" between management and labor where decision-making power is supposedly granted to the workers, is nothing more than a new despotism of the bosses meant to accelerate profits, reduce costs and introduce an unprecedented era of permanent displacement and enlargement of the unemployed rolls.

The remorseless and relentless trend of barbarously dismantling whole plants and industrial complexes does not by any means negate the scientific-technological revolution but on the contrary will intensify it. The breakup into smaller units (like mini-mills and so on) is not a progressive trend, as some in the camp of bourgeois sociology see it, toward small businesses or the dissolution of the monopolies and oligarchies. That is a ridiculous conclusion based on utterly false assumptions.

The trend toward small high-tech units is financed by the huge banks, the source of the recent wave of buyouts, corporate reorganizations and dissolutions. The net result is the further concentration of the wealth in fewer hands and strengthened monopoly. As even the liberal economist Lester Thurow has pointed out, only 1% of the population owns 48% of the stock in this country, and the rest is not owned by the workers except for a small, utterly insignificant sprinkling.

In all earlier phases of capitalist production, beginning with simple cooperation, the tendency had been to concentrate larger and larger numbers of workers under one roof or in contiguous areas. In the latest phase of development, however, there is the deliberate dispersal of the large concentrations of workers into widely spread geographical areas. Often this is not necessarily for immediate economic gain, especially by the huge multinational corporations, but for broad social and political reasons.

Large concentrations of workers are more susceptible to union organization and are more affected by the "contagion" of progressive, militant ideas. The other aspect is pure and simple racism—to get away from the areas of the country where oppressed people especially are concentrated. The Pentagon is a principal promoter of this.

The AFL-CIO study mentions "unstable labor conditions" but does not recognize the great importance in all this, that the technological revolution has broken up the old mold of labor relations.

The workers and their unions are trapped in an historic labor relations framework at a time when the structure of capitalist industry has undergone a wholesale transformation. This is to the great advantage of the ruling class, the bosses and bankers who own and control the industry, and to the tremendous disadvantage of the workers who have produced the industrial infrastructure, who laid the first bricks, forged the iron and steel, hammered in the first nails and have mastered it all, up to and including the very summits of the most sophisticated high technology.

There is no question that these changes constitute a revolutionary development which requires the development of a corresponding revolutionary strategy. It is required not only for the further development of a working class offensive to meet the anti-labor offensive of the bosses, but for the sheer survival of the trade union movement.

The great necessity is to reverse the anti-labor offensive. New forms of struggle are necessary.

Notes

1. "The Changing Situation of Workers and Their Unions," a Report by the AFL-CIO Committee on the Evolution of Work, February 1985.

2. Marx, Karl, *Capital*, Progress Publishers (Moscow, 1984), Vol. 1, p. 404.

3. *Ibid*, p. 321.

4. *Ibid*, p. 407.

Chapter 2

The Scientific-Technological Revolution

Technology and trade union tactics

An example from the distant past can be related to the present to help bring into focus the importance of technological revolutions in relation to the class struggle.

In 1789 an Englishman named Samuel Slater, an inventor by profession, devised a secret design for a machine to make textiles. As a result of this machine it was possible to set up textile factories.

British law at the time would not allow him to export the machine or to legally leave the country himself; if he were caught, he would be subject to imprisonment. That's how much importance was given to technology and its export at that time.

However, posing as a farmer in order to evade the emigration law, Slater was able to secretly leave the country. He memorized the design so that he would have no documents with him in case of investigation. That's how Britain at that time guarded technology and that's how the early ruling class understood the significance of technology in its world struggle.

That was almost two centuries ago. At present the struggle over high technology (that's what Slater's invention was at that time) has taken on an even more momentous aspect from the point of view of secrecy and the secret struggle within the bourgeoisie.

U.S. corporations have retained hundreds of spies abroad in order to garner the latest technological innovations while at the same time using the FBI as a virtual private army to track down their opponents, especially the Japanese.

Where does this technological struggle, the constantly and continually growing technological revolution, leave the workers and the unions? What does it mean under present circumstances?

What it has meant in the last few years is that the ruling class believes that the labor movement and the trade unions in particular are no longer necessary to the system. It sees the unions as an encumbrance, an obstacle in the way of further technological development.

Even the bourgeois liberals no longer feel they need liberalism as such and hence have turned away from an alliance with the labor movement. Liberalism as an ideology is no longer essential to the predatory, avaricious multinational corporations in the struggle for high technology, which is, under the present social structure, absolutely in conflict with the working class.

Plant closings and high-tech obsolescence

In the early 1960s, consumer groups began a campaign designed to point out that a great variety of commodities were deliberately produced to have a shorter duration of usefulness than might be possible given the same manufacturing equipment and technological know-how.

It was a case of planned obsolescence. Thus many products, ranging from home appliances to automobiles and even skyscrapers, were planned to endure for a shorter period than was necessary.

The scope of the products to come under the umbrella of planned obsolescence was legion. However, this did not include the heavy industries, the machines which produce machines; in other words, the industrial structure.

The Second World War, which caused so much destruction of human lives, also took a very heavy toll of property. Among the imperialist countries, it destroyed a considerable part of the infrastructure of Germany and Japan. Whole factories and buildings were bombed to the ground. This happened to a lesser extent in Britain and elsewhere.

The U.S., as is well known, was free from military attack and its industrial structure remained intact. Initially, of course, this was a tremendous advantage at the end of the war. However, in order to rebuild Europe and also Japan, the U.S. spent a considerable amount of money and some equipment under the Marshall Plan to revitalize European industry. The Japanese also started to rebuild along these same lines.

Since whole factories and industrial complexes had been destroyed, this gave a very important impetus to the development of high technology. In the U.S. the impetus for the development of high technology was almost immediately absorbed by the military-industrial complex, to the disadvantage of civilian industry.

In some ways the capitalists in both West Germany and Japan, and to a much lesser degree Britain, were given the opportunity to build whole new plants based on up-to-date and state-of-the-art facilities. The very destruction that was supposed to have broken the back of the capitalist competition from Germany and Japan gradually was turned to a large extent into its opposite.

High technology took off swiftly over there, particularly in Japan and then West Germany. Whereas earlier planned obsolescence had been applied mostly to means of consumption, from home appliances to construction materials and autos, it now took off and was applied to the industrial infrastructure, the plants themselves.

Accordingly, the life cycle of the new heavy industry, including steel and auto plants, grew increasingly shorter than that of older facilities in the U.S.

The life cycle of the technology in a steel plant by the standards of the 1950s and 1960s was about 14 years, if not longer. However, by the late 1970s, the life cycle of a Japanese plant was about 8 or 9 years, while that of U.S. plants remained somewhere around 14.

By virtue of the quantum jumps brought about by the application of computers and electronics, the very high-technology industrial units now last about two or three years before they become outdated by even more sophisticated technology, whose life cycle is even shorter. This process under the capitalist system is as ruthless as it is relentless.

Any efforts to manage this technology so as not to reduce the workforce turn to nil. Trade unionists who represent the workers must take note of this tendency and know that it is of an international character; that the life cycles of all technologies continually get reduced. The process was much slower but just as pervasive even at the dawn of the capitalist system, when technology first began to be widely applied with the use of machinery, the industrial revolution and so on.

High technology, especially in the era of computers and electronics, continues to take quantum jumps. A plant which just recently may have had ten years to go can now become obsolete as a result of the constant revolution of the means of production. The development of not only products and devices but of whole new technologies makes what otherwise would be a well-functioning, long-lasting plant with a stable workforce obsolete, but only in comparison to the new technologies.

This is what lies at the root of what has become an epidemic of plant closings. In part it is due to the capitalist cycle of production. But while it takes on a more aggravated and epidemic character in capitalist recessions, this tendency prevails as a characteristic of capitalist development in so-called good times as well.

Let's take a look at four fairly recent examples of changes introduced by the high-tech revolution and their effects upon the workers and the trade union movement. One deals with the communications industry, one with construction and earth-moving equipment, one with electronics, and one with automobiles. These four symbolize what is projected for industry in general, but is still in an anticipatory stage.

The end of the AT&T myth

The AT&T Systems Information Division announced in August 1985 that it would be eliminating 25,000 jobs at its various installations. This was the second major layoff at AT&T in less than two years. The significance of this sharp retrenchment of the workforce goes far beyond its numbers. Yet even so, about one-fourth of the 120,000 workers in the divisions involved have been laid off.

Until just recently, AT&T had a nearly absolute monopoly in its field of operations. It occupies a special place at the very summit of highly sophisticated technology.

Before the 1970s AT&T was regarded as relatively less sensitive to the vicissitudes of the capitalist economic cycle than other giant corporations. Jobs there, it used to be said, were much more secure than in other huge manufacturing companies or utilities. All the more has this unprecedented cutback come as a shock to many of AT&T's apologists.

It is a common error to believe that AT&T's recent divestiture, in which it is supposed to have spun off for good its local telephone companies, was all the result of public pressure, that it was a case of the government responding to the needs of the people and that a federal judge by judicial intervention had robbed AT&T of its monopoly status.

Nothing of the sort. It was the swift changes in technological development, the revolution in electronics, microwave radio transmission, the need to develop satellite communications and the leap into the Space Age beginning with the Soviet Union's launching of Sputnik which laid the foundation for AT&T's divestiture.

The development of a multitude of new technologies ushered in with the Space Age made it incumbent upon AT&T to look for a solution to its vast new problems by way of spinning off its local telephone companies over a period of time and utilizing the vast money thus derived to shield itself from other corporate competitors.

The continued existence of the AT&T monopoly in its old corporate framework was incompatible with the new revolutionary developments in technology. If it stayed the way it was, there would be a flight of capital away from AT&T into the areas of the satellite sciences, radio microwave transmissions and electronic developments of all sorts, particularly those geared to Pentagon needs. Either AT&T would have to begin the task of transforming itself or it would be outstripped by the newcomers outside its corporate framework.

AT&T is thus an illustrative example of how a giant corporation, no matter how huge, no matter how insulated it seems to be from the ravages of predatory capitalist competition, nevertheless ultimately either falls to the mainstream or becomes successfully dismembered by competing dynastic financial and industrial cliques.

We see illustrated here what Marxism has always taught: that it is the development of the productive forces which changes the economic conditions. The ruling class politicians and judges who seem to have ordained the AT&T breakup were merely responding to new economic conditions facing the ruling class.

Capitalism never fully carries through any of its economic tendencies to the very end. This is remarkably illustrated by the tendency of capitalist competition to turn into monopoly. This tendency is never fully realized. While the general epoch is that of monopoly capitalism, contradictory trends in capitalist development have demonstrated that competition exists side by side with monopoly.

In the last two decades some of the greatest monopolies, like AT&T and others which seemed so monolithic and omnipotent, have all shown a tendency to break up and re-form again and again. This applies to the greatly exaggerated power and supposed monopoly of the OPEC countries, too. The dominant relationship between the oppressor and oppressed has never ceased for a moment to be a fundamental factor in the situation.

The tendency to disintegrate, break up and re-form again and again is a characteristic feature in the struggle between competition and monopoly. Huge corporations turn into conglomerates, later spin off some of their divisions, and again break up and re-form. The underlying element in all this is that capital tends to flow to wherever the rate of profit is higher, but retreats as soon as the tendency toward lowering the profit rate makes itself evident.

The divestiture of AT&T and its deregulatory aspects are merely a reflection of what has been taking place in the anatomy of the capitalist economy resulting from the growth of the productive forces. The growth of the productive forces always upsets established relationships in the constellation of conflicting forces and groupings in the ruling class.

The havoc AT&T wreaked on the workers by unloosing such devastating cutbacks mirrors the general crisis which the high-technology establishments are experiencing. High technology was supposed to be if not altogether immune from unemployment, then at least only marginally affected. Now this myth has been thoroughly demolished. There are now severe cutbacks not only in high-technology companies like AT&T but in all the semiconductor establishments as well.

Mass layoffs have taken place all around Silicon Valley in California and there have been significant slowdowns in other high-tech regions of the country as well, such as in the Boston area around Route 128.

This experience demonstrates how false is the notion that unemployment has been plaguing only the so-called Rust Belt in steel, mining, other metal industries and coal. One is supposed to forget that there has also been a tremendous erosion of jobs in textiles, housing, lumber and agriculture.

Of all the arguments that have been advanced to embellish the so-called new information society, the most banal one is that it tends to increase the demand for more and more scientific personnel, that it requires more and more skilled workers, and that these together with management personnel constitute a base that is sheltered from the crisis of capitalism.

It is true of course that some elements of the capitalist economy respond to capitalist economic stagnation and crisis earlier than others. But it is simply a matter of timing.

What is afflicting AT&T today will surely surface tomorrow in IBM. Moreover, it will make its way (if it has not already done so) into the broad service sector which has been indirectly fed by high technology in the first place.

Mass layoffs at Caterpillar

The Caterpillar Tractor Company is the world's largest producer of earth-moving equipment, which is mostly used in construction projects of all kinds, oil drilling and mining. In early December 1985, investment analysts praised Caterpillar for announcing plans to further reduce its workforce, which had already been cut from 90,000 in 1979 to 53,000. The company wanted to lay off 10,000 additional workers over the next five-year period, while maintaining the same output.

This posed a strategic problem for the unions involved. The Caterpillar workers had already gone through a six-month strike, and these big layoffs made such struggle even more difficult.

Caterpillar's plans called for transforming the step-by-step assembly line system in its existing plants to a system where work is done in stages in various factory areas. These "factory cells," it is claimed, would speed production and lower costs through automated materials handling and processing. This plan is an example of a new manufacturing philosophy called "down-sizing" which also lends itself to more outsourcing of component parts.

Another element to its $600 million automation program would focus on robotics and computer-aided manufacturing systems which would involve not only more automated materials handling, but also more robots in welding and foundry work.

Such a drastic reduction in the workforce to less than half in only ten years, which evokes such praise from the banks and investment houses, is another prime example of what is in store for the workers. This profound transformation in manufacturing methods, which is still only in its early stages, will be felt by all the unions and indeed constitutes a classwide assault on all workers and oppressed people.

It should also be noted that these layoffs came at the height of the so-called capitalist recovery, when the crisis was supposedly over and companies should have been rehiring. This is supposed to be the pickup in the economy brought about by the Reagan program. But if this was true, and these layoffs were occurring in a period of recovery, then what will happen in a downturn?

The implications of this for overall trade union strategy are extremely serious, and demonstrate once again the need for new strategic conceptions.

The GE-RCA merger

As the largest non-oil merger ever, costing over $6 billion, the merger or acquisition of RCA Corporation by General Electric will have far-reaching effects on a global scale. It is especially important that the workers involved understand the significance of the merger historically and as part of a broad social process that goes beyond local or even national boundaries.

By virtue of their vast facilities, often in other countries and not unionized, these corporate monsters have gained broad social, political and diplomatic leverage against single unions. These concentrations of capital are classwide organizations to which the workers in the unions have to develop a classwide perspective, nationally as well as internationally, in order to be able to get a firm handle on how to fight the companies.

The unions have to both go beyond the strictly legalistic character of union contracts and go outside of the capitalist-labor property relations in order to be able to combat the corporations effectively. This is more important than it was 60 years ago, when both these giant companies were rapidly expanding the workforce. Now they are contracting it, a fact which is statistically undeniable.

Even during the 1970s, GE reduced its U.S. employment by 25,000 and RCA cut its domestic workforce by 14,000.[1] It is no answer that they increased employment abroad. That merely illustrates the continual flight of capital from one area to another, depending on both economic and political conditions, for capital will go wherever the rate of profits is highest at a particular moment.

It is also not true to say that the flight of capital is from the Frost Belt of the U.S. to the Sun Belt, because statistics now show a flight of capital from the South back to the Northeast and the Midwest (see Appendix A). However, this is accompanied by higher technology and lower wages.[2] The fact that there has been a certain upturn in the capitalist economy only emphasizes that when the downward cycle begins again, the process of dismantling these so-called new plants will become just as barbarous as it has been with the older ones.

One of the many important lessons that can be learned from the GE-RCA merger is the need for the workers to establish vigilance committees, which can ferret out information in advance of mergers, acquisitions, layoffs and so on, in order to prepare the workers for sudden turnabouts by these predatory giants. Even greater is the necessity, even if only in embryonic form, for the absolutely indispensable education of the workers: the development of union consciousness into class consciousness, and with it an appreciation of international cooperation between all the workers.

Furthermore, a truly classwide perspective in relation to such important mergers or acquisitions shows that, notwithstanding all the suffering they impose on the workers everywhere, the basic content of these developments is to lay the solid and indestructible foundation for socialism. The objective economic content of the scientific-technological revolution is that it socializes the labor process with virtually lightning speed, showing the ripeness and maturity for a socialist takeover by the workers of the means of production so they can be used for the benefit of humanity and not for private profit.

This GE-RCA merger in particular has an economic and technological significance which could potentially have great social value in the struggle for socialism. GE and RCA may overlap, but they could be integrated so as to have great sociological importance. Their merger lays the material foundation for genuine socialist construction.

In the old days, when a steel company bought an iron ore mine, constructed a railroad to transport its raw materials, or acquired coal mines, it became an integrated entity, and from the perspective of socialist construction was progressive. It organized production in such a way that workers' control would potentially be able to function more efficiently.

It is an altogether different matter when a steel or other company buys a gambling casino, a racetrack, a tourist resort or other entities that are wholly unrelated to the development of its original specific purpose. This kind of buying and selling is for the sole purpose of garnering huge profits, particularly in a wildly speculative period which is characterized precisely by such deals.

Many mergers are motivated solely for the purpose of manipulating the cash acquired from one of the corporations. In these cases, there is sometimes not the remotest connection between the productive processes of the companies involved. For that reason, there soon develop divestiture procedures or spin-offs, which happen when one of the corporations either is milked of its cash or puts up some of its valuable assets to be sold for cash. In the past, both RCA and GE have in this way spun off parts of their acquisitions acquired in other mergers.

In the 1960s, a characteristic form of the concentration of capital was the conglomerate. A variety of different and unrelated businesses were absorbed into a consolidated company. The diversity of products thus brought under one corporate roof was believed to shelter the conglomerate from capitalist economic crisis.

What made this attractive for a short period, however, was the fact that the 1960s was a time of relative capitalist stability and prosperity, due most of all to the Viet Nam war. Under these conditions, the unions did not perceive much of a threat to their position coming from the conglomerate trend.

The buyouts and acquisitions of recent years, however, are quite different. Not only have they come in a more downward phase of the capitalist economic cycle, but the top priority of the cost reduction aspect of this newer concentration of capital is the elimination of jobs.

All this brings into sharp focus the urgent need for the workers to be able to pass from rudimentary trade unionism, based on trade, plant or industry, to a classwide understanding of their key role in production.

Saturnization

Ever since the General Motors Corporation announced that it would build a new Saturn plant in Tennessee, and even before the actual site for the plant was chosen, there began a widely heralded and unprecedented publicity campaign that this would be the technological miracle of the latter half of the 20th century. Indeed, it is claimed that this type of plant will lay the basis for the U.S. to win the race in low-cost cars with the Japanese and other competitors.

There are two aspects to this question: that of labor relations in the new plant, and the public presentation by the company of its technological and competitive significance from the viewpoint of efficiency and low-cost operation.

How it will affect the workers is given secondary consideration in the capitalist press. What is stressed in most of the major capitalist newspapers and electronic media is that it will inaugurate a new era in labor-management relations, that indeed it will be the answer to what they call the fruitless confrontational aspects of the collective bargaining process, and that what will result from the UAW-GM agreement is a new spirit of cooperation. This is supposedly based on the new, more modern concept of involving the workers in decision making and of doing away with monotonous, repetitive and, needless to say, extremely arduous work by combining several operations.

Outside of the UAW ranks themselves, the popular impression is that this will modify if not undermine the rigid division between the managerial staff and the workers. The workers themselves will have more of a say in what they do and what they produce.

View of UAW militants

Needless to say, the militant workers in the UAW immediately saw through all this. A summary of what was actually being proposed by the company was leaked to the press on July 9, 1985. It was analyzed by Jerry Goldberg in *Workers World* newspaper.[3]

The contract not only set a base pay at about 80% of what workers at traditional plants will earn later in this decade, but the Saturn plant will operate with only one unskilled job classification and three to five skilled classifications. By contrast, traditional plants have as many as 100 classifications.

The Saturn contract makes no room for work rules and lets management transfer workers more easily within the plants, allowing the company to eliminate many jobs. The *Workers World* report gives these details:

"Pete Kelly, who is a member of the UAW International Executive Board, had this comment to make: 'Saturn at its core is a threat to the union.' The new agreement eliminates the union shop committee. There will be no union representatives on the shop floor to handle grievances and other worker problems. At Saturn a union-management consensus system will replace the shop committee.

"The proposal eliminates seniority except for unusual circumstances when worker abilities are equal.

"Under Saturn, all workers will be salaried. Raises for each individual will be based on meeting productivity, quality, production and attendance goals, as well as profit sharing. As Kelly correctly pointed out in objecting to those provisions, 'The union fought for 40 years to get rid of incentive pay.'

"Supposed job security is a key element of the deal. Some 80% of the workforce will receive 'guaranteed employment' unless 'severe economic conditions' or 'catastrophic events' occur [in other words, a recession—S.M.]. The other 20% of the workers will be 'associate members' who will not receive blanket protection from layoffs. 'That creates a second class of citizens in the UAW,' Kelly said.

"For the past five years the union leadership has swallowed the company line that foreign imports represent the greatest problem facing the autoworkers. 'Buy American' is the UAW's main slogan. In taking this line the union leadership has accepted the company argument that to become competitive with the Japanese the companies must cut U.S. labor costs $2,000 per worker."

There is no question that these terms are extraordinarily onerous and are a break with the UAW's traditional progressive stance over the many years the union has been in existence. However, at the time of this writing the agreement is only an executory contract. It will take many months if not a couple of years before the plant becomes operational, at which time the contract would go into effect.

Thus, what the company and the labor officialdom propose, the workers may very well dispose. There's many a slip between the cup and the lip.

Another 'Ford revolution'?

The way the Saturn project has been presented as constituting a technological breakthrough has led many to anticipate nothing less than a second auto revolution, having effects as profound as those Ford introduced with the mass production concept.

It is worthwhile examining this for the project is being presented to the public as a big boon. It is bound to create a tremendous number of jobs by the sheer volume of investment projected—$5 billion according to some estimates.

It is said that the Ford Motor Company, by introducing new methods and a new concept, was able to create hundreds of thousands of jobs which ultimately made work for millions. Is it not possible that the Saturn project could result in similar accomplishments with another radical departure from the accepted norms in labor relations and production techniques?

Let us see.

What was the essence of the Ford Motor Company's concept and technique? It introduced mass production. It brought a new principle into the production process.

There's no new principle in the Saturn project, an analysis shows. Henry Ford's mass production methods were based on two general ideas: 1) division and specialization and 2) the use of tools and machines in the production of standard, interchangeable parts. The total production operation was carefully divided into specialized tasks made up of relatively simple, highly repetitive motion patterns and the minimum handling or positioning of the workpiece.

This permitted the development of human motion patterns that were easily learned and rapidly performed. The simplification and standardization of component parts permitted large production runs of parts which were readily fitted without adjustment.

Smaller tasks and more finely delimited methods reduced the variability in technique. The worker became more removed from responsibility and the authority to integrate his or her task was left to others.

The assembly line epitomizes the whole Ford concept and practice. There's no need to go into the exhaustion, boredom, hazards and hardships of the assembly line. That should be well known. But the Ford revolution also had a progressive social aspect to it.

The Ford introduction of mass production, what amounted to micro-division of labor in the plants, dramatically reduced the cost of a motor vehicle and was followed by a vast expansion of employment. Ford was also able to pay the highest wages and introduced the five-day week.

Because the Ford concept enabled the production of many millions of vehicles, it fostered and cultivated the growth of satellite industries and generally constituted a significant contribution to capitalist production in the U.S.

It was on that basis that the Ford Motor Company until the late 1930s was preeminent in the auto field on a world scale. It became a tremendous multinational corporation with its own sources of raw materials and so on.

The Scientific-Technological Revolution   21

The Ford method and concept therefore led to an expansion of capitalist production. The Saturn project, however, is based on a contraction of the existing workforce.

The Ford concept and strategy resulted in wiping out the old craft unions to a large extent. The problems that skilled workers had in the early days are documented in the struggles of the Mechanics Educational League, which was an organized expression of the skilled trades in the auto industry. It later dissolved and became the skilled crafts part of the UAW.

The Saturn project is still in the planning stage, is only an executory contract which still has to be put into effect. The intention, however, is to wipe out as many as 100 job classifications. Even if only half that is consummated, it will amount to a vast contraction, in other words, the opposite of what happened in the earlier Ford concept.

The concept behind the Saturn project is calculated to undermine the older, standardized, minutely calculated micro-division of labor and supplant it with multiple operations by workers, who it is claimed will be working together with more cooperative methods.

Of course, cooperation and division of labor are not specifically capitalist aspects of production. Division of labor has existed over the ages, and so has cooperation. This was so even in ancient times, long before the dawn of the modern age. The Egyptian pyramids were built on the basis of division of labor and cooperation. It is impossible to conceive of any production not having some degree of division of labor and cooperation.

What makes the Saturn project different from early forms of cooperation and division of labor is that it is done on a specifically capitalist basis, the aim of which is the chase after profits based on commodity production.

It remains to be seen in what respects the Saturn production concept will differ from the old Ford-GM method. A great deal is being said about how the introduction of sophisticated and even exotic technology will do incredible things, of how intelligent workers cooperating in groups will have renewed pride in their work, and that this will result in a better car.

Some of this is sheer propaganda by the company. But won't the new technology be so effective that it produces an even greater number of vehicles at lower cost? Wouldn't a new technology superior to that of the Japanese, Germans or Koreans help close the gap with them?

The GM-Hughes merger and military technology

The truth of the matter is that GM is relying not so much on new technological inventions and scientific developments from its own laboratories and science centers as on the transfer of technology from its acquisition of the Hughes Aircraft Corporation.

What is involved in the GM-Hughes merger is a very deep and profound shift of the civilian industry toward the military-industrial complex. It strengthens the hand of the Pentagon in its long-standing attempt to become the central organizer of the capitalist economy.

Up until the day of this acquisition, General Motors was the number one civilian producer in the country—the largest auto manufacturer and the largest complex of industrial facilities. As of June 1985, it became not just the number one auto producer but the number one defense electronics company as well.

By merging with or buying out Hughes Aircraft, General Motors became inextricably bound up with the production of missiles, satellites, radar, surveillance, guidance and other military products. It thus became integrated with the military establishment on a really large scale.

While before this buyout defense contracts were only 1% to 1.5% of GM's gross production, it is now estimated they will make up more than 6%. More important than the percentages, however, is the direction of this development. It is a qualitatively different kind of merger. It marks a giant leap of civilian industry into the arms of the military-industrial complex.

Even though General Motors is so huge in comparison to Hughes Aircraft, one must reckon with the fact that it is not Hughes (that is, an individual giant corporation) which will exercise influence over General Motors. That would be absurd. Rather, it is the Pentagon, which has at its disposal hundreds of billions of dollars and therefore towers over any corporation, including GM.

It should be noted that the Ford Motor Company has also become involved in military production. This will compel more and more civilian producers to follow the trend. It is part and parcel of the Pentagon's effort to militarize U.S. industry.

For a long time the auto industry, in particular, was viewed by a variety of liberal thinkers concerned with the struggle against imperialist war as a mainstay for peaceful coexistence with the USSR and other socialist countries and as a brake on the Pentagon. This was regarded as the material basis for the existence of a moderate grouping within the bourgeoisie, with economic roots in the civilian sector. This merger comes as a severe blow to this view.

However, it is part of a longer-term trend. The principal motivation for the GM-Hughes merger and its most immediate basis can be directly traced to the Star Wars project, which has been pushed so feverishly by the Reagan administration. It is important to take into account this extremely significant political development, which gave the final stimulus to the GM-Hughes merger.

In this "most open of open societies," the most important economic and political processes are carried out in secret. Only when they are completed are they brought out into the open as an accomplished fact. The GM-Hughes merger was a textbook example of this.

This extraordinary development could not have been achieved without undercover cooperation among the holy trinity—high industry, finance and the government. What its effect will be on the auto workers and the Hughes workers remains to be seen. It most certainly will entail layoffs for many thousands sooner or later.

It shows how the most important decisions governing the direction of the economy and affecting millions of people are decided by a handful of business executives who are not elected by the people and who are not even subject to veto by the government.

We know now that the deal between Hughes and GM was long in the making. But it is the political process that gave it such a huge lift. Once the appropriations process in the Star Wars scheme was terminated with the presidential signature, the Pentagon opened up the process of bidding for research and development. Then began an explosive scramble by all the elements of the military-industrial complex to grab whatever they could of these most luscious contracts, where super-profits are most extravagant.

It must be understood that we are dealing not with a "few" billion dollars worth of military contracts, but with hundreds of billions. Such is the dimension of the Star Wars project. No large corporation, not even such an enormous one as General Motors, could stand outside the orbit of this magnetic attraction for super-profits.

Aside from anything else, this merger illustrates how utterly hypocritical are the assertions of giant corporations like GM that they are opposed to the government having a hand in private enterprise, that they are against bail-outs or government assistance or involvement. Certainly GM has been the loudest in proclaiming its independence of the government. Now it is completely intertwined with it.

This deal is so enormous that it certainly warrants being used for more than the transfer of technology. More important for General Motors at the moment is that, in purchasing Hughes Aircraft, it enhances its profitability, precisely because Hughes is a huge prime military contractor.

In fact, a formidable problem arises when the deal is viewed as a source for the transfer of technology from aerospace to auto manufacturing, as the company has claimed. The transfer of military technology on a mass scale to civilian auto production in particular may present insurmountable problems, at least for a considerable period of time, if the aim of reducing the cost per vehicle is taken into account.

Experience has shown that the transfer of military technology to civilian production, on the basis of production for profit, has brought about enormous problems. Several examples come to mind that are detailed in Seymour Melman's book *Profits Without Production*.[4]

"Until now," says Melman, "no major military-serving enterprise has demonstrated an autonomous ability to carry out the sort of occupational switch that is needed to go civilian."

Conversion means changing over the physical resources, the skills of all workers and the ways of organizing work to serve civilian rather than military goals. "Organization [of a conversion] is a problem area because of certain characteristics of military industry. The decision goals and occupational practices of [military] industry encourage cost escalation. Cost maximizing is feasible because subsidies from the federal government offset extraordinary increases."

Hughes Aircraft is not the exception to this, but the rule. The government's largess to Hughes Aircraft is well known, as it is with other military contractors.

"Military products are often designed to increase military 'capability' regardless of cost," says Melman. "Given that priority, reliability takes second place, as do such considerations as ease of maintenance and minimum cost for accomplishing a given function."

Melman gives two well-known examples of military industry contractors who attempted to change over part of their production facilities and even labor force to civilian work: the Rohr Corporation of Chula Vista, Calif., and Boeing-Vertol, a division of Boeing Company.

Rohr built the cars for BART (Bay Area Rapid Transit) in San Francisco, as well as for the Washington, D.C., subway system. Boeing built the MBTA (Massachusetts Bay Transportation Authority) buses. In both cases the costs were enormous. The systems didn't work well and took long years for proper operation. There were frequent vehicle derailments, malfunctioning of the air conditioning system, cooling motors and fans when the motors burned out too quickly, and so on.

There is another recent example of the difficulty created when technology developed by military contractors is used for civilian purposes. In the New York City area, Grumman buses, like those of the MBTA in Massachusetts, soon became notorious for improper functioning, compelling the city to sue the company.

When GM announced the acquisition of Hughes, the capitalist press mentioned here and there the difficulties that might be incurred because of the different "lifestyles" of the two companies. But none mentioned the real problem: how to transfer the exorbitant costs of maximized technology to civilian production, where the objective is to produce a low-cost competitive vehicle.

As a Pentagon protege, Hughes, like the other principal prime military contractors—General Dynamics, Boeing, and Rockwell to name a few—is not concerned with minimizing costs but with maximizing them. Therefore, when its military technology is transferred to civilian production, the burden of this cost will first be put on the workers in the Saturn plant. We thus see that the new technology is bound to be far more costly and that the workers will have to pay for it.

Furthermore, the auto industry historically is the one last area where civilian competition has existed on a wide international basis. These new technologies, whose shorter life cycles add more to the costs, spur on the tendency toward conversion to military production.

This is what Saturnization means.

Military reorganization of the economy

Aside from the profit motive involved, where does the steam come from for all this? Who pushes the scientific-technological revolution at such a feverish pace? The AFL-CIO report discussed in Chapter 1 makes no mention of it, but automation, workerless factories, and all the rest are being pushed vigorously by the Pentagon. The Star Wars program is the prime example of and an outgrowth of this phenomenon.

Right after AT&T announced its imminent layoff of tens of thousands of workers, a company spokesman said it was now ready to forge ahead with Star Wars research. "Can computer software handle anything Star Wars throws at them?" was the question posed by members of the Senate Armed Services Subcommittee on Strategic and Theater Nuclear Forces. "I believe the answer is yes," replied Solomon Buchsbaum of AT&T Bell Laboratories.[5]

The Pentagon since before 1983 has been attempting to make a quantum leap into an area which was previously regarded, at least in peace time, as off-limits. It is attempting to become the central organizer, not merely of the war industries, but of the capitalist economy as a whole.

The term "centrally organized economy" has generally been applied by bourgeois economists only to socialist countries. The very term has been anathema to big business. For decades bourgeois economic dogma has held onto the fiction that in the U.S. individual corporate enterprises are dominant; that "free enterprise" and capitalist competition reign supreme; and that it was only the Rooseveltian New Dealers and their latter-day administrators of the capitalist state who injected the government into what is normally regarded as the private sector.

The truth of the matter, however, is that monopoly capitalism in the U.S. has been steadily and relentlessly fusing with the capitalist state for decades, and is intertwined with the military in a thousand and one ways.

It was General Eisenhower who coined the term "military-industrial complex" to describe the infrastructure that was set up during World War II and that was never really demobilized after the war. What is now contemplated by the Pentagon is not merely adding to the existing structure, which has expanded enormously over the years, but creating a new concept altogether. It envisions the organization of the basic elements of the capitalist economy under the aegis of the Pentagon in so-called peace time.

There is a struggle, a virtual war, going on over whether and how to do this. A glimpse of this was aired in 1983, on a special segment of the PBS program "Frontline" entitled "Pentagon Inc."[6]

The program dealt with the existence of a little-known group that has tremendous power and authority. It is called the Manufacturing Technology Advisory Group (MTAG) and it includes representatives of both the military and the principal defense contractors. The ambition of this group is to become the MITI of the United States. (MITI is the ministry set up by the Japanese capitalist government which is said to direct the goals of the Japanese economy.)

Air Force General Bernard Weiss explained how the military views MTAG: "To me," said Weiss to a meeting of MTAG that included many military contractors, "I look upon all of us here today in your organizations that you work for as the MITI that will take the U.S. out of the position that it's in today in productivity and quality and move it back to being preeminent in this world."

Now, that requires a considerable reorientation of U.S. industry and commerce. It means that this group would, in the words of the PBS narrator, "set the direction for our industrial future. They make up an economic apparatus every bit as rich and elaborate as MITI. But it is the military here controlling the money and the goals are set by military men."

In Japan, of course, only a very small percent of its gross national product is involved in military research and development as against the huge expenditures in the U.S.

Another speaker at the MTAG meeting shown on PBS was a General Skantze, whose title "Head of Manufacturing Command" was not explained, nor were his job classification and scope of authority.

General Skantze was more specific than General Weiss. "Since our warfighting equipment comes from the industrial base," he said, "the condition within that base must be addressed and corrected. We now have an effort underway to provide a **planning system that will guide our industrial base investments** and will eventually integrate technology, opportunity and business investment planning. It is a top-down approach we call 'Industrial Base Planning.' " (Our emphasis.)

"We plan to maximize application of mechanization and automation," he continued, "and we plan a paper-free factory with planning, scheduling and control by the latest computer hardware and software techniques. We thus expect a factory that can perform at least one full shift per day unmanned."

The Scientific-Technological Revolution

What all this signifies is that the Pentagon is aiming at capitalist regimentation of industry, high-technology industries in particular, and the capitalist economy in general. The whole purpose of it, the Pentagon made clear through these spokesmen, is not to coordinate and plan for useful, cooperative production for the people. It is, as they make very plain, to compete not only with Japan but the whole world, militarily and economically.

Planning while retaining the ownership in the private hands of the capitalist class and having the Pentagon as the central planner is the very opposite of the centrally planned economies in the USSR, China and other socialist countries.

There production is planned for use. Here, as the generals make very clear, the planning is to strengthen competition, which leads to struggles abroad, intensifies antagonisms among the capitalist cliques here, and above all lays the basis for not a capitalist boom but for an even more devastating capitalist crisis, which the brass think they can contain through military regimentation.

Mussolini, Hitler and Tojo thought so too. They did not succeed very well, as we all know. Neither will the Pentagon.

It was a frequent theme in the middle 1950s, that is, between the Korean and Viet Nam wars, that because of the Pentagon's enormous power to maximize costs and its authority to hand out lavish and extravagant contracts for defense orders, the capitalist state thereby acquires the ability to abolish capitalist economic crises altogether.

Of course it is all too true that the capitalist state can accelerate military contracts and thereby temporarily stave off an economic crisis. But it is also all too clear that when that fails, they resort to military adventures. In fact, the 20th century is full of examples of militarism giving a temporary respite to the capitalist system, only to later bring on a deeper and more profound economic crisis.

In fact, there is no scientific basis for the view that militarization of the economy can avoid capitalist crises. The capitalist state is only the collective organizer on behalf of the individual capitalists. Insofar as its economic function is concerned, it appropriates an additional portion of surplus value or unpaid labor from the workers above and beyond what the individual capitalists have the power to extract. It thus intensifies the exploitation of the workers by the capitalists, adding more burdens as a result of its political role, including that of collecting taxes, and its special role as a repressive instrument against the working class and oppressed people. None of what the Pentagon and the capitalist state do alters the fundamental relations between the classes.

The whole purpose of the capitalist state is to enhance the accumulation of capital. But the biggest obstruction to abolishing capitalist crisis is capital itself and the private ownership of the means of production. However the capitalist state may seek to intervene in the organization of the economy, it leaves unaltered the fundamental relation of exploitation. And it is this which generates the chaos and anarchy in capitalist production.

Liberal thinkers are often blinded by what appears to be the omnipotence of the capitalist state because of its power of repression. But while it has tinkered with the economic laws of motion governing capitalist society, it has been unable to alter them in a way that would purge the system of crisis. It only succeeds in delaying the crisis, which is then even more disastrous when it comes.

The crisis in agriculture

The very acute agricultural crisis the U.S. is experiencing at the present time, which is deeper and more profound than any other crisis in agriculture since the early thirties, is not merely the result of capitalist over production. Contrary to widespread popular misconception, it is also very much the product of the scientific-technological revolution. Some aspects of this began well over a decade ago.

"Agriculture's preoccupation with scientific and business efficiency has produced a radical restructuring of rural America and consequently of urban America," wrote Jim Hightower, a former USDA official, in his book *Hard Tomatoes, Hard Times*.[7] "There has been more than a green revolution out there. In the last 30 years there literally has been a social and economic upheaval in the American countryside. It is a protracted, violent revolution and it continues today."

This revolution, says Hightower, has been fueled by "funds to the land grant college complex" which "has been the scientific and intellectual progenitor of that revolution."

Hightower quotes the *Des Moines Register* to show that the land grant universities have devoted "the overwhelming portion of their research and educational funds to the promotion of agricultural technology in the service of the highest income farmers and bypassed poor farmers and rural communities."

Thus, the huge profits go to large corporate enterprises, particularly the huge corporate farms and ranches, what Hightower calls the "vertically integrated and conglomerate corporations," which own "the seed, feed, chemical, credit, machinery and other 'input' industries and the processing, packaging, marketing, distributing, retailing, exporting and other 'output' industries.

"Increasingly, agricultural production is vertically integrated. The markets are concentrated and dinners are prepackaged by corporate America. ITT serves up Gwaltney ham and Wonder bread. The turkey comes from Greyhound Corp.'s Armour division. Dow Chemical brings the lettuce, while Tenneco provides fresh fruits. Count on Boeing for the potatoes and American Brands for Mott's apple sauce. Coca-Cola serves orange juice, and for dessert there are strawberries from Purex.

"Ralston Purina, Del Monte, Tropicana and Safeway are taking control of agricultural production, reducing farm laborers to contract laborers. Commodity after commodity is being groomed under vertically integrated contract, including 95% of the broilers, 75% of processed vegetables, 70% of citrus, 55% of turkeys, 40% of potatoes and 33% of fresh vegetables.

"These percentages," the author adds, "are increasing every day."

Every lever in this scientific-technological revolution in agriculture is controlled by the same industrial and financial plutocracy which is so well known for its stranglehold on industry in general. While it has been regarded in the past as divorced from agriculture, in reality it has absorbed most of the agricultural sector.

Two articles written more than a decade later have verified this trend. The first was in the *Wall Street Journal* and proclaimed that "U.S. agriculture is in the midst of a radical restructuring. Middle-sized farms are vanishing; the growers are going high-tech; some sectors are robust and developing, some are sickly and dying. None are what they used to be."[8]

"Medium-sized farms," continued the Journal, "generally defined as having $40,000 to $100,000 in annual sales, are shaping up as big losers. Large enough to be awash in debt but too small for the maximum in technology and efficiency, such farms are increasingly being squeezed out of business.

"Snapping up much of their land are bigger, more efficient operators. About 12% of U.S. farmers now account for 63% of farm sales. The largest farms, those with sales over $250,000, rose 54% in number from 1978 to 1982."

The article cited a bank economist from the Kansas City Federal Reserve Bank, a constituent part of the national Federal Reserve Bank, who gave his judgment on the course of the agricultural crisis and the scientific-technological revolution: "We will see a greater and greater concentration of the assets of agriculture in fewer and fewer hands."

A continuation of this trend was reported in another article more than a year later in *USA Today*.[9] It cited a January 9, 1986, Census Bureau report that "more people left U.S. farms in 1985 than in any year since 1976, bringing U.S. farm population to its lowest level ever. The report comes at a time of crisis in U.S. agriculture. The Census Bureau said 399,000 left farms in 1985—bringing the percentage of farmers in the population to an all-time low of 2.2%. The departures are mostly younger families forced out because of economic adversity, forcing them to sell off or go out of business. The farm population peaked at 33% in 1916, but dropped steadily until the late 1970s. Other reasons are declining birthrates, aging farmers and technological changes."

In a general way, everything said in these two articles is correct. However, they obscure what is truly fundamental and crucial for an understanding of agriculture in the U.S. in general and the agricultural crisis in particular. This is especially true of the way the Bureau of Labor Statistics (BLS) gathers and reports data.

They leave out of consideration the basic characteristic of capitalism in agriculture: the private ownership of land and its relationship to **wage labor.** This omission is of critical importance. Reading these two articles as well as much of the general literature on farming, one gets the impression that the fundamental factor in U.S. agriculture is the so-called independent, individual property-owning farmer. This leaves totally out of consideration the vast and often uncounted agricultural workers, the wage earners–some of whose wages are so meager they can scarcely be called that.

The other fallacy in much of the popular literature on the agricultural crisis is to divide farms into large and small depending on acreage. This leaves out of consideration that a farm may be relatively small in terms of the number of acres but have great intensity in the application of capital, machinery and high technology. It may also employ huge numbers of agricultural workers. There are many such farms spread throughout the length and breadth of the country, from California to Florida, Arizona to New Jersey and all the way up to Maine and the state of Washington.

Since its dawn, the capitalist system has been characterized by a sharp contrast between town and country, between rural and urban life, between the workers on the land and those in the factories. While the scientific-technological revolution has done much to blunt this grave contradiction, it has at the same time sharpened the contradiction between the working class as a whole, including agricultural workers, and the capitalist class.

Unity and solidarity between those who work under the sun and those who work under the factory roof are more urgently needed than ever. A great deal of attention especially needs to be paid to putting the so-called "illegal," migrant workers within the framework of the organized trade union movement, which such organizations as the United Farm Workers (UFW) and the Farm Labor Organizing Committee (FLOC) have set out to do.

Writing more than 70 years ago on the development of capitalism in agriculture in the U.S., Lenin wrote: "Hired labor is the chief sign and indicator of capitalism in agriculture."[10] How striking this is, considering that even today in the U.S., the movies, television, literature and songs dwell on the family farm, leaving the wage laborer largely invisible!

"The development of hired labor, like the growing use of machinery," said Lenin about the U.S., "is evident in all parts of the country, and in every branch of agriculture."

In his painstaking study and statistical analysis of agriculture in the U.S., Lenin pointed out that in the 1910 U.S. census, all the farms were divided according to areas, just as had been done in the 1900 census. But unlike that earlier census, the one in 1910 did not divide the employment of hired labor according to the same classifications. Thus, wrote Lenin, "we are deprived of the opportunity of comparing the small and large area farms according to the number of hired laborers they employ."

The effort continues to hide the significance of wage labor. Little attention is paid to the special exploitation of the agricultural worker, who more often than not is a migrant worker. Many are Black, the legacy of the sharecropping and tenant farming to which Lenin gave considerable attention in his study. Perhaps the majority, however, are so-called "illegal" immigrants from Mexico, Central America and the Caribbean. "Illegal workers make up an estimated 50 to 70% of the nation's migrant workforce on the farms," according to the *Wall Street Journal*.[11]

Unless the agricultural crisis and more specifically the scientific-technological revolution in agriculture is put in the context of the capital-labor relation, as we did earlier, one gets a completely distorted viewpoint, not only of the current agricultural crisis, but of the nature of capitalist agriculture in general.

Agriculture is now experiencing the same phenomenon observed in industry generally, where high technology is displacing workers and the substitution of lower-paid for higher-paid jobs is taking place. There has been a proportionate loss of jobs by comparison with previous periods. As Table 1 (see Appendix B), taken from the study series on "The Underbelly of the U.S. Economy" shows, "employment among farm workers (including farmers and farm managers, farm laborers and supervisors) declined in actual numbers from 4.2 million in 1964 to 3.1 million in 1974. From 1979 to 1982, the number declined by 15,000 to 2.7 million. Thus farm workers have declined as a percentage of total employment from 6.1% in 1964 to 2.7% in 1982. After 1982, the BLS no longer reported on this category of worker. [Not much has changed since Lenin!—S.M.] Overall employment in agriculture, however, has continued to decline from 3.4 million in 1982 to 3.3 million in 1984."[12]

The scientific-technological revolution in agriculture should also be seen against the historical background of the centuries-long struggle to maintain the family farm, owned by the individual proprietor, free from the onslaught of capitalist development. The Homestead Act, passed in 1862 by the U.S. Congress, provided for the transfer of 160 acres of unoccupied public land to each homesteader on payment of a nominal fee. This was to fortify and strengthen the individual farmer in the face of the onrushing development of capitalist accumulation in industry. It was supposed to be a shelter against the big landgrabbers, the industrial and real estate magnates, the railroads. (Of course, all this was done with no regard for the sovereign rights of the Native peoples.)

But as Marx explained long ago, and as Lenin was to repeat many times, capital subordinates to itself all the varied forms of land tenure and reorganizes them in accordance with its needs, not the needs of the individual owner. Marx in *Capital* analyzed the extremely varied forms of land ownership, such as feudal, clan, communal, and state forms, and demonstrated how each in its own time became subjugated to the concentration of capital in the hands of a few and stronger capitalists. In the present monopoly stage of capitalist development, the historical mission of the scientific-technological revolution resulting from the law of capitalist accumulation is to facilitate the socialization of agriculture in the same way it has socialized industry, that is, while at the same time retaining the private ownership of the means of production, which is in irreconcilable contradiction to the social character of production.

What role does the state play in this? The capitalist state tries to counteract the effects of large-scale production, which becomes ever more concentrated as a result of the scientific-technological revolution. The state does this by intervening on behalf of the capitalists while giving the appearance of continuing to enhance the socializing trend of capitalist industry. It takes over an increasing number of bankrupt enterprises, especially the huge ones, and bails them out as was done with the Chrysler Corporation and with Continental Illinois Bank and hundreds of smaller banks.

Even the Reagan administration has allotted billions in subsidies to agriculture, the purpose of which is frankly stated: to strengthen the "viable enterprises," meaning the huge monopolist agribusiness corporate owners and controllers, and to facilitate the death of the smaller ones. On the other hand, the capitalist state has been forced all over the imperialist world to disgorge a great deal of what it formerly nationalized or subsidized and return it to the individual capitalists. This is done as a means of strengthening and intensifying capitalist exploitation over the workers and opening up new avenues of exploitation, especially in the oppressed countries, under the aegis of the strongest and most powerful multinational corporations.

Nationalization, denationalization and deregulation are all functions of the capitalist state as an oppressor and exploiter. These tendencies transcend conservative and liberal administrations, reactionaries and progressives, so-called socialist administrations as in France, Spain and Greece, so-called Labor governments as in Britain, Norway, Sweden and Belgium and blatant, unrestrained reactionaries like the Reagan administration.

It is instructive to compare the way the bourgeoisie has lamented over the collectivization (socialization) of agriculture in the USSR, China, and other socialist countries, especially the so-called forced collectivization, and contrast it with how they have welcomed the capitalist "collectivization" of farming communities here, which is done with much cruelty and is so remorseless and relentless. The apologists for the capitalist monopolies find only the highest praise for this kind of collectivization or socialization. It is progress. It is the future.

But viewed in another light, viewed from a revolutionary perspective, this trend has laid the objective basis for socialism. Seen over a longer period, it has facilitated the task that the workers will have of reconstructing society. Decaying capitalism, with its perennial economic crises of capitalist overproduction, its billions upon billions of bushels of "surplus" corn, wheat, soybeans, etc., can find no better solution than to foreclose farms, making agricultural communities more destitute and compelling rural people to flee to the cities to increase the vast pool of the unemployed. As the article in *USA Today* showed, they are leaving the farms in droves, at a rate of close to 400,000 a year in 1985. They will become more and more integrated with the working class.

Notes

1. Bluestone, Barry and Bennet Harrison, *The Deindustrialization of America*, Basic Books (New York, 1982).

2. *New York Times*, Dec. 22, 1985.

3. *Workers World*, July 25, 1985.

4. Melman, Seymour, *Profits Without Production*, Alfred A. Knopf, Inc. (New York, 1983).

5. *USA Today*, Dec. 9, 1985.

6. "Frontline," Public Broadcasting System, Feb. 21, 1983.

7. Hightower, Jim, *Hard Tomatoes, Hard Times*, Schenkman Publishing Co. (Cambridge, 1973).

8. *Wall Street Journal*, Dec. 9, 1984.

9. *USA Today*, weekend edition, Jan. 10-12, 1986.

10. Lenin, V.I., "Data on the development of capitalism in agriculture," *Collected Works*, Progress Publishers (Moscow, 1964), Vol. 22.

11. *Wall Street Journal*, May 15, 1985.

12. Morehouse, Ward and David Dembo, "The Underbelly of the U.S. Economy: Joblessness and Pauperization of Work in America," Special Report No. 3, Council on International and Public Affairs (New York, 1984-85).

Chapter 3

The Ups and Downs of the Capitalist Economy

How cyclical crises affect trade unions

It should be recognized that trade unions are a limited form of organization. This does not mean that they are limited to only taking up purely economic tasks arising from the conditions at work. In recent years the unions have taken on more and more political activities.

But the unions are limited in a different way, in that there is only so much that can be done within the limits or the framework of the capitalist relationship between workers and bosses. Thus the economic cycle of capitalist development is often decisive in determining what workers can achieve through a union or what they may have to concede. **The cycle of capitalist development dictates the objective conditions in which the unions operate and in turn puts an obligation upon them, the workers and their leaders, to develop both tactics and strategic plans to combat this problem.**

As long as the relationship of exploiter and exploited is retained within the framework of the capitalist system, the unions necessarily remain hemmed in and at the mercy of the capitalist cycle of development.

One of the most pervasive myths regarding the standard of living of the workers is that it has gradually improved over the years. It is true that much has been gained by the workers. But the ravages of a capitalist crisis have often hurled them back.

Everyone knows that the great capitalist crisis of the 1930s created havoc with the workers' standard of living. This happens with nearly every significant capitalist depression. It is only in periods of a capitalist upswing, or what is known as prosperity, that the workers are able to recover what was previously lost and perhaps gain more as a result of new opportunities for struggle.

The capitalists attempt to take advantage of every capitalist crisis to carry out both indirect and frontal attacks against the working class as soon as they get the opportunity. "The origin of the crisis of the cities," we wrote in the middle of 1975, "lies therefore in the general crisis of capitalism in this country. The capitalists are trying to overcome their crisis by a general assault on the mass of the [municipal] workers, striking at the weakest link first—health-care, social services, education, fire and sanitation."[1]

We noted at that time, however, that "a broad frontal attack on the **organized** working class, especially in basic industries, is at the present time not possible though it is precisely what the ruling class has in mind." (Emphasis in original.)

The frontal attack did come several years later and began with the demand for concessions from the organized working class, especially in the basic industries. Cutbacks and plant layoffs became the order of the day. The assault was one of the most venomous in the history of the U.S. working class. It not only struck the basic industries, mining and metal, it struck all manufacturing. The bourgeois state gave it added impetus with the breaking of the PATCO union of air traffic controllers. This concerted assault has tended to lower the wages of the higher-paid, thus leveling the standard of living of the workers as a whole. It has also destroyed the jobs of millions.

During the 1970s the employers, unable to carry out a frontal attack on the workers, had to resort to more indirect means by fueling the fires of inflation. But the deflationary process that began in the 1980s necessitated a frontal attack.

As can be seen, the capital-labor relationship puts the working class in a vise-like condition with respect to the employers. As long as they accept that relationship, the workers are in the subordinate position and their opportunities are limited by the very nature of the trade union organization, whose fundamental purpose is merely to bargain over the wages and conditions of employment (the price of exploitation).

Members of a revolutionary working class party, as we'll go into more fully in Chapter 8, differ from mere trade unionists in that their goal is the abolition of the relationship of exploitation. But there is still another fundamental difference that is closely connected with this. They regard the antagonistic relationship between the employers and the workers as an irreconcilable one. This dictates an entirely different attitude in labor relations, negotiations and even grievance proceedings.

Militant workers almost always instinctively understand this irreconcilable character of their relationship to the bosses. As a *Wall Street Journal* article on the 1985 Wheeling-Pittsburgh Steel strike observed, when the workers were speaking about labor relations they referred to "a struggle between us and them." It is a clear-cut example of how the objective relationship of exploitation sinks into the consciousness of the workers as a struggle between "us and them."

Capitalist recessions have lengthened

The problem facing the trade union movement is how to effectuate strategy during times of chronic depression, of protracted capitalist overproduction which gives the employers the upper hand, at least on a narrow economic front.

Capitalist recessions in the United States a century ago, such as the "panics" in 1873 and 1893, were relatively short by comparison with the current ones. It was generally assumed at that time that the workers' movement, especially in Europe, was capable of resuming its upward swing politically and would soon make up what it could not win economically during periods of capitalist recession.

On the whole, capitalist recessions were not as chronic and protracted in the last quarter of the 19th century as they are now. The illusion of capitalist stability and the resulting revisionism of Marxism toward the end of the 19th century came about as the result of this.

But the period following the Second World War has been punctuated by longer-lasting recessions. No one can accurately estimate how long the earlier periods of relative capitalist stability would have lasted had the imperialists not created two world wars and innumerable counter-revolutionary interventions.

All of these retarded the capitalist crises, at least temporarily. There is no question that the crises might have resulted in the overturn of class relations in at least some of the capitalist countries, had it not been for the intervention of war.

All of this is very important in relation to strike strategy, which has a lot to do with the duration of the capitalist economic crisis. If the capitalist crisis were to last only a month or two months, the workers would be in a more advantageous position.

Marx says that the most favorable time for the workers is a period of rapid capitalist accumulation. That aspect of Marxism every trade union bureaucrat will agree with.

So the problem arises, what can be done during periods of capitalist recession when the workers are on the defensive? How should they react if the recession turns out to be protracted and the employers can seemingly hold out for a long time?

The 1979-82 capitalist recession, which is certainly not over for the manufacturing industries, has also been accompanied by political reaction, by the most reactionary intervention of the capitalist state against all workers. The Reagan administration has generated reaction in all fields of social life. But separate and apart from the Reagan administration, the capitalist recession has had a universal effect. "Socialist" governments in Spain, France and Greece have been forced by the capitalist crisis to carry out almost the same austerity measures that the Reagans and Thatchers have imposed on the workers.

So it is not really the form of the capitalist state which determines how the rulers respond to the capitalist crisis. The capitalist system engenders both social-democratic and outright reactionary forms in the administration of the capitalist state. It continually throws up a variety of political formations, few if any of which address themselves to the fundamental ills of the capitalist system or promote a revolutionary perspective.

The lengthened character of the capitalist recessions imposes on the working class in general and the trade unions in particular the necessity to develop a defensive strategy. The working class as a whole can, after a period of time, transform this into an offensive. There is no way this can be done, however, without attempts to break out from the accepted bourgeois conception of the capital-labor relationship. Otherwise the workers are kept in a kind of stranglehold which they cannot get out of by economic means alone and which leads to a continuing stream of concessions to the employers.

Campaigns for prenotification

One such defensive strategy was first raised around 1956 in the upstate New York area. Those were not years of capitalist recession, but nevertheless the Ford Motor Co. closed its stamping plant, organized by the UAW, and Wickwire Steel, a plant owned by Colorado Iron and Fuel, also closed down around that time.

Earlier, of course, there had been a tendency for plants in the North to flee to the South, where not only was labor cheaper but the climate was viciously anti-union. Many states in the South were still governed by so-called right-to-work laws. But when plants did relocate, it was generally with about the same kind of equipment and technology as in the North.

It was in 1956 that militants in the Buffalo area for the first time in U.S. labor history introduced the idea of prenotification, designed to stop plant closings. Since then, prenotification has become widely publicized, even though the trade unions have been slow to avail themselves of this weapon in the struggle. Many local and state bills have been introduced which in one way or another contain prenotification provisions to halt the spread of plant closings. Few if any, however, have really been implemented into law.

Prenotification usually means that before a plant can close, it is required by law to give the workers a notice of one or two years, depending upon how strong a legislative campaign the union and progressive movement have conducted. The tactic is to have hearings on the legislation. This halts the plant closings pending the hearings, which of course take place over an extended period. Penalties against the company designed to protect the workers and the community are assessed on the basis of public hearings.

It cannot be stressed too strongly that the unions have to link up with the rest of the community, which has a great stake in this. For a company to move out and close a plant inflicts incalculable damage on a community as well as on the workers.

In almost all communities the corporations are given subsidies in the form of tax breaks for locating there. Small homeowners and others, by comparison, seldom get any tax relief. Therefore penalties must be assessed in the event these companies want to pull out. This is a deterrent to plant closings.

Of course, political pressure has to be applied at all levels of government, and in this respect the union also has to mobilize the masses politically in order to sustain the struggle and see that irreparable damage is not inflicted upon the communities.

Wherever possible, injunctive relief should also be sought in the form of temporary restraining orders. In other words, the judicial process should be utilized, notwithstanding the fact that the judges are generally more reactionary than the legislators. But publicity around this type of case is a form of pressure and can mobilize the workers for more direct action. Just as farmers have learned to stop farm foreclosures, in some cases with overwhelming might, this has to be done on an industrial basis.

Also state and federal legislators should be urged to introduce legislation declaring a moratorium on plant closings and where possible unions should collaborate with the legislators in framing the legislation. All this would be immensely educational and at the same time enhance trade union activity.

There are now whole groupings of enlightened environmental groups which could also lend their support. They have come to realize the value of having an alliance between the working class and all progressives concerned about the damage that is inflicted upon the environment and society as a whole by the reckless pursuit of super-profits by the capitalist class.

Pentagon plant closings

It is often assumed that plant closings happen only in the civilian sector of the economy. It is further assumed that with the growth of the military budget and the consequent expansion of the Pentagon's operations, plant closings should not be a problem. However, this is not so.

There are now 37,000 industrial firms serving the Pentagon as prime contractors, and three times as many subcontractors, according to Seymour Melman.[2] This means that at least 100,000 industrial units operate to serve the Pentagon in one capacity or another.

When the Pentagon decides to close out an operation, it of course is not motivated by the same considerations as a civilian production unit or plant. The latter is fundamentally concerned with maximizing its profit. That's the basis for its existence in the first place.

It is altogether different with the Pentagon. They don't have to be concerned with profit or loss. The endless stream of appropriations grows ever larger as each new Congress gives the Pentagon a virtual carte blanche on how to dispose of billions of dollars. Occasionally the mere whim of the military bureaucracy can decide when and if to close down a plant or relocate it.

The Pentagon has historically chosen to locate its business in areas away from a labor force which would be susceptible to union organization. Many times it forces the closure of plants out of purely racist considerations, always claiming a military rationale and using national security gobbledygook to cover itself. Most often, it prefers locating in rural or suburban areas away from the centers of contagious labor militancy that characterize the metropolitan areas of the country.

There is also the matter of obsolescence, which often leads to layoffs and plant closings. It ranks high in the Pentagon as a means of producing sophisticated or exotic new technologies. But often these can be rapidly discredited, especially when one considers the sheer number and variety of weapons the Pentagon is involved in producing.

It is well known how when legislators fail to vote for the Pentagon's appropriation requests, the military threatens to close military bases in their area. This practice is even more common when it comes to closing military production units.

Should there be a sudden shift in weapons development, the closing of defense plants could become a far more serious development than it is now. The vast bulk of the subcontractors in particular are smaller units and mostly unorganized. However, they can be just as susceptible to and just as much in need of union organization as those in the civilian sector.

In this connection, it should be borne in mind that in the first years after the Second World War, as well as after the Korean and Viet Nam wars, there were several public campaigns by progressive organizations to convert military production to civilian use. Of all the international unions in the country, the International Association of Machinists (IAM) was the only one to present a plan and attempt to publicize it in order to educate the public on the need for conversion of military production to public use.

Since then, no other union has so far broached the subject, notwithstanding the staggering unemployment and the growth of the military.

Notes

1. Marcy, Sam, "Capitalist Economic Stagnation and the Revolutionary Perspective," *Workers World*, Aug. 8, 1975.
2. Melman, Seymour, *Profits Without Production*, p. 252.

Chapter 4

The Changing Character
of the Working Class

During the early phase of the Cuban Revolution, Che Guevara came to New York to attend a UN General Assembly session. During his brief stay, he arranged some private meetings with progressives.

In the course of conversations about the U.S. and Cuba, he was asked whether changes in the administration here would deter U.S. aggression against Cuba. He replied that a great deal depended on changes in the U.S. working class.

These remarks were all the more interesting because at the time Guevara was regarded only as a popular and victorious guerrilla leader. It didn't appear that he was in a position to take into account the condition of the working class. What the progressive elements in this country, especially the militants among the youth, were concerned with then was a rebellion of oppressed people in alliance with progressive elements. Most of them discounted the working class as such. It is significant, therefore, that Che saw great changes in the U.S. to be contingent on great changes in the working class.

At that time (December, 1964) the U.S. was in a period of so-called capitalist prosperity. Aside from some minor capitalist recessions, it continued until the steep economic crisis of 1974-75.

Whether there would be fundamental changes in the consciousness of the U.S. working class has been a topic of debate for many years. Most anticipation of change in class and political consciousness has been geared to the ups and downs of the capitalist economic cycle.

Of course, for most of this century, if not for the entire course of capitalist development, that's the way it has been. Political attitudes have changed with economic conditions. The ups and downs in the cycle of capitalist economic development have been seen as the fundamental driving force in changing political consciousness, outlook and participation as a whole.

The new social composition of labor

There is, however, a new and fundamental trend which has to do not only with the ups and downs of the capitalist economic cycle, but with the social composition of the working class. It is an objective trend that arises out of the changes in the technological structure of capitalist industry, which in turn have changed the working class itself.

We have written elsewhere[1] about the change as it pertains to the growing proportion of Black, Latin, Asian, Native, women and undocumented workers. That, however, could be interpreted as a mere numerical change, or one that is related to "ethnicity," as they phrase it in bourgeois sociology.

But the change in social composition goes beyond that. It involves a relative reduction in the percentage of skilled workers and a tremendous increase in the number of semi-skilled. Also, on an overall scale, it means the creation of lower-paying jobs as against higher-paying ones. It means the decline of the traditionally more privileged workers and industries with higher wages and the creation of a vast pool of lower-paid workers. This trend is still surfacing and has yet to be given any kind of independent political expression.

From a class point of view, it is truly one of the most profound, socially significant trends to emerge. The number of lower-paid workers is bound to increase at the expense of the more privileged workers.

Since we wrote on this subject in 1984, much data has appeared substantiating the shift in social composition of the working class. It is worth repeating a section of our earlier document here.

Today the working class is of a thoroughgoing multinational character. The significance of this profound change has yet to be fully assessed.

Statistics appear almost daily in the bourgeois press which show how much of the working class today is Black, Latin, Asian, Native as well as women. The most recent study shows that white males are no longer predominant in industry. The workforce is already composed of over 40% women. And notwithstanding the heavy Black and Latin unemployment, their percentage of the workforce continues to increase significantly. All of this is readily admitted in the bourgeois press.

But what has not been pointedly brought to the attention of the public is that the working class as a whole in the U.S. has changed dramatically in another sense. The predominance of the skilled over the unskilled, of the higher paid over the lower paid, has narrowed continually. . . .

Marx pointed out in *Capital* that, even at the height of capitalist development, during a period of upsurge, labor productivity increases as a result of the introduction of labor-saving devices and this tends to diminish the number of skilled members of the working class as against the unskilled. This has the effect of changing the social composition of the working class.

It matters a great deal because, in terms of political struggle, the objective basis is laid for political leadership to be assumed by the more numerous segment of the class.

If we take into consideration that the working class has changed both socially and from a socio-ethnic-national point of view, one can say that there has taken place a wholesale change in the social composition of the working class.

The highly skilled have long predominated politically over the unskilled. This is not necessarily confined to the crafts such as carpenters, plumbers, electricians and so on. The rise of the basic industries such as steel and auto in the earlier decades also had the effect of retaining the influence of the higher paid, particularly in what were regarded as heavy industries.

What has happened, particularly in the last decade, is that the very speed of the introduction of high technology, the very sophisticated type, has undermined the privileged sectors of the working class (such as those in steel and auto) on a world scale and has begun a leveling process which has undermined the living standard of the working class as a whole.

However, it has shifted the objective basis for political leadership in the working class movement away from the more privileged sectors of the working class toward those very numerous working class elements which have had little political influence and been less articulate over the years.

What high technology has effectuated, therefore, is a sharp shift from higher-paid jobs to lower ones. It is not to be wondered at that the phrase 'high tech creates low-paying jobs' has now become vogue. And therein lies the essence of the transformation of the social composition of the working class.

To be sure, it is not a finished process by any means, nor can such a process be finished. But it is a basic trend in the evolution of the working class. While it continues to ravage the living standards of the workers, at the same time it lays the objective basis for the politicization of the workers, for moving in a more leftward direction and for organization on a broad scale. The political consciousness that ought to correspond to the new material conditions of life has lagged behind, as it almost always does.

During the stormy, near-revolutionary working class struggles of the 1930s, it was unthinkable that hospital workers would be organized or that they could carry out an effective strike, as more than 50,000 hospital workers are now doing in New York City. That the hospital strikers are more politically conscious and a more militant element of the working class can easily be verified by even a chance acquaintance with them.

In almost all of the service industries, particularly those in food processing, department stores, grocery chains, transportation, the large wholesale and retail businesses throughout the country, as well as the so-called new industries which have sprung up as some of the old ones have decayed, there is a growing preponderance of new, low-paid workers. The labor force has shifted from what it was decades ago—a mostly urban white working class—to one that is of a multinational character, which does not at all enjoy the privileges which accompanied the earlier rise of the capitalist system in the U.S.

So when we talk of the working class as a class today, it is a different class than what existed a hundred years ago or even 30 years ago. The bourgeoisie tries to hide the profound social and political significance of this transformation of the working class. The bourgeoisie tries to portray the growing number of so-called service workers as 'white collar,' 'administrative,' and even 'middle class.' In other words, it tries to divorce the service and clerical proletariat from the rest of the working class.

Again and again their continuous flood of statistics is tendentiously interpreted against the proletariat, as though the service workers are not wage workers who are exploited along with the rest of the working class. But this is a fallacy. . . .

Since this was written, many articles, studies and reports have verified this basic trend. One of the most comprehensive and at the same time most concise was the special series of reports we mentioned earlier by the Council on International and Public Affairs entitled "The Underbelly of the U.S. Economy: Joblessness and Pauperization of Work in America."

These reports showed that unemployment in the U.S. is grossly understated by the Bureau of Labor Statistics (BLS) because it routinely does not count "discouraged workers" who have given up hope of finding a job and because it does not take into account the wages lost by those who can only find part-time work. More pertinent to the point at hand, however, was the section on pauperization of work, which included the following:

Joblessness is only one aspect of the changing nature of work in America. The pauperization of work is increasingly evident. According to a recent BLS study, for example, of the persons who lost full-time jobs during the recession and were able to find reemployment, 45.7% were only able to find part-time or lower paying jobs than the ones they lost. Of the 5.1 million reported on in the BLS study who lost jobs during the recession, 45.1% were unable to find jobs at all.

Most of the new jobs created during the recovery, furthermore, have been low-paying, while high-paying jobs, especially in manufacturing, have continued to decline. Since 1982, 87.8% of new jobs created have been in the service sector. Of these, 73.7% have been in the lowest paying categories of that sector—namely, retail trade and health and business services. A full-time job in the retail trade (many are part-time) pays only $9,251 a year, well below the 1984 poverty line of $10,610."[2]

This report contained a number of tables containing data to substantiate these observations. The table on "Comparison of weekly earnings in manufacturing and retail trade" shows how the shift away from manufacturing has affected wages. As the report explained, "The discrepancies are substantial between the service-producing and the goods-producing sectors. Thus, the hourly wage in the retail trade is only 62.8% of the hourly wage in manufacturing, while the discrepancy in weekly earnings is even greater (retail is only 45.7% of manufacturing). This higher discrepancy is a reflection of the incidence of part-time work in the retail trade. In September 1985 workers in manufacturing averaged 40.7 hours a week while those in the retail trade averaged only 29.6."

The report continued, "These 'pauperizing' trends in wages, furthermore, now affect an increasing proportion of the labor force—and those sectors that are growing the fastest—while the number of workers in the high-wage sectors is either flat or declining."

One bourgeois theory has it that the change in the social composition of the working class is due to the capitalist industrial cycle. They attempt to show that the service sector, as they call it, and high tech are relatively immune to the capitalist crisis, and are therefore able to grow while the "smokestack" sector of the economy is shrinking. However, no sector of the economy is immune to capitalist economic crisis. It affects all industries sooner or later. It's just a matter of time.

The very protracted banking crisis, which has been in the process of development since 1981 but has been artificially avoided by monetary devaluation and government takeovers, is sure to break out eventually and accelerate the overall crisis. This will not be confined to the industrial sector but can take on vast international proportions.

Automation in large insurance companies and other so-called financial service organizations is eliminating thousands of what were once considered secure white-collar jobs. Even middle management people are being discharged wholesale in corporations like Ford and General Motors, while every merger leads to the elimination of hundreds of office as well as production workers.

The "feminization" of labor

For more than a century, women in increasing numbers have worked in industry in this country. Employers never objected in principle to hiring women when there were profits to be made off their labor. Even before World War I, women were employed in large numbers in such industries as textiles, where working conditions were abominable and wages barely above starvation level. It was in response to these conditions that in 1908 tens of thousands of women workers demonstrated in New York City on March 8, and this led the Socialist International two years later to proclaim that date as International Women's Day.

Protective legislation for workers was especially weak with regard to the sweatshops that employed women. Over 140 women textile workers, most of them very young, died in the Triangle Shirtwaist Company fire in 1911 because of the woefully inadequate safety codes regulating industrial buildings in New York and other manufacturing cities.

Not only women but children were cruelly exploited in those days (as they continue to be in agriculture up to this day). Wages were so low that whole families had to work long hours in the factories just to put food on the table. From 1916 to 1933, three different attempts were made in Congress to legislate an end to child labor, but all three were declared unconstitutional by the Supreme Court. It wasn't until after the tumultuous labor struggles of the 1930s that industry finally accepted the Fair Labor Standards Act of 1938, which set a minimum age of 16 for work in most industries.

The labor shortage created by World War II was what finally opened up the higher-paying industrial jobs to women. The war tremendously spurred the development of the capitalist economy, and for the first time such services as daycare centers were set up to facilitate more women being able to work full time. When the war ended, a major propaganda effort was made to get women to leave the factories and return to the home, yet in 1948 32.7% of women were in the labor force.

The further development of the processes of capitalist production has forced many more women out of the home and into the work force. It is these objective trends more than any subjective factors which have broken up the old family structure headed by the male bread winner. The pauperization of labor, which we have already discussed, has made it imperative that women work.

Much has been written about the "feminization" of labor, most of it bemoaning the demise of the "white male prototype." In 1983, for the first time, "white men, the prototype of the American worker since the beginning of the nation, no longer [made] up the majority of the country's work force."[3] The chauvinist view is that women and Third World workers have taken away the jobs of white men. But this reactionary formulation of the question is also demonstrably false.

As a further report in the "Underbelly" series by Morehouse and Dembo shows, "While men have certainly been dropping out of the labor force, their relatively high paying jobs, mostly in manufacturing, have simply disappeared, not been taken by women. Instead women have flocked to low paying, often part-time jobs in the service sector, many below the poverty line or in the 'poverty zone.'"[4]

By early 1986, women made up nearly 44% of the civilian employed population. But the jobs available to them were generally so low paying that more and more women and their children were falling below the poverty line, in spite of the fact that more women were working than ever before.

Taking into account what they call the Jobless Rate, which factors in the effect of part-time and seasonal employment, Morehouse and Dembo conclude that "The increased participation of women in the work force, often because of increased overall Jobless Rates as well as quality and pay of jobs secured by women, has done nothing to alleviate the poverty of women and children, and in most cases has paralleled a worsening in their condition. Thus, the number of females below the poverty level has increased both in absolute numbers and as a percentage of women in the population, from 14.1 million (13.8% of all women) to 20.1 million (16.8%)." (See Table 4 in Appendix B.)

It is the objective processes of capitalist production, accelerated as we have seen by the great changes introduced by the scientific-technological revolution, that are responsible for this significant pauperization of the work force. Capitalist commentators, however, often persist in putting the cart before the horse and blaming women for lowering wages.

The trend described in the "Underbelly" report continues, as a column in the financial section of the *New York Post* in February 1986 confirmed.[5] Entitled "Lower wages paid to women reduce real average earnings," it showed that real wages had been dropping ever since 1978, and that this was linked to the fact that more women had joined the work force than men.

"Between 1980 and December 1985," said the article, "the number of males in civilian employment rose from 57.2 million to 60.2 million—an increase of 5.2%. In contrast, total female employment rose from 42.1 million in 1980 to 48.0 million in December 1985, an increase of 14%, or about three times the proportionate rise in male employment."

Explaining that the new women's jobs were almost all in the lower-paying service sector, the article concluded that "the reason for the decline in average real hourly earnings as a whole may be the increased presence of females in the employment growth figures. This failure of real wages to remain constant may explain in part the failure of real economic growth in the U.S. in recent years. The rise in employment, about which the administration has congratulated itself, has not produced a proportionate rise in real GNP because so much of the employment increase has been in the form of female employment at substantially below average hourly earnings."

These figures can help one appreciate the tremendous significance of the struggle that women have launched for "comparable worth"—the concept that jobs which require a comparable level of skill, training and intensity should receive equal pay. When applied in areas like public service jobs, where secretaries and typists have always been paid much less than maintenance workers, for instance, it has meant a substantial raise in pay scales for women, that is, for those workers traditionally in the lowest-paid categories.

The struggle for comparable worth has broad implications for labor as a whole, since it is an effort to level wages **upward** by increasing the wages of the lowest-paid at a time when the whole thrust of the capitalist economy is to level wages **downward**.

Changing composition of capital

We want to demonstrate that the more or less constant growth in the reservoir of lower-paid workers is precisely the result of the loss of skilled jobs and growing unemployment as well. It's not possible to understand this problem, let alone adopt a correct trade union and working class strategy, unless one comes to grips with its economic origins.

The bourgeois press is full of the wonders of high technology and the introduction of robots in almost fully automated factories. But they neglect to mention an extremely important element in the economic laws of motion governing capitalist society: robots do not produce surplus value.

As Marx demonstrated long ago, machinery or constant capital is the result of past labor and past surplus value. Profit does not come from machinery itself. It is the labor of a worker, known in Marxist terms as variable capital, that produces surplus value, from which profit is derived. Workers produce a greater value than they receive back in wages, and it is the unpaid portion of their labor that produces surplus value. But a robot is not a worker. A robot is fixed or constant capital, which does not produce profit. Only unpaid human labor produces profit.

With fewer workers and more constant capital, the organic composition of capital changes, resulting in a falling rate of profit. This is an invariable law of the capitalist process of production. It cannot be gotten around.

The more dead or constant capital and the less human or variable capital used in production, the higher the organic composition of capital. This invariably leads to a decline in the rate of profit.

Despite this, the individual capitalists are driven to substitute labor-saving machinery for workers because it gives them a competitive advantage. For a certain period, the capitalist who is able to utilize the new technology and lower the unit cost of his product can actually enjoy a greater profit because the market reflects a generalized cost still based on the old technology. Eventually, however, the new technology itself becomes generalized and the rate of profit falls.

The advantage to a higher composition of constant capital is always temporary. Moreover, it spurs on destructive competition, in which much equipment that could still be socially useful is made prematurely obsolete.

In order to compensate for the falling rate of profit, the owners are forced to increase the volume of profit. This can only be done by further increasing production.

The world steel industry is probably the best example of how the decline in the rate of profit, which results from the changing organic composition of capital, leads to a glut of steel, contributing to another cyclical capitalist crisis.

The decline in the rate of profit leads to a flight of capital to where the rate of exploitation of the workers is higher. This does a lot to explain why the capitalist government is forever pushing a drive for exports in order to escape the diminishing rate of profit in the home market.

The Reagan administration, for example, has strenuously pushed the export drive while at the same time trying to put up high tariff walls, or ban imports, with a variety of weapons including monetary manipulation.

However, the point we want to make is that the modernization campaign here and in other capitalist countries amounts to an intensification of the exploitation of labor, with the introduction of higher and more sophisticated machinery until we reach the robot stage.

Much of the economic literature deals with the displacement of jobs as the result of the introduction of high technology, but it does not deal with the decline in the rate of profit from the long-range point of view. Technology is a double-edged weapon.

Furthermore, automation does not solve the problem of the capitalist contradiction that leads to economic crisis. On the contrary, it exacerbates it precisely because of the decline in the rate of profit.

High technology does not produce high profits. It increases the productivity of labor, but decreases the proportion of labor used in production in relation to the amount of fixed capital. Without labor no amount of high technology can produce surplus value, which is the unpaid portion of labor.

How can there be unpaid labor without laborers in the factories? Robots are dead labor. For the production of surplus value you need living labor.

While this may have little immediate significance from the point of view of profit, it has immense long-term significance.

Decline in trade union strength

The trade unions are the strongest, most formidable and fundamental organs of working class struggle and have a tremendous potential to lead the mass of workers in this country (more than 106 million as of 1985). According to the AFL-CIO study referred to in Chapter 1, "Unions represent over 20 million working men and women in the U.S. Organized labor remains a vital force for progress in this nation. . . ." The union movement has made tremendous strides in the struggle for higher wages and better conditions and has fought over the years for progressive labor and social legislation, notwithstanding the hostility of various U.S. administrations of both big business parties.

However, the report added that "union membership has shown a decline in absolute numbers as well as in percentage terms. The proportion of workers who are eligible to join a union and who in fact belong to a union has fallen from close to 45% to under 28% since 1954; using the measure of percentage of the entire workforce, the decline has been from 35% to under 19%."

Of course, the objective basis for this has been the ravages of two capitalist crises—one in 1974-75 and one which began in early 1979 and, with slight ephemeral upturns, continues to the present day. These crises have been accompanied by an anti-labor offensive which, as we said earlier, was in full swing even before the Reagan victory and became unmistakable with the breaking of the PATCO strike. Those are the objective factors.

However, there is also the subjective factor, the traditional labor relations policy, the collective bargaining approach which is summed up in the AFL-CIO report: "Organized labor believes that each worker is entitled to a fair day's pay for a fair day's work; that pay should include a share in the profits the worker helps to create, and thus unions seek a larger share of those profits than 'market forces' might dictate."

This century-old, vague, ambiguous formula disregards the most basic and fundamental reality of labor relations: that the relations between the employer and the employee, the boss and the worker, have their foundation in the existence of irreconcilable class antagonisms. These antagonisms do not lend themselves to solution by such vague terms as fairness and justice when each class views morality and justice from a different perspective. These different and opposing conceptions are based upon the struggle over the paid and unpaid portions of labor.

This formula, furthermore, ties wages to the vicissitudes of the capitalist market with its ups and downs. The tremendous toll this takes in a capitalist recession is responsible for the long stream of concessions forced on the workers. In the wake of a capitalist crisis, the bosses have a free hand to fix wages to their sales, and to demand higher productivity, which can only reduce the workforce.

In its section dealing with advancing the interests of the workers, the AFL-CIO report suggested that workers "in some bargaining units may not desire to establish a comprehensive set of hard and fast terms and conditions of employment but may nonetheless desire a representative to negotiate minimum guarantees that will serve as a floor for **individual bargaining**, to provide advocacy for individuals, or to seek redress for particular difficulties as they arise. In other units a bargaining approach based on solving problems through arbitration or mediation rather than through ultimate recourse to economic weapons may be most effective." (Our emphasis.)

Of course, even the most militant and aggressive unions have had to resort to mediation and/or arbitration when the situation required it. But coupling this with individual bargaining foreshadows a weakening of collective bargaining, which instead must be strengthened.

As the report further showed, there are about two million workers in unionized plants who are not members of any unions. The weakening of the collective bargaining process as outlined in the above quote will do nothing to bring this large body of workers into the union fold.

There are recommendations in the AFL-CIO report which are helpful and attempt to improve the situation of the unions, but as we have mentioned above it does not go to the gut issues of the problems. Its view of the evolution of work totally ignores the reality of exploitation and the private ownership of the means of production by the bosses.

All the more conspicuous is the absence of any reference to the special exploitation of Black, Latino, Asian, Arab and Native workers, women, lesbians and gay men, disabled and undocumented workers. It is supposed that all are included in the generalizations made in the study, but unless these special oppressions are given special attention, it can only be seen as utter neglect.

A more detailed report on overall union membership, summarized in the *New York Times*[6] showed the shift away from skilled jobs in concrete terms.

The United Steel Workers (USWA) "had 572,000 members as of June 30, about half as many as it had in the 1970s. Membership in the United Auto Workers (UAW) was down 35% to 974,000. The union had more than a million and a half members in the 1970s." The Rubber Workers declined by 33% to 106,000, the report said, down from 158,000 in the 1970s. The International Association of Machinists (IAM) had 520,000 members, a decline of 22% from as late as 1979, when it had 664,000 members, and a decline of 37% from 1969, its peak year with 850,000 members.

Membership in the ILGWU was down to 210,000, a 40% drop from 1977 when it stood at 350,000. Also the International Typographical Union (ITU) had fallen more than 50% in the previous 15 years from 89,000 in 1969 to 38,000 in the first six months of 1985.

By sharp contrast, however, "the Service Employees International Union (SEIU) has undergone a dramatic growth. The union, which had 505,000 members in 1977, had 688,000 members this year."

It is this highly significant shift from the higher paid to the lower paid which is dramatically changing the social composition of the working class, greatly increasing the importance of the so-called ethnic composition of the working class, that is, the number of Black, Latin, Asian, women and other oppressed groups, particularly the millions of undocumented workers. Inadequate attention is paid by the AFL-CIO to this multinational composition of the working class.

It is this aspect of the changing situation of the workers and their unions which has to be given great prominence as the most important significant phenomenon to have emerged from the development of the scientific-technological revolution. This profound change is not only unseating traditional labor relations but has made obsolete the prevailing conceptions and strategic approaches of the official labor leadership of the trade union movement.

Moreover, the bosses are trying to exploit the inertia in the officialdom, especially the top echelons, of the trade unions and take advantage of a lack of bold, truly progressive and militant innovation to put across their own formula for change, which is to deepen dependency and conformity to the will of the bosses and to insist on thoroughgoing cooperation with management.

Prospects for a classwide movement

Up until now when the word movement was used, it could mean either the Black movement, the Latino movement, the civil rights movement, the anti-war movement, the lesbian and gay movement or the women's movement. But the term seldom if ever referred to the working class movement. By and large the progressive movement as a whole was more or less separate from the working class.

Now, however, the change in the social composition of the working class lays the objective basis for a movement of the working class itself, of which these movements will become so many constituent parts.

When we speak of the women's movement or the anti-war movement or the Black movement as part of the working class movement, it doesn't mean they won't have an independent character. Of course they will. But they will be part of the working class movement because it will have come alive as the fundamental class in society which alone can weld these movements together in a genuine anti-capitalist and progressive struggle, a struggle both for democratic rights and for socialism.

The change of consciousness which has so long been delayed could not have come earlier merely as a result of episodic turns in the capitalist cycle. But it is bound to come as the result of deep-seated, profound changes in the social composition of the working class.

The bourgeoisie have initially viewed this trend as a favorable sign for class collaboration. But they will soon become disillusioned.

Notes
1. Marcy, Sam, "The Changed Character of the Working Class."
2. Morehouse, Special Report No. 5.
3. *New York Times*, July 31, 1984.
4. Morehouse, Special Report No. 4.
5. *New York Post*, Feb. 26, 1986.
6. *New York Times*, Oct. 5, 1985.

PART 2

Technology and National Oppression

Chapter 5

Black Labor from Chattel Slavery to Wage Slavery

The scientific-technological revolution has affected and will continue to affect Black workers much more significantly than is commonly acknowledged by the capitalist press. Automation takes even more than its usual toll when oppressed people are concerned. It intensifies racist oppression and increases unemployment among Black people even when a capitalist economic recovery is said to be sharply on the rise, as in 1983-84.

But the impact of the scientific-technological revolution on Black people is not only a recent phenomenon. It has historical roots that go back to the beginnings of the slave trade.

The compass and the slave trade

The speed and momentum with which the scientific-technological revolution has taken off in recent years has tended to shrink into insignificance inventions which exercised a profound influence on developing social relations in the early stages of the capitalist system. Take the compass, which is regarded today as a basic direction-finding device in navigation. It is not a capitalist invention. It is said to have been discovered as early as the year 1100 in China, and may have also been discovered independently in Europe somewhat later; it was used by Arab sailors in the early 13th century.

Its development and perfection over the years became indispensable to world trade. While not invented in a period of capitalist development, the compass and other navigational instrumentation were appropriated from earlier modes of production by capitalist shipping companies at the very crest of the period of colonization, what is called the "age of discovery." It gave a tremendous impulse to world trade and commerce.

But what was the content of this trade? Why is it important in relation to our study here? Because as trade became a world phenomenon, it was essentially an international trade of slaves.

Millions upon millions of Black people were kidnapped, tortured, and brought on slave ships to the vast new continents of the Western Hemisphere.

The slave trade began in the mid-15th century when Spain and Portugal began importing a significant number of Black slaves to their plantations on the Canary and Madeira islands. Most of the very same leading imperialist powers that are today concerned with maintaining the South African regime in the face of the revolutionary mass movement there earlier participated in, promoted and in fact fought ferociously to maintain the slave trade and obtain a monopoly over it.

Modern transnational monopolies differ fundamentally in their economic content from those days, but they still show the same greed and avarice, the utterly unprecedented cruelty and barbarous treatment which characterized the slave trade. This is what lay behind the flourishing of world commerce, and laid the development for what Marx later called the primitive accumulation of capital. The word primitive was not a characterization of the many millions of people captured as slaves. The term primitive was applied to the fiendish method by which the early capitalists accumulated the primary, original capital that was so indispensable for the development of their system of oppression and exploitation. Not only Spain, Portugal, England, France and Holland, but also Denmark, Sweden and Prussia participated, garnering fabulous profits as a result of the slave trade.

The compass was one of the things that made the slave trade possible, but it alone can't be held responsible for the transportation of this vast number of human beings from one continent to another thousands of miles away— away from their homeland and loved ones to a strange new country where the whip and the gun held them at bay. Scandinavian people had made a transoceanic voyage earlier, in the 12th century. They too may have had a compass of a sort, for it is well known that the Vikings undertook long voyages and established settlements in Iceland, Greenland and even Labrador.[1] But these voyages differed fundamentally in that they were oriented toward settlements in the northern part of the world in harmony with the climatic conditions of the Scandinavian countries.

Until the development and perfection of navigational instrumentation such as the compass, the Western world was mainly confined to the Mediterranean and the coastal areas of the Atlantic so far as maritime commerce was concerned. The new era of discovery and colonization opened up the Atlantic for the first time. This could not have been done without the necessary technological improvements in navigational instrumentation as well as in the making of ships.

By 1745 the English inventor Gowin Knight had perfected a method of efficiently magnetizing needles of harder steel. He designed a compass with a single bar needle large enough for a cap resting on the pivot to be screwed into its center. He thus greatly improved the compass.[2] This significantly shortened the time of voyages, increased the safety of the ships and, what is of greater social and political significance, increased the volume of slavery.

As Marx was to write, "It is slavery that gave the colonies their value; it is the colonies that have created world trade, and it is world trade that is the precondition of large-scale industry. Thus slavery is an economic category of the greatest importance."[3]

The contract for supplying slaves to the Spanish colonies was called the Asiento. While British slave traders provided the necessary laborers for their own plantations, Spain contracted with the slave traders of other nations to supply its needs. The first Asiento was granted in 1518 to a Flemish company, and it specified that a certain number of tons (!) of slaves be delivered to the Spanish colonies.[4]

The Portuguese were the first traders to hold the Asiento, but the other rising capitalist powers were not to be outdone. The Dutch broke into this very lucrative form of trade around 1640 and Spain, France and Britain followed soon after.

The war for the Asiento continued until the Treaty of Utrecht (1713) when the English triumphed over their competitors. The English bourgeoisie from then on maintained control of the slave trade through the Royal African Company. This slave trade covered not only the English, French, and Dutch colonies in America and the West Indies but also the vast land of Brazil. It was in this way that such a vast portion of the African people were uprooted and thrown into the vortex of capitalist slavery.

In connection with Holland it should be noted that earlier, in the years 1636-37, the Dutch had engaged in a flourishing trade and development of tulips, for which they are still world-famous today. But that trade attained extraordinary speculative proportions so that at one period just one tulip was valued at thousands of dollars. Eventually the market broke and the Dutch bourgeoisie turned from trafficking in "a thing of matchless beauty" to the slave trade, one of the most odious, foul and certainly the most inhuman forms of commerce ever seen in history. This illustrates with what ease and facility the capitalists can plunge from one area to another in their insatiable appetite for profits, without any regard for human values whatever. The latter are totally irrelevant in the process of capitalist production. Capital simply flows to wherever profits are highest.

The banks and the drug trade

The world slave trade has been superseded by the world drug trade. It has been widely reported that today marijuana, whose cultivation is illegal, has become the single most valuable cash crop in U.S. agriculture. This should not surprise anyone in light of the fact that some of the biggest banks have been fined millions of dollars for laundering money, that is, disguising deposits from the criminal underworld engaged in the sale of not only marijuana but heroin and cocaine. The age of telecommunications has made it possible for the banks and the criminal underworld to work as partners.

The underworld, even if not part of the establishment, can't help but integrate themselves with the banks. They want the interest on their money! Drug busts used to yield amounts in the hundreds of thousands of dollars. This then escalated into the millions. Recently some drug busts have netted loot worth more than a billion dollars! It has escalated because it is so lucrative—like the slave trade. And what is the interest on a billion dollars? At just 6%, it comes to sixty million dollars. The banks have to get involved in the drug trade, because it is a lucrative source of deposits which are then loaned out at a profit.

The summits of high finance are involved. Among the banks caught red-handed have been Bank of America, the biggest in the country, and the First Boston Corporation. Bank of America was fined $4.75 million and First Boston half a million. Chase Manhattan, Manufacturers Hanover Trust, Chemical, Crocker National and Irving Trust Company have had to pay civil penalties ranging from $210,000 to $360,000 for reported violations.[5] What are they hiding? The deposit of profits from the criminal underworld engaged in destructive drug trafficking which takes an especially great toll in the oppressed communities. Legality and illegality coexist under the capitalist system and always have. Even after the slave trade was outlawed, it continued despite harsh penalties, as does the drug trade.

At a time when the banks are so heavily involved in unrecoverable loans worth hundreds of billions of dollars in connection with the indebtedness of oppressed countries, how many would not resort to this most modern and technologically advanced artifice to support their credit positions?

The observations made over a century ago by a certain T.J. Dunning, and quoted by Marx in *Capital*, ring all too familiar today: "With adequate profit, capital is very bold. A certain 10% will ensure its employment anywhere; 20% certain will produce eagerness; 50%, positive audacity; 100% will make it ready to trample all human laws; 300%, and there is not a crime at which it will scruple, nor a risk it will not run, even to the chance of its owner being hanged. If turbulence and strife will bring a profit, it will freely encourage both. Smuggling and the slave-trade have amply proved all that is here stated."[6]

The invention of the cotton gin

While the compass as a technological device in the field of navigation was appropriated by the developing bourgeoisie from an earlier mode of production dating back many hundreds of years, the invention of the cotton gin in 1793 belonged strictly to the era of capitalist development. Its invention was called forth by the development of capitalist trade and commerce. Its influence on slavery was stupendous.

A great deal has been written about Eli Whitney as the inventor of the cotton gin and as a great scientist, which he certainly was. However, according to some accounts,[7] the first gin made in Mississippi was constructed on the basis of a crude drawing by a skilled slave. This was probably not very unusual in light of the fact that even among the first slaves brought to this country from Africa, many were skilled craftsmen. Also in both the South and the North there were skilled free Blacks. Since the slaves were never recognized in law as persons, the slave owners could appropriate their property as well as any inventions they might conceive of.

The cotton gin has often been described as the very soul of simplicity. However, it should be borne in mind that cotton has been spun, woven and dyed from the earliest times. Cotton formed the staple clothing of India, Egypt and China. Hundreds of years before the Christian era, cotton textiles were woven in India with matchless skill and their use spread to the Mediterranean countries. In the first century, traders brought fine muslin and calico to Italy and Spain. The Arabs introduced the cultivation of cotton into Spain in the 9th century. By the 17th century, the East India Company was bringing rare fabrics from India.

Before the arrival of the Europeans in the Americas, cotton was skillfully spun there and woven into fine garments and dyed tapestries. Fabrics were found in Peruvian tombs that even belonged to pre-Inca cultures. Cotton was first planted by the Europeans in Virginia's Jamestown Colony in 1607.

The so-called Cotton Belt in the U.S., where cotton has historically been the main cash crop (now marijuana is!), extends through North Carolina, South Carolina, Georgia, Alabama, Mississippi, west Tennessee, east Arkansas, Louisiana, east Texas, and south Oklahoma, and also in smaller areas of southeast Missouri, southwest Kentucky, north Florida, and southeast Virginia. But prior to the invention of the cotton gin, cotton production was at a very low level. It was almost insignificant in the prevailing Southern economy. The plantation system rested mainly on tobacco and to a lesser extent on rice and indigo.

Rarely has an important technological development taken place which was as simple as the cotton gin. It separated the seeds from the cotton through a process using a cylinder with bent spikes sharpened to form hooks. They were set in a ring and revolved through slots in a bar. The teeth pulled away the lint, which was then cleaned from the teeth by brushes. A hand crank operated the whole machine.

What did this machine accomplish? As Eli Whitney himself explained in a letter, "The machine makes the labor 50 times less without throwing any class of people out of business."[8] Of course, the slave economy was not characterized by unemployment, unlike wage slavery.

The cotton gin tremendously increased the productivity of Black slave labor on the plantations. The figures in cotton crop production speak for themselves. In 1790, before the use of the cotton gin, the cotton crop of the U.S. amounted to 1.5 million pounds. By 1800 it had risen to 35 million pounds. By 1810 it had soared to 85 million pounds and by 1860 it reached the astonishing sum of 2 billion pounds.

The introduction of the cotton gin thus brought about a profound social revolution. A machine that could increase the productivity of labor 50 times was nothing less than sensational. It thoroughly revolutionized Southern agriculture as well as Northern production methods.

Furthermore, it was in response to the tremendous social transformation evoked by the Industrial Revolution in England, which had brought about a skyrocketing demand for cotton and a sharp price increase. As Marx explained it in broader terms, "A radical change in the mode of production in one sphere of industry involves a similar change in other spheres. This happens at first in such branches of industry as are connected together by separate phases of a process, and yet are isolated by the social division of labor, in such a way, that each of them produces an independent commodity. Thus spinning by machinery made weaving by machinery a necessity, and both together made the mechanical and chemical revolution that took place in bleaching, printing, and dyeing, imperative. So too, on the other hand, the revolution in cotton-spinning called forth the invention of the gin, for separating the seeds from the cotton fiber; it was only by means of this invention, that the production of cotton became possible on the enormous scale at present required."[9]

But how did it affect slavery itself, this "peculiar institution" as it was called at the time? Did the sensational, spectacular development in technology retard slavery or expand it?

From the time school children attend their earliest classes they are taught about the wonders of modern science and what a liberating influence it has. Did the cotton gin at the time help to weaken slavery, as the general conceptions cultivated and promoted by the bourgeoisie maintain? As we shall see, it strengthened slavery. And this happened at a time when it appeared (although it was only appearances) that slavery was in a decline.

Here it is necessary to look at the currents of thought which gave political expression to this phenomenon. For instance, the Continental Congress of 1774 proposed that the practice of importing slaves be stopped. Rhode Island and Connecticut passed laws providing that all chattel slaves brought within their respective provinces be freed, and Delaware prohibited the importation of bondsmen in 1776. Later, Virginia, South Carolina, Georgia, North Carolina and Maryland all forbade the importation of slaves.

The slave trade itself, of course, was finally prohibited in the U.S. more than a decade after the introduction of the cotton gin, in 1808. But it should not be forgotten that the Constitutional Convention of 1788 wrote a clause into the Constitution making it impossible as a matter of federal law to abolish the slave trade on a national basis before 1808.

The demise of the slave trade has to be viewed in the light of class interests, first of the slavocracy itself. Why would they as slaveowners be interested in abolishing it? Why, for instance, would George Mason of Virginia, himself a slave owner and supporter of slavery, condemn the slave trade as "diabolical itself and disgraceful to mankind"?[10]

Only by piercing the veil of capitalist hypocrisy, only by going behind the political rhetoric and seeking out the materialist interests of any given class, only by applying the materialist interpretation of history and analyzing social and political phenomena in terms of class interests, can we understand the politics, the social and political values. Thus the basic reason behind abolishing the importation of slaves even in the above-named Southern states and castigating the trade as a "disgrace to mankind" was the fact that there had been a huge influx of slaves. Like the excessive influx of any commodity governed by the law of supply and demand, this cheapened the price of a slave. The reasons behind it were economic in origin, masked in moralistic phraseology.

A surplus of slaves in some of the Southern states motivated the agitation against further importation. Most of this agitation, it should be noted, was before the use of the cotton gin really took off on a mass scale, producing unprecedented profits.

But there was also opposition to the slave trade motivated by an entirely different set of circumstances. This was a thoroughgoing revolutionary development which is highly obscured in U.S. history, particularly as it relates to the early struggles of the Black people before the Civil War. This revolutionary development fired the imagination of the enslaved Black people in this country and frightened the ruling class, both North and South.

The Haitian Revolution and U.S. slave revolts

This inspiring event was the successful revolution in Haiti led by its famous hero, Toussaint L'Ouverture. This great revolutionary development overthrew French colonial rule and then defeated massive British, Spanish and French interventionist forces in one of history's really brilliant political and military upsets. Unfortunately, the significance of this great revolutionary development has been obscured and dimmed in this century, especially over the past few decades, by the existence of the U.S.-supported Duvalier dictatorship over the Haitian people. Now that the Haitian masses are once again rising to shape their own destiny, the significance of the Haitian Revolution is sure to be rehabilitated.

Both in France and here in the U.S., the master class referred to the Haitian revolutionaries as "Black Jacobins," after the most radical and determined party in the French Revolution which had helped to inspire the Haitian Revolution. The Jacobins had attempted to go beyond the confines of the emerging capitalist system in France.

The Haitian Revolution of 1791-1803 established the first republic in the vast colonized area of the Caribbean and Latin America. But it remained isolated. It wasn't until this century that the Mexican Revolution, the brilliant achievements of the Cuban Revolution, the developing revolution in Nicaragua, and the many national liberation efforts throughout the Western Hemisphere began the long-delayed overthrow of imperialist domination in this hemisphere. This struggle has yet to come to completion and finish the processes begun by the great revolution in Haiti.

The American Revolution itself had unloosed a progressive current against slavery as part and parcel of the independence struggle. Genuine revolutionaries like Thomas Paine and others, unlike many among the "founding fathers," opposed slavery from the viewpoint of real freedom of the people and were not beholden to either the Northern industrialists or the Southern slavocracy.

But the most basic reason why some slave owners and others among the growing bourgeoisie felt the need for restraint on the importation of slaves and even the elimination of slavery was fear of domestic insurrection. This important motivating factor behind the opposition to slavery has not been given the attention it rates. For many, many decades the heroic slave insurrections were completely minimized and given scant attention.

The insurrections given the most detailed accounts in modern literature were those of Gabriel in Virginia (1800), Denmark Vesey in Charlestown, S.C. (1822), and most famous, that of Nat Turner in South Hampton County, Virginia (1831).[11]

However, a great many insurrections took place which are only beginning to be taken note of. The Civil War itself demonstrated many instances of insurrections by the Black people. The Black masses under slavery were not the passive, docile force imagined by bourgeois historiography, especially in the literature predating the mass movement of Black people in this century.

Black rebellions go back in history to the very beginnings of slavery in this country. As early as 1687, "one year previous to the Glorious Revolution in the mother country," the revolution in England that consolidated the power of the bourgeoisie as against the old feudal aristocracy, there was "widespread revolt throughout the colonies and at a time when the Negro population of the Old Dominion was about equal to that of whites. . . . That was the attempted insurrection in Northern Neck."[12] All were executed when the plot was discovered and the revolt was crushed.

How interesting, in light of present-day developments in South Africa, that the Virginia Council placed a ban on public funerals for the dead slaves in fear that they would bring out mass demonstrations and might even provoke another rebellion!

One thing to remember in connection with the early slave insurrections is that they were influenced politically by the English Revolution and, much more profoundly, by the French Revolution. The great revolutions of this century (especially in Russia, China, Cuba, Viet Nam, and Angola and now the emerging revolutionary struggle in South Africa) have also had the most profound effect among the exploited and oppressed masses everywhere.

The spectacular success of the cotton gin in raising the productivity of labor of the slaves tremendously strengthened the South, strengthened slavery and impelled the slaveholders to become not only more aggressive and bellicose but, far more important, more expansionist. Slavery drove into the Southwest and everywhere it could in order to expand its plantations and garner in unprecedented profits. Cotton production was extensive in character, appropriating more and more land, rather than intensively applying mechanical devices. It drove the slaves harder and harder, often beyond endurance.

But the very invention which had become such a tremendous advantage to the Southern planters, like all social phenomena, soon began to develop one of the sharpest social contradictions which ultimately would undo the slavocracy altogether.

Slavery vs. capitalist production

The South was a slavocracy based on an ancient mode of production within the geographical confines of a new world social order, the bourgeois social order with its own mode of capitalist production. One of the fundamental differences between the bourgeois mode and older modes of production so eloquently brought out in the *Communist Manifesto* is that "The bourgeoisie cannot exist without constantly revolutionizing the instruments of production and thereby the relations of production, and with them the whole relations of society." [13]

How does this stack up with the Southern slavocracy? Marx continued, "Conservation of the old modes of production in unaltered form was . . . the first condition of existence for all earlier industrial classes." The South tried to retain the old slavocracy not only in unaltered form but in extreme rigidity. It was therefore on a collision course with the new bourgeois order, with the process of capitalist production and its tremendous growth in the North.

Another and more flagrant contradiction was that one of the fundamental characteristics of the capitalist mode of production is wage slavery, which means a free proletarian, that is, a worker free to sell his or her labor on the capitalist market. Capitalist production and the extraction of surplus value in the interest of further capitalist accumulation is virtually impossible without a free working class, free to be exploited and oppressed, free to be unemployed. Chattel slavery was thus thoroughly incompatible with wage slavery.

Slavery as an economic institution has everywhere proved itself uneconomical. This is especially true when it depends on one great crop such as cotton, with diminishing reliance on sugar, rice and other products. The South was turning into a monocultural economy.

Overall, the spectacular leap in technology on which the Southern planters depended so heavily to maintain slavery was only one of many scientific and technological developments in an era which was rapidly turning them out in greater and greater numbers. In this respect the South was falling far behind the North.

The North was making all the great strides in science and technology. It built up great universities which became centers for basic research. Whatever prominence the South had had in science in the earlier days, it was losing to the North. Seen in terms of the contemporary struggle in technology of the U.S. against Japan and Western Europe, the South was steadily losing ground to the North in what we would call today the technological race.

As a competing form of economic and social system compared to the social system based on capitalist production, slavery was hopelessly out of place and had no chance, save by the use of sheer force. Slavery was static, fixed and extremely rigid in its form of production. It was also characterized by the most outlandish forms of cruelty and brutality. The capitalist system, on the other hand, while certainly not characterized by either compassion or humanity, was nevertheless "revolutionizing" its means of production, that is, it was advancing science and technology. The change from chattel slavery to wage slavery was a profoundly revolutionary change, a tremendous social transformation. But historically it constituted a change in the form of exploitation, not its abolition.

Thus we see that while the first phase of the scientific-technological revolution brought fabulous profits to the South and gave it the power to expand, it ultimately undid slavery. Just as technological change undermined the Southern slavocracy, so will it make obsolete the present industrial-financial plutocracy with its system of wage slavery.

Black scientists and inventors

It is beyond the province of this study to give an accounting of the many scientific inventions made, particularly during the last half of this century. The modern epoch in which the bourgeois system of production has predominated has been abundant in scientists and inventors whose contributions have laid the material foundation for present-day society.

However, there has been a systematic attempt in the U.S. to omit the very significant contributions of Black scientists. Popular science books available to the public contain the names of only a small number of Black inventors and scientists.

There are 14 Black scientists who are acknowledged to have made outstanding contributions to science, yet the *Encyclopedia Britannica* (1980 edition) lists only four. Conspicuously absent is Norbert Rilleux (1806-1894). He is one of three Black scientists who actually revolutionized an industry. In Rilleux's case it was sugar refining. By inventing the vacuum-pan evaporator, he transformed the sugar industry of the world.

That his name could be forgotten in a country which produces and consumes more refined sugar per capita than any other is hard to conceive of except on the basis of flagrant racist prejudice.

Until 1846, sugar cane juice was transformed into sugar by a very primitive, costly and slow process. Rilleux's invention replaced the manual operation with a mechanical one. As Louis Haber tells us in his *Black Pioneers of Science and Invention*,[14] slaves had formerly transferred the sugar cane juice from one boiling kettle to another by means of long ladles. With Rilleux's device, a single worker could operate the completely enclosed machine through outside valves. It was Rilleux and George Washington Carver (1860-1943) who rescued the South from being transformed into a hopelessly backward agricultural adjunct to the North, similar to the role played by the southern part of Italy until very recently.

Carver, however, is much too well known throughout the world for his reputation to be obscured. It was Carver's work in soil improvement and the diversification of crops which made him famous. He discovered hundreds of uses for the peanut, the sweet potato and the soybean and thus stimulated the culture of these important crops. He also derived many products from cotton wastes and extracted blue, purple and red pigments from local clay.

Many industries sprang up as a result of the use of peanut products. It helped to stimulate the Southern economy to the extent that many farmers found it more profitable to engage in the production of peanuts than tobacco.

Carver also demonstrated that from the pecan, which grew well in the South, could be extracted 75 different products. When there was an overproduction of cotton, Carver showed how it could be used to make insulating board, paper, rugs, cordage and even paving blocks for highways.

Carver's achievements were perhaps best summarized by President Franklin D. Roosevelt, who said upon his death: "The world of science has lost one of its most eminent figures and the race from which he sprang, an outstanding member. . . . The versatility of his genius and achievements in diverse branches of the arts and sciences were truly amazing. All mankind are the beneficiaries of his discoveries in the field of agricultural chemistry. The things which he achieved in the face of early handicaps will for all time afford an inspiring example to use everywhere."[15]

A third great Black scientist who transformed and revolutionized an entire industry was Jan Matzeliger (1852-1889). Although much less known than his two eminent fellow scientists, he invented what at the time seemed an impossible feat—a machine which would mass-produce shoes. Matzeliger accomplished for the shoe industry what Eli Whitney's gin did for the cotton industry of the South.

While it's true there were a number of machines in use in the shoemaking industry around the time of Matzeliger's invention, none seemed to have been able to connect the upper to the sole of the shoe. It was believed such a thing could not be done.

Matzeliger's machine did it. It could turn out a complete shoe. At first the machine made a record run of 75 pairs of women's shoes in one day. Later Matzeliger's machine made as many as 700 pairs of shoes a day. It also reduced the cost of shoes by half and was soon being applied on a worldwide scale.

In industry there were at least four more Black scientists who made very significant contributions to the development of science and technology but are little known. One was the man who invented the automatic lubrication of machinery, Elijah McCoy (1844-1929), whose work gave rise to the expression "the real McCoy." Before his time a machine had to be stopped in order to be lubricated.

Then there was Granville T. Woods (1856-1910), who developed so many electrical inventions that he was known as the Black Edison. There was also Lewis H. Latimer (1848-1928) who advanced electric lighting and Garrett A. Morgan (1877-1963) who invented the traffic light.

In this century a number of Black scientists have made outstanding contributions in the field of health and medicine. Charles R. Drew perfected techniques to preserve blood plasma which made possible the use of blood banks. Percy L. Julian developed synthetic cortisone which, among other applications, is helpful in combating the pain of arthritis. Lloyd A. Hall found ways to sterilize foods and medical supplies. Ernest E. Just became a leading authority on cell physiology. Louis T. Wright made advances in critical antibiotic research and Daniel Hale Williams performed the first open heart surgery.

There was, however, one early Black scientist whose special importance, aside from his inventive genius, was in the field of political struggle against oppression and for equality: Benjamin Banneker (1731-1806). In most texts he is described as the surveyor who laid out the city of Washington. But he was much more than that.

Banneker was a scientist, astronomer, mathematician, clockmaker and surveyor. Earlier we alluded to Samuel Slater, the Englishman who invented a textile machine and who, when prohibited from bringing his plans for the machine to this country, memorized the blueprints and then reconstructed the machine from memory. Benjamin Banneker was able to lay out the city of Washington after memorizing much more detailed plans to which he had had only limited access as an assistant.

Originally a young Frenchman had been given the job of planning and laying out the capital. Banneker was one of his three assistants. The young Frenchman got into a dispute with Thomas Jefferson and as a result took his plans and left for France, leaving Jefferson in the lurch. Banneker stepped forward and volunteered to do the job on the basis of what he retained in his memory. That's how the city was finally laid out.

Banneker made the first clock ever built in the United States. He built it entirely of wood and carved each gear by hand. The clock kept perfect time and people from all over the country came to see it. Banneker should also be remembered for the almanac he prepared in 1792 and each year thereafter for ten years.

What is politically significant in Banneker's history is that he was the only contemporary of Thomas Jefferson to challenge him on the issue of equality. Every school child is taught that Thomas Jefferson wrote the Declaration of Independence which contained this famous sentence: "We hold these truths to be self evident, that all men are created equal, that they are endowed by their Creator with certain inalienable rights, that among these are life, liberty and the pursuit of happiness."

But Jefferson was also a wealthy slave owner, and even though he sold off all his slaves toward the end of his life his concept of equality did not extend to Black people. He had also written that "the Blacks are inferior to the whites in the endowment both of body and mind." This was no chance statement. The collection of Jefferson's works demonstrates that these sentiments appeared widely in his writings.

Even though the 18th century became known in history as the Enlightenment, especially the years following the revolutions in the U.S. and France, Jefferson held to his reactionary, racist view of Black people. None of the outstanding leaders at the time directly took Jefferson to task for the flagrant contradiction between the florid language he used in the Declaration of Independence and the ugly practice of slavery, which in fact was validated in the Constitution.

It remained for Banneker to use his almanac for this purpose. He attached to it an eleven-page handwritten letter that systematically took apart Jefferson's lofty proclamation of inalienable rights while at the same time condoning the vicious practice of slavery. This was one of the few, perhaps the only, direct attacks on Jefferson, the man who to this day along with Andrew Jackson is honored by the Democratic capitalist politicians at their annual Jefferson-Jackson Day dinners as a symbol of democracy and freedom.

Banneker's letter to Jefferson did oblige the latter to back off somewhat. In a letter dated August 30, 1791, Jefferson thanked Banneker: "I can add with truth that nobody wishes more ardently to see a good system commence for raising the condition both of their [Black people's—S.M.] body and mind to what it ought to be. . . . I do see such proofs that you exhibit that nature has given to our Black brethren, talents equal to those of the other colors of men and that the appearance of the want of them is owing merely to degraded condition of their existence both in Africa and in America."

Jefferson said he was taking the liberty of sending Banneker's almanac to the French Academy of Sciences because he considered it a document "to which your whole color has a right for their justification against the doubts which have been entertained of them." It is only because of Banneker's struggle for equality and against oppression that Jefferson, who held such an eminent position in U.S. history as a liberal, was forced to retreat somewhat from his racist views.

By way of acknowledgment, it should be said that Louis Haber in his book *Black Pioneers of Science and Invention* has done as much to popularize what was so little known about the achievements of Black scientists as Paul D. DeKruif did for biologists more than a half century ago in his lucid exposition, *Microbe Hunters.*

The individual scientist in the modern era of the scientific-technological revolution faces a vastly different world than the one in which Banneker or even Thomas Edison at a later date lived and worked. The role of the individual scientist has been diminished by the emergence of capitalist collectivism in the big business laboratory. Today's vast laboratory complexes are organized and controlled by the mighty corporate giants and employ thousands of scientists. The giant corporations compel all scientific personnel to sign contracts that any inventions they may develop in the course of their work are the property of the company.

Superimposed on them is a labyrinth of laboratories directly controlled by the Pentagon. The great universities of today are intimate collaborators of the Pentagon and few have real independence as to how to allocate their scientific investigations.

One of the truly important scientific inventions of modern times was the transistor. True to the age in which we live, it was developed in the laboratories of Bell Telephone Company in 1948 by American physicists John Bardeen and Walter H. Brattain. How many hundreds of scientific workers helped lay the basis for it is not really taken into account.

When mass layoffs take place, such as we've described with AT&T, what happens to the laid-off scientific personnel? How does it affect the pursuit of their scientific career? In that highly significant layoff, no breakdown was given as to how it affected Black scientific workers, women or other oppressed people. There's not a word as to whether affirmative action has been a factor in the employment of Black, Latin, Asian, Native, Arab and women workers, or whether the layoffs took place in accordance with affirmative action guidelines.

The Third World brain drain

The scientific-technological revolution has had a deleterious effect on Third World scientific personnel and the development of science and inventions. Immediately after the Second World War the U.S. embarked on a vast campaign to pirate both the technology and the scientific personnel of the other imperialist countries. It also started to drain the budding development of science and technology in the oppressed countries.

With respect to the imperialist countries, it is well known how right after the war the U.S. brought captured German scientific personnel here to work on rockets and space flight. But it wasn't only from Germany. The British government under Labor Prime Minister Harold Wilson finally restricted what was later called the brain drain by an agreement that limited U.S. pirating of scientists, at least from that area.

While U.S. government policy has been to restrict immigration and imprison and deport so-called illegal, undocumented workers, it has at the same time enticed Third World scientists to the U.S. On the one hand, imperialist policy through a variety of foundations like those endowed by the Fords, Rockefellers and others seems to be constantly exhorting the oppressed countries to modernize, to become innovative and inventive and thereby aid their industrial and technological development. But the truth is that every chance they get to entice Third World scientists to the U.S., they do so, in complete contradiction to the proclaimed policy. They not only extend the stay of visiting students and professors and encourage them to become citizens but also offer them various monetary inducements.

It is one thing to defend the democratic right of individuals to choose their own domicile. It is another matter if this is part and parcel of a policy of monopoly capitalism to pillage and plunder the resources of Third World countries.

The scientific personnel of less developed countries are in many respects their most precious resource. The brain-drain aspect of the scientific-technological revolution has enhanced, not diminished, U.S. imperialism's intense exploitation of the oppressed people.

Black labor today

Extrapolating from the population figures provided in the 1986 annual report of the National Urban League on the "State of Black America," there are about 28 million Black people in the United States. That's larger than most African countries and larger than most middle-sized countries represented in the United Nations.

By always referring to Black people as a minority, the bourgeois press obscures the class significance of the Black population, which is overwhelmingly working class and which therefore, especially when taken together with the Latin, Asian and Native population, adds a very significant dimension to the whole character of the working class here.

To regard the Black struggle strictly from the viewpoint of minority-majority is to lose much of its profound social and political implications. What should interest working class students of the Black struggle, however, is that even these figures, which are probably understated, disclose a social viability which has strong revolutionary potentialities given the conditions we believe are developing that will give a fundamentally altered social composition to the working class.

To understand the current state of Black labor in the United States, it is necessary to look first at the mass migration of Black people to the North which took on momentum early in the 20th century and reached considerable proportions at the end of the First World War. Mass production industries in the U.S. like auto (especially Ford) and steel were in a period of high capitalist development. When this culminated in the First World War it opened the gates of some industries and fields of economic endeavor to Black labor, notwithstanding rank discrimination and entrenched racial barriers.

These were not relaxed. Instead artificial classifications were created so that Black workers doing almost exactly the same work as whites got far lower wages. Nor were barriers lifted in the skilled trades and AFL craft unions. These were as rigidly racist in their approach as they had been before the First World War. But Black labor continually found ways to gain skills and get skilled jobs despite government, employer and union racial discrimination.

It should always be borne in mind that even the first boatloads of slaves who arrived in this country from Africa brought with them useful skills which were developed even in slave times. In cities like New York and Philadelphia, before the mass migrations from Europe started, there were a considerable number of Black workers in industry who had developed skills. But as more and more white labor from Europe became available, Black workers began to be relentlessly driven out of industry.

These mass migrations from Europe undermined whatever leverage the Black workers might have had in industry notwithstanding discrimination. Things got more and more difficult for them.

Capitalism as the involuntary promoter of the development of the working class also caused the mass migration of Black agricultural workers from the South to the North. Notwithstanding the racial barrier or the unemployment as a consequence of the capitalist economic cycle, more and more Black workers got into Northern industry even as the pool of Black unemployed grew.

That most of the central cities of the North and now some in the South have a majority or a very large minority of Black people is objectively due to the transformation of capitalist industry with the First and Second World Wars. World War II in particular was a much longer war for the U.S. and entailed the construction of many defense facilities. In fact, the entire U.S. industrial apparatus was converted for war purposes and for the first time full employment became an artificial phenomenon dependent on war spending.

These two objective factors—the First and Second World Wars—also found an echo beginning in 1950 with the Korean War. In the early 1950s and again during the Viet Nam War employment was artificially propped up by the continuing growth of the defense industries.

If today in cities like Detroit, Chicago, Newark, Philadelphia, New York, Atlanta, Memphis and Birmingham there are large Black populations with some political power, it is not due to any attempt by the ruling class to ameliorate the condition of Black workers or to lighten the burden of discrimination. Rather it comes as a result of objective development arising out of the organic functioning of the capitalist system and the inevitability of imperialist wars and military interventions abroad. This is not to say that the whole industrial structure of the U.S. is due entirely to imperialist wars, but without them it is difficult to conceive how there could have been such a rapid social transformation in the condition of Black and also white workers.

The mass migration from the South—and back to the South, especially during times of unemployment—is among the objective factors affecting the development of Black labor. The subjective factors arise from the freedom struggle, especially the struggle of the 1960s.

The Black freedom struggle

It is utterly impossible to understand the contemporary role of Black workers in this country and particularly their situation in the trade union movement without considering them in a broader political framework. A study of

Black labor, especially over the last 25 years, that omitted the general political struggle, the freedom struggle of the Black people as a whole, would make for a very constricted and even distorted view of both the great achievements of Black workers in the trade union movement and the equally great if not greater drawbacks of their situation.

Racism has permeated every layer of capitalist society; the trade union movement from its earliest times up to the present has been permeated with chauvinism and vicious discriminatory practices. The trade unions are the most formidable working class organizations in the country. Aside from temporary retreats and taking into account the long duration of the political reaction, they are bound to become organs of the great struggles for emancipation from both racist oppression and capitalist class exploitation.

But all of this has to be considered in the broader arena of the overall political struggle of Black people, in which the trade unions have certainly been a significant part, but only a part. In reality, what happens there is a reflection of what is going on in the Black struggle as a whole. The great battles of the 1960s and 1970s in particular must be considered in evaluating and analyzing how this reflected itself in the unions.

Just to take one example out of many: In April 1969, some 500 Black workers shut down production at the Ford plant in Mahwah, New Jersey, for several days. The workers walked out because a foreman called one of the workers a "Black bastard." Although the official UAW leadership urged the workers to return to their jobs, they nevertheless stayed out until the foreman was ousted from the plant. This was the famous so-called wildcat strike at Mahwah organized by the United Black Brothers, and it represented a significant victory for all the workers.

If this significant victory for the UAW at that period is seen only in the trade union framework, it could present an oddity. But when seen in the larger framework of the overall Black political struggle, one gets a far truer measure of its significance for the local struggle as well as nationally.

There were other significant developments in the UAW that came on the heels of the great 1967 rebellion in Detroit and ushered in a series of electoral victories for the Black workers in the UAW. "Suddenly the UAW leadership stopped the practice of mobilizing opposition to Black candidates in local elections. Within a few months after the formation of the League of Revolutionary Black Workers, Black workers were elected as presidents of Local 900 (Ford's Wayne plant), Local 47 (Chrysler Detroit Forge), Local 961 (Chrysler's Eldron Gear), Local 7 (Chrysler), Local 51 (Plymouth), and even Local 1248 (Chrysler Mopar), where only 20% of the plant's 989 workers were Black. A Black was elected for the first time as vice-president of Briggs Local 21. ..."[16]

Before the Mahwah struggle took place, there were a considerable number of political rebellions and insurrections of Black people. There was the Harlem rebellion, followed by Watts, Newark, and Cleveland, to name only a few, and of course the largest of the mass insurrections took place in Detroit. Following the assassination of Martin Luther King in 1968 there were a total of more than 500 rebellions throughout the whole country.

How then can the struggles of Black workers for equality be seen as strictly trade union struggles? Few if any of the very significant gains made by Black workers could have been attained without the so-called outside struggle, that is, the general political struggle put up by Black people. That was the real catalyst, the basic generator for the trade union gains, many of which were not only vital but indispensable, considering the long and difficult task to attain equality which still goes on.

What is said about the Black struggle applies equally and to some extent even more to the Latin struggle, the women's struggle and the gay and lesbian struggle. Any gains made in the unions must be related to the broader struggles which generated them. It would of course be fruitful to speculate on how different it could have been had the struggles been initiated by the trade union movement rather than being forced upon it. But this is the music of the future, not of the past.

There are about 110 million workers in the U.S. today. In the mid-1980s, only about 17.3 million belonged to unions, as we've discussed earlier. However, there can be no doubt that the union movement will become the fundamental lever for working class struggle. The anti-labor offensive which has been sweeping the country for several years is bound to produce one of the truly great upsurges of the working class, and this time the union movement will not be in the rearguard but in the vanguard of the struggle as regards Black, Latino, Asian, and Native people, women and lesbians and gay men.

The tardiness of the working class response to the offensive of the ruling class in the face of such profound political and social reaction can be explained in part by the lack of a mass political party of the working class. The response from the working class, both organized and unorganized, is likely to come as the result of spontaneous outbreaks which will take the form of trade unionism but not necessarily in the way the trade union officialdom presides over the union movement. What more concrete form it will take we have to leave for events themselves to reveal.

Suffice it to say that the very intensity of the political reaction, generated by the Reagan administration and prepared earlier by the Carter administration and its predecessors, has created the conditions for a tumultuous social upheaval, not a controlled one that could be easily manipulated by contemporary bourgeois politicians and the trade union bureaucracy. The very tardiness in preparing a party of the working class, which in Europe and other areas has taken generations to build up, makes inevitable that the pent-up rage at the oppression and exploitation endured by all strata of the working class will break out in another form. It would seem to emanate most easily from the workplace and from the vast pool of unemployed. The special oppression of women, Black, Latin, Asian, Arab and Native workers will make them a magnet for one another.

A former science adviser to Reagan in late 1985 told a Cable News Network (CNN) interviewer that "unemployment in Western Europe constitutes the greatest danger to Western civilization." Of course, it's true! But not only in Europe. The capitalist "recovery" here in the U.S. has been taking place amidst some 15 million unemployed, if comprehensive calculations are made. Social peace cannot be maintained on such an explosive material base.

The impact of high tech on Black postal workers

In attempting to evaluate the impact of the scientific-technological revolution on Black workers as well as other oppressed people, it is best to avoid focusing our analysis on a narrow sector of industry. Also, while the influence of high tech has been most profound in industries such as auto, electric and steel, we have already dealt with these areas in some measure.

We are also deliberately avoiding areas where racist or sexist discrimination is most pronounced, or where Black, Latin and women workers still constitute only a very small portion of the workforce. A broad sector of the economy, where there are a significant number of Black, Latin and women workers, is more appropriate for this study.

By taking a sector of the economy where so-called optimum conditions prevail, where racist and sexist oppression is generally regarded as less significant than in other areas, we are better able to illustrate our theme, namely, that high tech results in low-wage jobs and unemployment in all sectors of the economy. This explains why we have chosen what seems like an unlikely area, the U.S. Postal Service, for this study. Furthermore it is probably the oldest service industry in the country, being created around the time of the U.S. Constitution in 1789.

Though racism may be a less significant factor in the Postal Service than in some other areas, nevertheless this is the current situation for Black postal workers:

"Blacks appear to be concentrated in less future-oriented Postal Service jobs. When racial concentration versus dispersal of employees in the Postal Service is analyzed, Blacks appear to be concentrated in the lower range and low-paying jobs (levels 1-6). In contrast, in grade levels 7 to 38, 90% of the postal employees are non-minority. Thus the mode of substitution in this case is by a targeted racial distribution in which Blacks are concentrated in the jobs most likely to be affected by technology, particularly the nine-digit zip code, automated mail processing and flat sorting technology and the electronic message systems."[17] The same is true for Latin and other oppressed people.

During the depths of the Great Depression, work at the post office was considered the best and most secure job for anybody from a working class family. Even today, assuming there are openings, it probably offers more job security for a young person from a working class family than other areas. However, a great transformation is underway here too, although it is not publicly recognized.

In 1970, during the Nixon administration, Congress enacted the Postal Reorganization Act (PRA). With this new law the government took decisive steps that were to have far-reaching significance for many millions of workers. For the postal workers it began a chain of developments concerning the dispatching, processing and delivery of mail which ultimately resulted in a loss of almost 100,000 jobs as of 1983.

The PRA was the first early warning of what has become a virtual daily phenomenon, the so-called deregulation of industry, whose principal aim and function, despite claims of modernization by the ruling class, is to ditch restraining and protective labor legislation and to get into private hands anything they feel can be profitable.

The PRA made a so-called independent agency of the Postal Service, which had been regarded as a full-fledged arm of the government with representation in the Cabinet since way back in 1828. The act reduced the status of the post office and turned it into an agency of the executive branch with an eleven-person board of governors, nine of them appointed by the President with the approval of the Senate, and a Postmaster General who is responsible to the President.

The whole idea was to gradually shrink the vast and complex network of postal services, introduce a series of technological innovations and put it on a so-called business basis. The income and outgo of funds were to be equalized and eventually a net surplus was to be produced in the same way as in private industry.

What has really happened since the PRA went into effect?

Despite the decline in the number of postal workers from 756,000 in 1970 to 660,000 in 1983, the Postal Service has increased its piece volume by more than 20 billion. In 1981 alone, mail volume reached a record 110 billion pieces.

Despite this growth in productivity, however, in the last contract, announced on December 24, 1984, the government through an arbitration panel imposed a notorious two-tier wage pattern on the American Postal Workers Union and the National Association of Letter Carriers. This meant a 25% wage cut for workers hired after a certain date. In time this lower wage may apply to all workers unless a combined effort of all the unions, not only the postal unions, is mobilized against it throughout the country. (The two-tier system of wage levels first got a foothold in none other than the Boeing company, one of the pillars of high technology in the aerospace industry.)

At the same time, notwithstanding the government's bold talk about private enterprise standing on its own feet, it has continued a long line of luscious contracts to the big corporations which supply the materials to the Postal Service. In addition, the government is trying to weaken the "no-layoff clause" in the postal workers' contract.

The unions have a real job on their hands whenever they have to face the government in high-tech negotiations, particularly with the restriction on their right to strike and after what the Reagan administration did with its vicious union busting against the air traffic controllers (PATCO).

The new relationship of the government, particularly Congress, to the postal workers can be seen in the drastic decline in postal appropriations and share of operating expenses over the fiscal years 1971-83. A reactionary Congress and a reactionary White House have combined through the Nixon, Ford, Carter and Reagan years to steadily cut down the amount of appropriations for the post office and let the broad public carry the weight of financing postal operations.

Of course, in those years all other vital services by federal and state governments were also cut down. But what is necessary to distinguish here is that the entire strategy has been geared toward investment in the mechanization of the dispatching, processing and delivery of postal services. A significant portion of the appropriations has been devoted to the automation of mail processing—the installation of optical character readers and bar code sorters in major post offices. All this is bound to squeeze out more workers.

The aim of this automation is to save nearly a billion dollars a year in labor costs—which means that the jobs of many more workers, especially Black, Latin and women workers, are at peril. An official history published by the Postal Service itself says that "After the introduction of ZIP+4 in 1983, the first delivery phase of the new OCR (optical character readers) channel sorters and BCS (bar code sorters) was completed by mid-1984. When fully implemented and used with the expanded ZIP+4 codes, the automated system will save an estimated $960 million annually in labor costs alone."[18]

What happended to the electronic mail delivery service is instructive for seeing how the big corporations allow new technologies to be developed at government expense only to take them over themselves. The U.S. government first developed electronic computer-originated mail (E-COM), which went into service in 1982. It allowed large-volume mailers to transmit messages via computer to selected post offices, where they were printed out, placed in envelopes and delivered by letter carriers. But then a group of large private multinational companies including UPS, Federal Express and Western Union instigated the anti-trust division of the Justice Department to file a suit charging the Postal Service with unfair competition because of the low rates charged. Although the post office won, the so-called independent Postal Rate Commission then demanded that the E-COM rates be doubled, which finally forced the government to abandon that part of the delivery of electronic mail which pertains to domestic use. However, the government continues to maintain the service called Intelpost, which is an electronically transmitted international service.

The struggle by the big carriers to dismantle the Postal Service was foreshadowed by a big business-inspired article in the June 1979 *Forbes* magazine entitled, "Do we really need the postal service?"

Here it is necessary to demonstrate the close link that now exists between the Postal Service and the entire telecommunications industry. Real competition from any number of services in private industry operates as a goad to the Postal Service management to follow suit with each and every new mechanical innovation showing promise of reducing costs and hence the unit cost of labor. Essentially that is what really lies behind all cost-reducing programs.

In the period of the late 1960s and early 1970s, when the PRA was passed, AT&T carried out one of its devastating assaults on the mass of telephone operators, which took a huge toll on Black, Latin and women workers especially.

What happened at AT&T has exceptional relevance to the situation of the postal workers. Even at that time it had become clear that the telecommunications industry had tremendous influence in the government, and that the enactment of the PRA would begin active competition between private industry and the postal service, in the process liquidating many thousands upon thousands of jobs.

However, the postal workers saw the Postal Reorganization Act in an entirely different context. They had just gone through their first and most important strike, which despite some concessions had won legitimacy for their union. This was accomplished even though Nixon sent the U.S. Army into the post offices of the great metropolitan areas of the country in an effort to intimidate and break the workers' resistance. That the postal workers were able to survive this and grow in strength explains why they won subsequent gains and concessions from the government.

In all this, the historical background of the Postal Service should not be forgotten. Like other institutions of U.S. capitalism, it has been profoundly segregationist since the beginning. It was not until 1865, the last year of the Civil War, that the laws prohibiting, yes prohibiting!, Black people from carrying mailbags from stagecoach to post office were abolished.

Racism has continued during the many decades thereafter, partly as a result of outright discrimination by white organized unions. The founding of the National Alliance of Postal Workers in 1913 marked a milestone in self-help organizational mediums by Black workers when the leadership of white organized unions would not open their doors to Black workers.

It was not until the 1940s that Black, Latin and women workers were more freely admitted to the unions under the impact of many profound social changes, most important of which was the civil rights struggle and the upsurge of the labor movement as a whole. This finally made it possible for Black, Latin and women workers to take advantage of employment opportunities in the Postal Service.

Even now, despite attrition and pending future layoffs, "minorities [since 1978] have steadily increased as a proportion of total Postal Service employment." Thus in the fiscal year 1981, a year of big layoffs as a result of the capitalist recession all over industry, "the Postal Service hired 10,064 Blacks, 2,765 Hispanics and 2,289 other minorities for a total of 15,118 or 27.6% of new employees."[19]

Of course, with anticipated future employment reductions, the picture is not encouraging, particularly if one takes into account the direction the government is taking in pushing the replacement of workers with sophisticated technology. It is more and more geared to the telecommunications industry, of which the government is the principal supporter and promoter.

However, the future of women is a different matter. Female postal employment is predicted to rise while the proportion of Black workers as a whole is expected to remain constant.

The dispatch and delivery of mail are a component of the transportation and communications industry. Like railroad workers, truck drivers and waterfront workers, postal workers participate in the freight-handling process. Transportation facilitates the circulation of capitalist commodities and the scientific-technological revolution has accelerated this process. What automation has done in the Postal Service is another form of what containerization did in the shipping and maritime industries. The postal workers must view themselves as part of the communications, telecommunications and transportation industries with whom they have so much in common.

The employers and the capitalist state have a sustained and abiding interest in artificially keeping the workers in these industries apart and separated. They do this all the more to divide Black and white. However, the scientific-technological revolution has forged a new link between a variety of industries which hitherto seemed to be very separated. It has opened up a new vista, a new horizon which lays out and broadens the basis for working class solidarity.

The capitalist system in its early stages needed a government postal service in order to develop capitalist industry and communications as a whole. It could not have developed the productive forces without almost two centuries of a government-sponsored postal service. Now, with the development of telecommunications, the government wants to ditch that part of the service which is no longer lucrative for big business and high finance, and retain that portion which still facilitates big business, while holding a club over the heads of the postal workers through compulsory no-strike mediation and arbitration.

Union leaders must make particularly clear that there is absolutely no valid reason why the capitalist government should be able to dictate the wages and working conditions of the postal workers and at the same time deprive the workers of their right to strike. The Postal Service is but one segment of the telecommunications industry, as are RCA, GE or AT&T. It is really one connected industry and the demand should be made to remove the anti-strike clause against the postal workers.

Notes

1. Hogben, Lancelot, *Science for the Citizen*, Allen & Unwin (London, 1956), p. 620.

2. *Encyclopedia Britannica*, 1982 ed., Vol. 4, p. 1040.

3. Marx, Karl, "The Poverty of Philosophy," *Marx and Engels Collected Works*, International Publishers (New York, 1976), Vol. 6, p. 167.

4. Ki-Zerbo, Joseph, *Histoire de l'Afrique Noire, d'Hier a Demain*, Librairie A. Hatier (Paris, 1978), p. 211.

5. *New York Times*, Jan. 22, 1986.

6. Marx, *Capital*, p. 712fn.

7. Aptheker, Herbert, *American Negro Slave Revolts*, International Publishers (New York, 1974), p. 238.

8. Struik, Dirk, *The Origins of American Science*, Cameron Associates, Inc. (New York, 1957).

9. Marx, *Capital*, p. 362.

10. Hill, Helen D., *George Mason, Constitutionalist*, as quoted by William Z. Foster in *The Negro People in American History*, International Publishers (New York, 1954).

11. See Joseph C. Carroll, *Slave Insurrections in the United States, 1800-1860*, Chapman & Grimes (Boston, 1938), reprinted by New American Library (New York, 1969); and Aptheker, *op. cit.*

12. Carroll, *ibid.*

13. Marx, Karl and Frederick Engels, "Manifesto of the Communist Party," *Collected Works*, Vol. 6, p. 487.

14. Haber, Louis, *Black Pioneers of Science and Invention*, Harcourt Brace Jovanovich (New York, 1970).

15. Quoted in Haber, *op. cit.*

16. Foner, Philip, *Organized Labor and the Black Worker, 1619 1981*, International Publishers (New York, 1982), p. 417.

17. Henderson, Lenneal J. and Charles Murphy, "Perils of Black Postal Workers in a Technological Age: Some Strategies for Survival," *Urban League Review*, Summer 1983, Vol. 7, No. 2.

18. *History of the U.S. Postal Service, 1775-1984*, published by the U.S. Postal Service.

19. Henderson and Murphy, *op. cit.*, p. 38.

Chapter 6

Latin Workers and Latin American Underdevelopment

The Latin struggle in the U.S.

All during the 1960s and 1970s, Latin workers in the U.S. fought a common battle against discrimination and national oppression along with Black, Native and Asian workers. Indeed, there has been a common struggle of all the oppressed and the working class against capitalism, imperialism and national oppression.

The Latin movement in this country has undergone a vast change in the last 30 to 40 years. It has grown in size, leading the bourgeois press to describe Latin-American people in the U.S. as the "fastest-growing minority." The changing character of the movement, however, is based not only on domestic but international considerations as well.

In the 1950s, for instance, the struggle for Puerto Rican independence acted like a magnet in attracting limited but very intense attention and feeling. This was exemplified by the struggles to free Don Pedro Albizu Campos, Lolita Lebron and other Nationalist political prisoners.

Those campaigns had about the same significance here as the campaign to free Nelson Mandela has in the 1980s. The struggle for Puerto Rican independence received a tremendous stimulant from the Cuban Revolution, in particular because of the bold and forward manner in which the Cuban government and Premier Fidel Castro raised the issues of Puerto Rican independence and the political prisoners and turned them into a continent-wide if not worldwide struggle.

However, following the Cuban missile crisis, the U.S. began a campaign to promote and cultivate a variety of counter-revolutionary elements and launched a campaign of terror in the U.S. as well as in Puerto Rico. It utilized Cuban counter-revolutionary mercenaries to mount regular campaigns of intimidation, terror and harassment which set back the Latin struggle in the U.S.

There is no question that U.S. imperialist reaction against the Cuban Revolution had its counterpart here and acted as a blight on the Latin movement in the U.S. The U.S. was steadily and consistently flattering and cultivating a host of counter-revolutionary exiles, until they finally became too unruly, even for the imperialists, and had to be checked somewhat.

Nevertheless, the Latin movement here lost some of its original momentum. It has not fully recovered from the reaction begun by the U.S. government, even though in the 1960s and 1970s there was collaboration with the Black movement, the women's movement and other progressive forces. The Puerto Rican struggle in the U.S. reached its high-water mark with the tremendous demonstration in Philadelphia in 1976.

U.S. economic hold over Latin America

In the previous pages we have discussed the effects of the scientific-technological revolution on Black workers and some historical aspects of the Black struggle as regards slavery. The common goal of all the oppressed and exploited can scarcely be denied. There are, however, some matters which have to be seen in a different perspective so far as Latin workers are concerned.

For instance, among Black workers there is an affinity to Africa and the African revolution based on the common historical legacy. From this has issued a struggle for international solidarity with all of the oppressed in Africa.

Of course, the same thing applies to Latin workers in relationship to their national origins in the Western Hemisphere, particularly Mexico, the Caribbean, and Central America. But where there is a difference is in the intimate economic ties which the U.S. exercises over the countries of Latin America. These have a profound influence both in the mother countries and on the vast Latin American populations in the States.

Of course, the U.S. has many imperialist economic ties to Africa. Its significant investments in South Africa have only recently come under close scrutiny. Black working class ties to Africa are important, but they are generally much more remote than the relations between Chicano-Mexicano workers here and workers in Mexico, for instance.

What has to be taken into account, particularly in regard to the future, is the effect of the scientific-technological revolution on these struggles, to which hardly any attention is paid. This is of critical importance and each passing day gives it emphasis. A great deal of attention in the progressive and working class press is given to the questions of unemployment, malnutrition and the severity of the domination of U.S. imperialism in Latin America. This is frequently given the priority attention it needs.

But it is really indispensable in this particular phase of monopoly capitalist development to show the effects of the scientific-technological revolution and to point out what it portends for the future and what remedies have to be applied which flow clearly from this latest phase of capitalist development.

This requires careful attention. Perhaps a few examples will illustrate the importance of the scientific-technological revolution as it relates to Puerto Rico and Mexico and by extension to the Latin population in this country.

Keeping high tech under lock and key

Earlier in our study we alluded to the Saturnization plan of General Motors and to the plant that it projects to construct in Tennessee. We demonstrated that by the militant standards of auto workers it was a retreat from progressive trade unionism and that it entailed significant concessions to the company. This foreshadows over a period of time the lowering of the wage standards not only of the auto workers but of all workers in the U.S.

However, prior to embarking on its technological venture to build this estimated $5 billion plant, GM invited all the states to bid for the site. Puerto Rico was not invited. Many governors literally tumbled over each other for the bid to construct this model automated plant. It was very conspicuous that Puerto Rico was not considered.

Now, it is one thing for the Puerto Rican people to reject any further imperialist investment. That could be a proper choice from the viewpoint of strengthening the struggle for independence. But it is another matter altogether for one of the principal industrial corporations, with all the scientific and technological apparatus it has at hand, to deny the Puerto Rican people the opportunity to avail themselves of the most modern, up-to-date scientific-technological elements which could constitute a significant part of the infrastructure needed to raise themselves from an underdeveloped to a developed country.

While the wage patterns and job classifications in the Saturn plant will in all probability be scaled down from what they are in other UAW plants today, nevertheless if established in Puerto Rico they would constitute a considerable advance. This plant is in many ways designed to be a symbol of scientific and technological excellence, the last word in research and invention. Its application will have a revolutionizing effect on the means of production to be used in the next era.

By deliberately excluding Puerto Rico and other dependent countries from such a development, the U.S. compels them to steadily fall behind in industrial development. As this example illustrates, it in fact dictates greater dependence upon imperialism by depriving them of the necessary means to overcome economic backwardness. This is not accidental. Japanese high-tech companies, auto in particular, when seeking out sites for construction of new plants have also deliberately avoided Puerto Rico. They have sought a haven in rural areas of the U.S. like Smyrna, Tennessee, and Marysville, Ohio, where there is a young, rural, white labor force. There is no question that the other imperialist powers, including West Germany and France, do the same.

It is an altogether different matter when these monopolist corporations establish assembly plants or auxiliary facilities that are just adjuncts to the basic manufacturing structures. Then they do seek out oppressed countries where wages and working conditions are low. But all these corporations protect with the highest security classifications the latest findings and developments of science and technology, which are decisive for development, particularly in the less developed countries.

The examples we have given of GM, Nissan, and others barely scratch the surface of what is going on. Important as the Saturn plant may be, it is nevertheless dwarfed by other developments in the scientific-technological revolution. For instance, there has been a notable tendency on the part of Bell Laboratories, RCA, GE, IBM and others to relocate or spread out their research centers and development facilities. We noted earlier how Bell Telephone laid off thousands and moved some of its facilities to other parts of the country. But none of these giant corporations have relocated their research centers to such areas as Puerto Rico.

In the early period of monopoly capitalist development, as Lenin described in his celebrated work on imperialism,[1] the first stage of imperialist penetration of the underdeveloped countries was characterized by the building of railroads, docks, the introduction of the telegraph, electricity, radio and so on. That laid the infrastructure for imperialist domination. It established a material basis for the special exploitation of underdeveloped countries, concentrating on the extractive industries. These allowed the imperialists to accumulate vast super-profits.

Matters are altogether different in the epoch of the scientific-technological revolution, which for the development of the dependent countries requires much more than just the importation of high-speed, sophisticated computers. What is needed is the scientific and technical training of hundreds of thousands of personnel to unlock the secrets which modern science has yielded. Instead of making this available, the imperialist corporations keep it securely under lock and key in the home laboratories and research centers.

Whenever these giant corporations build a new technological facility, they regard it as seed money toward future profits. None of this is ever made available to the underdeveloped countries. This policy continues to widen and deepen the gulf of dependence. It vastly overwhelms whatever technology is made available through the granting of aid or the construction of projects where low skills are involved.

The scientific-technological revolution has made it all the more essential to view the relations between imperialism and the dependent countries in a wholly different perspective than the earlier struggles. While the U.S. imperialists regard Puerto Rico, for instance, as under their juridical hegemony, they refuse to accord it the rights to which it is entitled under the Constitution of the U.S. After all, Puerto Ricans are supposed to be regarded as citizens and accorded due process of law, the same as other U.S. citizens.

The giant corporations have in fact maintained a conspiracy among themselves whereby the rights accorded to the states are flagrantly disregarded with respect to Puerto Rico, which juridically is entitled to the same considerations but is treated on a wholly unequal basis. Indeed, this is not the worst of it.

The U.S. government in 1984 signed into law the Bail Reform Act, which has been used particularly to target Puerto Rican political activists in the struggle for independence. It completely disregards 200 years of criminal jurisprudence in this country since it authorizes the government to detain people on mere suspicion and to hold them without bail. Its "preventive detention" provision, supposedly passed to stem the tide of so-called terrorism, is in reality used as an instrument of repression. This is exemplified by the arrest in August 1985 of 13 Puerto Rican defendants and the continuing detention of nine of them under this new law, about whom little has been said in the capitalist press.

The U.S. corporate giants want to have it both ways. They won't allow Puerto Rico to forge its own independence and seek out new relationships with other countries so as to get out of the vise-like colonial relationship which hinders it from acquiring economic and technological development which may be available elsewhere.

At the same time they won't make available what is necessary, which doesn't mean just food stamps or a few housing units here and there. It means obtaining the new tools that are necessary to train the young generation to deal with the newly emerging conditions. It's not just a question of importing new technology; it's a question of obtaining the know-how, training the personnel, acquiring the educational facilities, both in agriculture and industry. This is what is being withheld.

Loans for debt, not for development

What is said in connection with Puerto Rico applies equally to Mexico, but in a different form. The U.S. bankers not long ago showed great eagerness to extend loans to Mexico in connection with the extraction and production for sale of its oil. Oil seemed the answer to all the burning questions of economic development and the means to make a real leap forward from underdevelopment to becoming a developed industrial country. This has not happened.

The collapse of oil on a worldwide scale has only emphasized the monocultural aspect of oil production. It does not create in and of itself the necessary scientific and technological infrastructure to build a modern industrialized country.

Of course it is helpful for any country to find oil or any other natural resource. But as in the case of Nigeria, Venezuela, Indonesia and other countries (with the exception of Saudi Arabia and some of the Gulf states), the development of its oil resources did not make any substantial difference once the capitalist crisis overtook Mexico.

On the contrary, the introduction of capitalist technology has not decreased poverty but has disrupted existing social relations, accelerating the so-called illegal immigration of Mexicans into the U.S. The so-called immigration problem does not lend itself to solutions merely on the basis of the development of the oil industry, in which the imperialist countries, particularly the U.S., were most eager to participate. It should be remembered that the border itself is the product of a war of conquest by the U.S. against Mexico, and that millions of Mexican people inhabited the Southwest before it was annexed to the United States.

Oil is an extractive industry where the banks realize lucrative super-profits by making abundant loans readily available. The same does not apply when it comes to capital for the broad scientific and technological infrastructure needed to really develop the country given the contemporary stage of the scientific-technological revolution. The incubus of private ownership in the means of production, of subordination and control by imperialist monopolies, makes it prohibitive from the vantage point of imperialist interests.

Last year alone, the U.S. government forcibly deported a million workers to Mexico. The immigration problem cannot be solved on the basis of the contemporary imperialist relationship between the U.S. and Mexico. It requires a reorientation of the productive forces. But this is impossible when all of the great advances in science and technology are kept under lock and key in the citadels of imperialist power, which only occasionally let some of them trickle through and then only on the basis of continuing dependence.

What is said in respect to Mexico applies equally to the Caribbean countries.

The hodgepodge of aid, of grants, even of the "generous" kind, so-called, in the long run is of no avail in the face of the widening gulf between the dependent countries and the metropolitan imperialist centers. Only a thoroughgoing socialist revolution can overcome the effects of imperialist bondage and get rid of the incubus of monopoly-capitalist private property. This is the only way to unearth the secrets which science and invention are daily yielding up but which are misused by the vested, predatory, monopoly capitalist interests.

Notes

1. Lenin, V.I., "Imperialism, the Highest Stage of Capitalism," *Collected Works*, Progress Publishers (Moscow, 1964), Vol. 22.

Chapter 7

Native People Under the Gun

Gunpowder and mass production of firearms

The scientific-technological revolution has had the most devastating effect on the Native people of North America. The campaigns of extermination and plunder conducted by the North and South could scarcely have assumed the proportions they did had it not been for the weapons of destruction the settlers and colonizers brought with them.

As is well known, gunpowder had revolutionized warfare throughout Europe. Although first developed in China in the 9th and 10th centuries, it was not used as an explosive for military purposes on a wide scale until the 15th century in Europe. The bow and arrow and other earlier weapons could not compete with firearms.

The French had developed the most devastating form of gunpowder, superior to that originally used here by the English-speaking settlers. It was the DuPonts who brought the production of this more powerful type of gunpowder to the New World.

Much has been written about the early settlers and how they employed their guns, especially the Kentucky long-barreled rifles, in hunting squirrels and rabbits for food. But in reality these weapons were used mainly to terrorize the Native people and rob them of their land.

What gave the new ruling class its greatest advantage in the struggle against the Native people, however, and for that matter against all the oppressed and exploited, were the technological advances in the production of arms. The bourgeois state, no matter how much it is prettified, is basically an instrument of repression.

Eli Whitney, whom we mentioned earlier as the inventor of the cotton gin, also introduced into the U.S. a new principle in the production of arms. He originated the use of interchangeable parts for machines and their products, in other words, the first elements of mass production. This was over 100 years before Henry Ford got together the capital to apply this technique to the mass production of automobiles.

"When [Whitney] decided to undertake the manufacture of firearms for the U.S. government, he introduced a new principle—one destined to revolutionize production methods as his gin had revolutionized the social structure of the South, namely the use of interchangeable parts for tools, for machinery and for their products."[1]

As early as 1798, Whitney's principle began to supplant individual gunsmiths with factories for the manufacture of firearms. In order to have interchangeable parts, firearms now had to be standardized. As Whitney himself said, he had to "substitute correct and effective operations of machinery for that skill of an artist which is acquired only by long practice and experience." This required making the same parts of different guns "as much like each other as the successive impressions of a copper plate engraving."[2]

All this required the division of labor and the transfer of human skills to special tools and machinery. It took two years to produce and install the necessary machines, after which the production of muskets could proceed on a mass scale. This is what then enabled the European colonizers to defeat the Native people in an unequal struggle.

The standardization of arms production was a very early precursor to the development of the military-industrial complex in the epoch of imperialist wars. When Whitney developed his principle of interchangeable parts, there were no factories for arms production, only individual gunsmiths. However, he persuaded President Thomas of the utility of his idea and was able to obtain a contract for the production of 10,000 muskets. He then built an armory in New Haven, Connecticut, to produce this large number of weapons. It was thus the state that was instrumental in revolutionizing this industry from an inefficient, individual enterprise into a much more collective form of production. This helped to bolster the repressive power of the state as it struggled against the oppressed and exploited masses.

The earlier, handcrafted guns had of course been much more expensive. The new principle of incipient mass production enabled the U.S. government to equip large armies and expand the militia. This inglorious aspect of the scientific-technological revolution is frequently neglected by historians, as though the settlers had been born with weapons of destruction.

Expansion of slave plantations onto Native land

Both Northern capitalists and Southern slaveowners learned early on that, notwithstanding the very fundamental and irreconcilable contradictions between them, they nevertheless had a common objective in the suppression of the exploited and oppressed masses.

The expansion of slavery, which we have shown was largely due to increased cotton production, gave even more impetus to the drive to oust the Native people from their land. A path had to be cleared for the expanding plantations, and that meant expelling the Native people from areas where they had lived from time immemorial.

We mentioned earlier how every year the liberals in the Democratic Party pay tribute to Thomas Jefferson and Andrew Jackson as great democrats and men of the people. They don't mention that Jefferson was a racist and large slaveowner, as we said. The historian Arthur Schlesinger, viewed as a great liberal chronicler, wrote a book on *The Age of Jackson* which viewed the progressive era of Franklin Roosevelt as an extension of Jacksonian democracy. But Jackson's role in the extermination campaigns against Native people needs to be mentioned here.

General Andrew Jackson was one of the most vicious enemies of the Native people, and participated in campaigns to drive them out of their homes in Georgia, Alabama, Mississippi, Tennessee and Florida, all in the interests of expanding the slave plantations. His demand from the Creek nation in 1814 that they yield 23 million acres of their ancient domain was described by an early historian as "unequaled for exorbitance."[3]

His move from military to civilian politics had no softening effect on Jackson. "Later, when he became President, Jackson finished the job on the Creeks, Cherokees, Seminoles, and others. He forced them off their Southern preserves altogether and across the Mississippi River in 1835. They were finally rounded up, stripped of their hunting grounds, and confined in concentration camps known as Indian reservations. . . . The big planters got the cream of the wide and fertile Southern lands stolen from the Indians by the government."[4]

Any idea that contemporary imperialism has become more moderate and enlightened and less predatory toward Native people is dispelled by taking a careful look at how the U.S. government and the multinational corporations, especially the huge energy monopolies, deal with the rights of Native people today.

It took a virtual uprising at Wounded Knee in 1973 for the struggle of Native people to finally gain some kind of national recognition. But the desperate conditions highlighted in that heroic struggle continue to persist around the country today. Many of the leaders of that period have been assassinated or imprisoned. One of the most prominent, Leonard Peltier, has gained international support as an eminent political prisoner, but remains virtually unmentioned in the imperialist press of the U.S.

The government in cahoots with the energy monopolies is trying to force the relocation of the Dineh (Navajo) and Hopi peoples from their mineral-rich lands in Arizona. High unemployment, infant mortality, suicide and alcoholism on the reservations all attest to a ruthless disregard of the sovereign rights of the Native people.

Mass migrations from Europe and the Utopians

It was to try and achieve basic democratic rights that many millions came to the New World, fleeing the injustice, cruelty and oppression of the European regimes. However, these migrations, often spurred on by the breakup of the old feudal order, never took into account the rights of the indigenous people.

The character of this migration became a matter of sharp debate in the socialist movement in Europe, even though the controversy did not center on the question of the indigenous people, but rather on the idea that a socialist utopia could be established in the New World, a view that Marx rejected.

Frederick Engels in his celebrated work *Socialism, Utopian and Scientific* [5] examined the ideas of the great utopian socialists, from Thomas More and Saint-Simon to Robert Owen and Fourier. These early social reformers envisioned a variety of communal societies that would abolish class distinctions and bring about justice and equality. As Engels demonstrated, however, their experiments were bound to come to a sad end because they disregarded or were unable to see the development of the class struggle between the working class and the bourgeoisie, which is the driving force of modern society.

While they lacked a scientific analysis of class society, and could not see that the working class would replace the bourgeoisie only through a thorough-going socialist revolution, these early utopian socialists nevertheless made a contribution to what would later be developed by both Marx and Engels into a scientific, revolutionary socialist theory.

These early utopian socialists, however, must be distinguished from a variety of others who came along later when there was less justification for their erroneous views and who in fact were harmful to the developing workers' movement. We particularly are referring here to those who saw the Western Hemisphere as a land of great opportunity to build a free socialist society on the basis of mass migration from Europe. It appears that never for a moment did these utopians inquire as to the rights or even the existence of the Native people in making their calculations.

Marx took a dim view of mass migration as a panacea for building a socialist society. A young man named Hermann Kriege, who had worked with Marx for a short time, went to America and started a journal "for the propaganda of communism." But, says Lenin in an essay on this question,[6] "he conducted this propaganda in such a manner that Marx was obliged to protest very strongly."

Kriege had said in his journal that "If this immense area (the 1,400,000,000 acres of North American public domain) is withdrawn from commerce and is secured in restricted amounts for labor, an end will be put to poverty in America at one stroke. . . ." Marx had replied, "And who are the Europeans whose 'dreams' would thus come true? Not the communist workers, but bankrupt shopkeepers and handicraftsmen, or ruined cottars, who yearn for the good fortune of once again becoming petty bourgeois. . . . And what is the 'dream' that is to be fulfilled by means of these 1,400,000,000 acres? No other than that all men be converted into private owners, a dream which is as unrealizable and as communistic as the dream to convert all men into emperors, kings, and popes."

Although in this article Marx didn't refer to the Native population, in *Capital* he denounced the "extirpation, enslavement and entombment in mines of the aboriginal population" in America which, together with the looting of the East Indies and the slave trade in Africa, signaled "the rosy dawn of the era of capitalist production."[7]

When Marx answered Kriege, he was himself only 28 years old and had not yet fully developed the views which were to appear as matured Marxism in such later works as the *Communist Manifesto* and *The Poverty of Philosophy*.

Reactionary schemes of utopian socialism continued to plague the socialist movement almost until the turn of the century. Thus, in June 1897, when the railway union headed by Eugene V. Debs merged with the Social Democracy then being formed in Chicago, "leading the list of the Social Democracy's demands was the colonization plan which proposed to establish a socialist America by organizing a mass migration to a Western state, where cooperative colonies would be formed, from which the movement would spread throughout the nation and in due time create a socialist United States."[8]

What is striking about this and all other mass migration plans in the Western Hemisphere, particularly in the U.S., is that there was no recognition whatever of the rights of the indigenous people, whose land was to be appropriated.

Later a new wing of socialists more attuned to the teachings of Marx, as then understood and practiced in the U.S., gained greater influence in the Social Democratic organization. The colonization scheme was ditched and a split with these utopian socialists took place. However, in all this the criticism against the utopian socialists was based on the fantastic and impractical character of their schemes, not that the land was to be appropriated from the Native people. Moreover, this was a time when the cruelest oppression of the indigenous people was taking place.

Notwithstanding the inevitability of capitalist development and its triumph over previous modes of production, Engels paid a great deal of attention to the findings of Lewis Henry Morgan, who learned first-hand about the social organization of Native peoples in North America. The significance of Morgan's findings, which confirmed the existence of natural communism and pre-class society, was brought to light in Engels' famous work, *The Origin of the Family, Private Property and the State*, which was subtitled, *In the Light of the Researches of Lewis H. Morgan*.[9]

Marx, too, was enthused by Morgan's discoveries about the communal society of the Iroquois people, and wrote to a comrade in 1881 that the crisis of capitalism would only end "with its abolition, with the return of modern societies to the 'archaic' type of communal ownership, or, as an American author [Morgan] . . . says—the new system toward which modern society is tending 'will be a revival of the archaic societal type in a superior form.' One should not be frightened overmuch by the word 'archaic.'"[10]

Leninist stand on national oppression

It was not until the arrival of Lenin on the historical scene, however, that the whole question of national oppression, including that of Native people in this country, began to be taken note of by white progressive and working class organizations. It is a cornerstone of Leninism that socialism cannot coexist with national oppression; genuine socialist internationalism can only be achieved through the recognition of the sovereign rights of oppressed people. This is particularly true of the indigenous peoples, who have been uprooted around the globe, not just in North America.

The task of a revolutionary workers' party here is to promote the sovereign rights of the Native peoples. Some white progressives seem to worry about how this can be done in light of the advance of capitalist development, whether such a stand wouldn't mean turning back the wheel of history altogether. They would do better to think about how to fight imperialism's aggressiveness and predatory monopoly character.

The broad progressive movement has unfortunately had for its heroes men like Senators George McGovern of South Dakota and Morris Udall of Arizona, for many years two of the most luminous stars in the liberal firmament. But what about their record in relation to Native people, who have significant concentrations in both states? They are not heroes but rather the executors of the same old policy of colonial conquest. And when both men have run for President, they haven't so much as mentioned Native people.

The right of Native peoples to choose their own form of self-determination, including sovereignty, has not found its way into the programmatic demands of many working class tendencies in this country. Many who never give a second thought to how "practical" it may be for the U.S. to have annexed as its fiftieth state the group of Hawaiian islands far off in the Pacific are quick to declaim on the "impracticality" of sovereignty for the Native peoples because of the modern industrial development of capitalism.

Yet it has proven very practical in the USSR for a variety of forms of self-determination to be exercised by the indigenous peoples there, who belong to many different autonomous republics and regions. From Central Asia to the Soviet Near East to Siberia, there are many Soviet peoples who are not Russian and who since the Revolution have harmonized the development of their regions with their cultures and needs.

As we have shown, the effects of the scientific-technological revolution are more onerous on oppressed peoples. A very firm and clear stand on the rights of Native peoples and all oppressed nationalities is therefore of utmost importance for the working class vanguard in all propaganda and political activity.

Notes

1. Struik, *The Origins of American Science.*

2. Eli Whitney, quoted in Struik, *op. cit.*

3. Quoted in Foster, *American Trade Unionism.*

4. Foster, *op. cit.*

5. Engels, Frederick, "Socialism, Utopian and Scientific," *Marx/Engels Selected Works*, Progress Publishers (Moscow, 1970), Vol. 3.

6. Lenin, V.I., "Marx on the American 'General Redistribution,'" *Collected Works,* Foreign Languages Publishing House (Moscow, 1962), Vol. 8, pp. 323-24.

7. Marx, *Capital*, p. 703.

8. Foner, Philip, *History of the Labor Movement in the United States*, International Publishers (New York, 1980), Vol. 2, p. 388.

9. Engels, Frederick, "The Origin of the Family, Private Property and the State," *Marx and Engels Selected Works*, Vol. 3.

10. Marx, Karl, letter to Vera Sassulitch, March 1881, in *On America and the Civil War*, McGraw-Hill Book Co. (New York, 1972).

PART 3

Strategies for a
Working Class Fightback

Chapter 8

Defensive Trade Union Strategies

Difference between a workers' party and a trade union

What is the fundamental difference between a workers' party and a trade union? Of course, every party member in a union has a duty to work with all other progressive unionists and try to improve the wages and living conditions of the workers. It's true that party members can be distinguished by their militancy, aggressiveness, determination and the enormous energy they expend with other workers in the struggle against the bosses. These alone, however, are not what distinguish a party member in the trade unions.

The politically conscious worker must also attempt to educate the other workers in the spirit of the class struggle and promote the socialist goal. This goal is not an ideal as such. The socialist perspective is not something that is a matter of faith in the sense that someone holds some religious or political concept that is dear to them.

The ordinary worker is taught that his or her objective in the union as a worker should be confined to fighting for "a fair day's pay for a fair day's work." "Fairness" and "justice" are most frequently proclaimed by the trade union officialdom as the goal of the workers and the union. A party member, however, understands that this standard is based upon a moral conception of the relations between the workers and the bosses which is very vague and ambiguous and actually presupposes the acceptance of the moral values of the ruling class.

This conception disregards that in reality the relations between the workers and the bosses are governed not by the lofty moral standards proclaimed by the bosses, the government and the media, but by the objective economic laws of motion which govern the relations between capital and labor and are based upon the exploitation and subordination of the latter. What thus differentiates a party member from the general mass of the workers is that she or he **has an objective appraisal** of the relationship between the workers and the bosses.

Look at any union contract in the big industries such as auto, steel or electric and you will almost always come across a preamble similar to the one in the current General Motors contract with the United Auto Workers:

"The management of General Motors recognizes that it cannot get along without labor any more than labor can get along without the management. Both are in the same business and the success of that business is vital to all concerned. This requires that both management and the employees work together to the end that the quality and cost of the product will prove increasingly satisfactory and attractive so that the business will be continuously successful.

"General Motors holds that the basic interests of the employers and the employees are the same. However, at times employees and the management have different ideas on various matters affecting their relationship. The management of General Motors is convinced that there is no reason why these differences cannot be peacefully and satisfactorily adjusted by sincere and patient effort on both sides."

This clause is not there by accident. It is demanded by almost all companies. Indeed, this view is promoted assiduously by the capitalist press, media, government, schools and universities, their ideologists and politicians.

It cultivates the idea that there is an identity of interests between the workers and the bosses. Cooperation with this concept is considered mandatory. Of course, it is never to be interpreted that the employers have to cooperate with the workers. The identity of interests is based on the workers cooperating with the interests of the company and the bosses.

This is and has been the prevailing view ever since the dawn of the so-called free enterprise system. It means the subordination of the workers to the interests of the employers.

A workers' party must challenge and continually demonstrate the utter falsity and perniciousness of this idea. It must be continually demonstrated that the interests of the employers and the workers are diametrically opposed to each other, that the evolution of capitalist society demonstrates the existence of the class struggle rather than identity of class interests.

By accepting the identity of interests between employers and workers, the latter are forced into a subordinate position. The theory of the identity of interests inculcates in the workers the idea that the employers get their share, namely profits, and the workers get theirs, wages. Both supposedly get the fruits of their contribution to the product.

This is wholly erroneous. In reality the workers are subjected to exploitation while the employers reap the benefits of the unpaid labor of the workers. The difference between the class approach to the problem and even the most progressive trade union approach is that the latter would not acknowledge the objective significance of the relations between the employers and the workers.

Limits of trade union approach

The trade unions function as the collective bargaining agent for the workers. It is worth pondering on the meaning of the word bargaining. What it really means is to bargain over the sale of the labor power of the workers.

The bargaining process involves a struggle over the terms of the sale and purchase for a limited period of the one commodity the workers have to sell—their labor power. It is bargaining over the rates and conditions of the exploitation of the workers. The workers attempt to both limit the conditions of exploitation and increase their wages, which means to diminish the profit of the bosses.

No amount of effective bargaining negates the existence of the exploitation of the workers. It can change the conditions of the exploitation, of course, improving the working conditions and increasing the wages, but at all times it retains the exploitation relationship between capital and labor. This is the one invariable element in the relation between capital and labor, between workers and the bosses.

Party members must and do explain that in the struggle with the bosses their aim is to abolish the exploitation relationship. This then is the fundamental difference between them and other progressives whose views and conceptions are based on the existing ideology of the bosses which ties them to cooperation in the exploitation of the workers. No matter how good a union contract may be, it at best stabilizes the conditions of exploitation.

It is not just a struggle of divergent conceptions. It is a struggle to bring to the workers an objective, dispassionate evaluation of the real relationship which exists. This is the very opposite of what the employers do.

If you think the cooperative part of the preamble to any union contract may be accidental, let's look at still another and much more specific clause that appears in most big industry contracts and further defines the relationship from the bourgeois point of view. It is called "the management clause," and here is how it reads in the UAW-GM contract:

"The right to hire; promote; discharge or discipline for cause; and to maintain discipline and efficiency of employees, is the sole responsibility of the Corporation except that Union members shall not be discriminated against as such. In addition, the products to be manufactured, the location of the plants, the schedules of production, the methods, processes and means of manufacturing are solely and exclusively the responsibility of the Corporation."

The purpose of this clause is to bolster the exploitation relationship between the bosses and the workers by categorically stating that it is the bosses who own and control the plant. This is so the workers don't get any idea in the course of the struggle that they own the plant or that they are to operate it on their own. This clause too is not accidental.

This together with the preamble makes sure that the capitalist system of exploitation is sanctified in every union contract. And when that is of no avail, they resort to the courts, the capitalist politicians and even the military, as they have done on occasion.

Problems of the strike weapon

The effort to fight back against the offensive unloosed by the bosses cannot always be done in the more elementary form of strike struggles during periods when the capitalist cycle of development is descending. The bosses may be able to hold out longer.

One only has to look at what has happened in the last few years in strikes such as Brown & Sharpe, Phelps Dodge and Wheeling-Pittsburgh Steel. (We'll discuss these again later.) In all three, despite the fact that the workers put up glorious and heroic struggles, the unions were not able to win victories equal to the strength of their strikes.

Many years ago, Rudolf Hilferding wrote a book on *Finance Capital* with a chapter entitled "The Conflict Over the Labor Contract." [1] He described in vivid detail the formal aspects of the struggle over the union contract. What is interesting here is that he dwelt in considerable detail on the merits of strike strategy. He explained the necessity for the unions to educate the workers so that they will strike against the employers at a time most advantageous to the workers.

That time, he explained, is when the capitalist industrial cycle is in its upward, so-called prosperity swing. He said that when workers are making more money, making overtime, they may be less inclined to strike—although the advantage from the point of view of changing the balance of power with the employers is greatest then.

Unquestionably, this is all too true. Few union leaders would contradict this and most workers, especially those in unions, understand very well that from the point of view of strike strategy it's very important to call a strike at a favorable time. The bigger problem is, what if there are attempted lockouts, what if the employers **force a strike** during a period of capitalist recession? Unfortunately, Hilferding didn't deal with that.

The period since the Second World War shows that these capitalist recessions tend to be of a protracted character and capitalist overproduction can continue for a long period. Agricultural production, for instance, has been characterized by a glut since 1979. This has resulted in depressing effects in the food and processing industries for a considerable period. There's a glut in all kinds of metals and there is no question that there is a glut in world production of steel.

Some of the imperialist countries, most of all the U.S., are trying to solve this problem by putting up high tariff walls, which President Reagan enforced in 1984. This probably has resulted in an increase in steel production, for example. But that has not overcome the general condition of capitalist overproduction in steel.

If steel can be characterized as stagnant because of capitalist overproduction, all the more is this true in copper, tin and aluminum. Needless to say, iron ore has long been in a slump, and while coal mining has somewhat stabilized, it is nowhere near the level of the 1970s. The times are not propitious for a strike in coal on the basis of any upward cycle of capitalist production.

Business Week [2] has estimated that the glut in petroleum extraction could last well into the 21st century. And similar conditions persist in other industries, such as textiles.

Although some industries seem to be relatively more secure from protracted capitalist recession, such as health care and other service industries, this can generally be explained on the basis that the steep recession stage has not yet affected them. The bourgeois press has cultivated the myth that some industries are recession proof. But this is altogether fraudulent. There are no such industries. It is just that the crisis reaches them later or less severely.

Once the workers are frozen into the capital-labor relationship, once that is dogmatically accepted as the permanent condition of the workers, once this business of a fair day's work for a fair day's pay is the conception, it inevitably follows that the workers must make concessions regardless of whether the union is strong or weak. The issue becomes saving the company or industry.

In reality the company, if they mean by that the physical plant and so on, is in no danger of going under. No natural disaster is threatening it. It's only the **ownership** that may undergo some changes, from one individual to another, or to another group of employers in the case of bankruptcy.

So that the policy of concessions flows directly and inevitably from the acceptance of the capital-labor relationship, from the acceptance of exploitation as the permanent condition of the working class. The ideology corresponding to this can only be that of class collaboration. It is very deeply ingrained into the consciousness of the workers by the press, the media, the courts, the pulpit and the schools and universities.

At times the demand for concessions by the workers becomes almost hysterical. And yet the workers are not inclined to surrender to the hysteria. Their very instincts lead them to opposition. But again, by accepting the capital-labor relationship, they prescribe for themselves a very narrow field for the struggle: the economic struggle, which usually means strikes, stoppages which interrupt capitalist production.

These of course are very important and indispensable. There can be no denying the effectiveness of the strike weapon. The strike weapon, the weapon which interrupts production, is regarded as a calamity for the individual employers of the capitalist class, but not because it stops production as such.

There is still a great deal of production that goes on in contemporary society which the capitalist class does not get worked up about if it is interrupted—the work people do at home, on their own small farms, or generally useful work. The interruptions the capitalists are opposed to are the interruptions of **capitalist** production, which means the interruption of the source of their profits. When this happens, the strike weapon is regarded as a mortal enemy, especially if it is of a protracted character and at a time when it is inconvenient for the employers.

But, again, the strike weapon has its limitations, particularly in the period we are addressing: that phase of development which is characterized by protracted capitalist economic crisis. The strike struggle alone, confining the union to economic means, is inadequate.

Of course, the first and most important condition necessary to make a strike successful is to obtain united fronts with other workers and to maintain a solid working class front. This would hardly be opposed or denied by even the most casehardened bureaucrats, nor would they oppose political action as they see it, meaning to enlist "friendly" capitalist politicians with so-called pro-labor records. But this too is usually a drawn-out process and is rarely effective enough to determine the course of the strike in favor of the workers. It may be helpful, and often is, but in and of itself is not decisive.

What is needed is to supplement the strike weapon with additional weapons so as to have a variety of different forms of struggle in order to confront the ruling class.

The economic struggle, especially on a plantwide or industrywide basis, is too narrow if for no other reason than that the employers are able to line up the capitalist state on their side. The struggle is an uneven one.

Much more is needed in constructing a strategy for periods of chronic economic depression. These often culminate in a capitalist crisis which in turn could develop into a full-scale general political crisis of the system.

Barring that unforeseen development, it is necessary to take some first steps which may have the effect of breaking out of the capital-labor relationship. What is meant here is not disruption, physical sabotage or anything of the sort, but to break up the sociological scheme of the capital-labor relationship, which is one of exploitation.

Notes

1. Hilferding, Rudolf, *Finance Capital*, Routledge & Kegan Paul [London & Boston, 1981 (1910)].
2. *Business Week*, Nov. 12, 1984 .

Chapter 9

Offensive Strategies: Workers' Control

New forms of struggle necessary

New forms of struggle are necessary to meet the growing challenge and menace of the bosses. It's to be remembered that all great social movements in the history of the working class have first arisen from below. None ever came from labor consultants, bourgeois academic professionals or capitalist politicians. What's most important in all this is to recognize that the technological revolution has put the workers and their unions in a great crisis and is shaking them out of the old historic mold of labor relations in which they have been trapped.

The vast transformation which the structural framework of capitalist industry is undergoing makes new forms of struggle absolutely indispensable or the workers must become captives of management altogether. These new forms of struggle are an outgrowth and development of the older forms and an advance upon them.

What's needed is not to abandon the old militant methods but to recognize that the conventional, traditional weapons—including the indispensable strike weapon—have to be refined and supplemented by new methods which include the right to seize, occupy, take over and operate plants, equipment and industry.

Such very important struggles as exemplified by the strikes at Brown & Sharpe, Phelps Dodge and Wheeling-Pittsburgh were not guided or prepared by a general, overall, national strategy or policy at the central leadership level of the AFL-CIO. Instead, they were conducted like small isolated skirmishes in a guerrilla struggle, when what was needed was a general assault policy including at the very earliest opportunity the struggle to seize, occupy and hold the plants.

Great changes in strategic and tactical approaches develop slowly. They are most often the product of a long line of evolutionary development which includes not only phases of slow growth but leaps and giant forward strides.

The first such struggle was for the right "to think unthinkable thoughts," to think of organizing the workers. It had been regarded as a conspiracy—any combination of workers to organize a union, even to conduct meetings, had been regarded as illegal.

That won, the next struggle was over the right to openly proclaim the need for organization and the right to strike. But the thing to remember is that **the strikes came before striking was legalized**. That's the lesson of the 1930s. The great sit-down strikes, which were the heroic age of modern labor organization, came first. Then came the law that validated collective bargaining, the Wagner Act.

It's relevant to go over here a few points concerning the great historical experience of the occupation of General Motors by the workers in the 1930s. This militant action rocked the country, fired the imagination of millions and determined the course of labor history for years to come.

Historians and scholars will always be at odds on precisely how, but that it succeeded all the world knows. At that time the National Labor Relations Act (NLRA) was already in existence and the workers had a right to organize and strike. But the company, the courts and a vast horde of public officials were opposed to it and denied the right of the workers, even though this right was very clearly and unambiguously stated in Section 7a of the NLRA.

The workers had seen how police and state troopers attacked strikers on a picketline. Fear of the power of General Motors, then as now the largest manufacturer in the world, inhibited the workers from taking to the picketline. So after discussion they tried to accomplish the same thing in another way.

In the weeks and months before the auto workers occupied the GM plants, there were many public officials and community leaders who met with union leaders and many promises were made to the workers, but nothing came of all this. However, when the workers finally made a break for it and occupied the plants, Michigan Governor Frank Murphy became one of the central figures mediating the situation.

Interestingly, President Roosevelt's Secretary of Labor at the time, Frances Perkins, defended the right of the workers to occupy the plants. She did so not before the occupation, but toward the end of it. She said that the workers had a property right because of their jobs. And that is correct.

It would be foolish, of course, to take this action as a literal example of what must be done today. But it is relevant and enlightening as a bare outline and guide to how the workers can fight today to extend their rights to include the right to seize and occupy the plants. It is a logical and inevitable phase in the struggle of the labor movement, as imperative a necessity and as vital to the existence of the trade union movement as any of the preceding phases in its history.

Seizure and occupation of the plants

There are means by which the workers can go beyond the established capital-labor relationship, that is, the framework of capitalist exploitation. They can seize and occupy the plants and thereby force a new and different type of crisis on the ruling class, instead of remaining in a narrow, often frustrating endurance contest between the employers and the workers.

A strike can strain the meager savings of the workers and weaken their ability to withstand such a prolonged struggle. Seizure and occupation of the plants and other facilities have the effect of hastening a crisis in the relationship between the employers and the workers. It can be a transitional form when the opportunity and objective conditions arise to stimulate a wholly different type of working class struggle, one that does not drain the energy of the workers but on the other hand has the possibility of posing the question of a workers' takeover of industry as a whole.

It can change the form of the struggle, take it out of its narrow confines and impart to it a broader perspective. In truth, it brings to the surface a new working class perspective on the struggle between the workers and the bosses. It says in so many words that we are not tied to a one-dimensional type of struggle with the bosses at a time when they have the levers of political authority in their hands. The struggle, except in periods of capitalist prosperity, is much too unequal.

Even capitalist courts have at times recognized the inequality of that type of struggle and it is from that point of view that government concessions have been made to the workers in the form of unemployment insurance and other benefits, which incidentally came also as a result of struggle. Of course, plant seizures are one of a variety of methods of changing the relationship of forces.

Workers' control is a unique form of struggle in that it holds out the possibility of breaking up the sociological scheme of the capital-labor relationship. It was originally conceived as a transitional form toward the overthrow of the capitalist system and the building of a socialist state.

It was also first brought up during a period when capitalist society was in grave crisis and the working class was resorting, at least in some parts of the world, to revolutionary means to solve its problem. Workers' control was not expected to be a protracted state of affairs.

It should be stated that workers' control in the present state of the working class movement is merely a demand within the framework of the bourgeois system, but it has the possibility of overturning the capital-labor relationship in a huge plant or preferably, where it might be more successful, in an industry.

There are periods in the course of a struggle with a company when the workers initially go out on strike. Then it is seen that the company is bent on strikebreaking in a very real way and has unquestionably made plans for such an eventuality.

In such a case a protracted struggle could prove counter-productive for the workers. Occupation and seizure of the plant can be the best way to not only cut down casualties but prevent strikebreaking.

This is the lesson that should come out of the experience of the Brown & Sharpe strike, which as of this writing was over four years old. The picketlines have been withdrawn, but the struggle continues in the courts. However, a great number of scabs have taken over and company-provoked violence has resulted in many arrests.

This was certainly a case when the plant should have been occupied. It would have been easy after the first few weeks. The seizure of the plant and its occupation would have provoked a political crisis. Given the formidable membership and assets of the International Association of Machinists (IAM) and the solidarity which it might have created on a mass scale, the strike could conceivably have been won.

Even more instructive is the case of the Phelps Dodge copper strike, which started in July 1983 and has also lasted for several years. There, too, it became clear after a period of time that the company was bent on strikebreaking and unionbusting; it was utilizing its vast international resources and the hundreds of millions in its treasury. There, too, scab-herding on the part of the company was clearly on the horizon in the early stages of the strike. The company had its eye set on stimulating racial antagonisms, pitting white workers against the Latino and Indian workers.

It is one thing to try to expose the company's links to banks, insurance companies and so on, and to put pressure on them with demonstrations, etc. Some of this was done very well in the Phelps Dodge strike, particularly the activities organized in New York City and Boston to get solidarity support and awaken the broad mass of the public to the danger of strikebreaking.

But it is an altogether different matter to rely upon this form of struggle as a fundamental lever rather than on the strike itself, on the picketline and rallying mass support. Worse still is to rely upon persuasion or slick approaches to the management of banks and insurance companies as a means of winning the workers' battle as the steel workers' union did.

On balance, these two very important struggles, Brown & Sharpe and Phelps Dodge, lent themselves far more to plant occupation and seizure of the properties as the best form of struggle under the given historical circumstances.

Bankruptcy and workers' control

Often a case presents itself to the workers where a legal possibility for workers' control seems to be ready made. That is the case of bankruptcy. There are hundreds of thousands of bankruptcies that take place during times of prosperity as well as times of recession.

In bankruptcy the legal ownership of the corporation or company is cast into doubt by its creditors. For a time at least the employer is incapable of exercising the right of exploitation in his or her own name unless the court or the creditors agree.

This is an ideal opportunity for the workers to intervene on the basis that they are the principal creditor, on two grounds. One, they are indispensable to production. And second, they are truly the most important creditors to the employers because they alone advance something of real value—their labor power—before getting paid. Few if any employers ever pay workers before they submit to exploitation, whether that be for a day, a week or a month.

By comparison, if a bank advances an individual a loan for a thousand dollars, the bank collects its interest before any of the principal is considered paid back. It is otherwise with the workers. They advance credit to the employers by virtue of the fact that they advance their labor power for a period of time prior to getting paid. No other creditors do that, only the workers.

Marx commented on this state of affairs in *Capital*: "In every country in which the capitalist mode of production reigns, it is the custom not to pay for labor-power before it has been exercised for the period fixed by the contract, as for example, the end of each week. In all cases, therefore, the use-value of the labor-power is advanced to the capitalist: the laborer allows the buyer to consume it before he receives payment of the price; he everywhere gives credit to the capitalist. That credit is no mere fiction is shown not only by the occasional loss of wages on the bankruptcy of the capitalist, but also by a series of more enduring consequences. Nevertheless, whether money serves as a means of purchase or as a means of payment, this makes no alteration in the nature of the exchange of commodities."[1]

The important thing Marx showed is that the status of the worker as a creditor is not a fiction but a reality.

Take factory workers, as one example. According to the Bureau of Labor Statistics, the average factory worker makes $246 a week. That's a $246 loan from the worker to the company until payday. Since the BLS says that there are almost 17 million factory workers in the U.S., that amounts to over $4 billion a week. When the wages of all the other workers are added to this, it is an astounding sum.

It should also be noted that the workers have a claim on interest on the credit they have advanced. This becomes lost because of the timidity of the position that the workers are restricted to mere wages. But the wages concept has to be broadened to go beyond just that part which has been won by the workers over years of struggle.

The workers' legal right as creditors in bankruptcy has never been asserted by the trade unions. It is high time that they do so, particularly at a time when bankruptcies are on the order of the day. This may strike some as a novel and out of this world idea, but so was union organization many years ago when it was considered a conspiracy, restraint of trade and illegal. What made it legal was that the workers asserted themselves. There is no reason they cannot do the same with this.

The United Mine Workers, for instance, introduced a new concept in bargaining when they demanded portal-to-portal pay—paying the workers from the time they arrived at the top of the mine shaft to when they got down to the mine face. How many hours do workers waste in getting to work? Why is that not compensated? The miners have won it only because they have put up a fight for it. Otherwise, no one would have listened to this impressive and necessary argument.

Leading workers in bargaining committees and elsewhere have to be educated on the question of workers' control. There are many unanswered questions when dealing with a hypothetical case that lend themselves to reasonable explanations once they are applied to a concrete situation.

It cannot be over-emphasized that workers' control is not a socialist measure. It is a democratic measure, a transitional form of struggle against capitalist management.

The Wheeling-Pittsburgh bankruptcy

When a company is about to go bankrupt, what should the union do? It is hazardous to disregard the bankruptcy threat, since companies are continually bringing it up.

The solution for the union is straightforward. Because the company has chosen the bankruptcy route, the union can insist on and has the right to become the trustee in bankruptcy and to operate the plant in the interests of the workers. When a company files for bankruptcy it is no longer the legal owner; it surrenders its title. The union, as the principal creditor of the company, is therefore the de facto owner on behalf of the workers.

The Wheeling-Pittsburgh Steel Company is a classic case where it was not only possible but probable that the union could have come out with a victory if it had seized and occupied the plant under its rights as principal creditor of the company which had entered into bankruptcy. There was no possibility whatever of strikebreaking as in the case of Brown & Sharpe or Phelps Dodge. There was no imminent danger of liquidation and the dismantling of the plants; this was altogether a phony threat.

Wheeling-Pittsburgh, with 8,200 workers, is one of the top seven steel corporations in the country with some of the most modern facilities. The union knew that whatever happened at Wheeling-Pitt would have a profound effect on all other steel workers.

The company had inspired a campaign of fear over many weeks, utilizing inner company struggles. It typically set up a good guy-bad guy situation in management and a quick fight among stockholders where the "good guys" won out over "bad guy" Dennis Carney, whose outlandish demeanor earned him the eternal hatred of the workers but to whom the union had made three wage and benefit concessions. Another group of stockholders under the leadership of a multi-millionaire named Allen Paulson with varied interests in other multinationals was set up as the "good guy."

Even under the bankruptcy law as it presently exists the union had some important vehicles for mounting an offensive against the company. The union is in point of law and of fact the principal creditor of the company. In the case of Wheeling-Pitt, for example, the company owed 10,000 retired workers over $400 million in benefits.

The union's standing as the principal creditor can also and should be deduced from the fact that the workers have a property right in their jobs. No operations can be or have been conducted by the company without the workers. Their labor is indispensable to the operation of the company.

This fact, so patently clear to anyone who has his or her eyes open, must be made a part of the bankruptcy proceedings, which are in reality a political struggle. As principal creditor, the union has the right to be appointed as the trustee in bankruptcy, if bankruptcy is the route that the company seeks to travel.

What is a trustee in bankruptcy? It is a person or group of persons that a court must appoint to take charge of the affairs of the company because it has filed for bankruptcy or reorganization. The trustee's duties and obligations are to operate and run the business. Once the union has become trustee it would have the right to recall the workers and begin to operate the business on the basis of the original union contract.

But how can the union undertake this initiative? The workers and the union have to take concrete steps to perfect their de facto ownership by possession and occupation of the plants or their rights will be disregarded.

A separation of ownership from possession cannot long exist. And the question of possession is critical to defending the union's right to trusteeship as the principal creditor.

The workers might have seized the plants and held them in the very early stages of the struggle at Wheeling-Pitt. This would have created the conditions to protect their rights as the principal creditors and therefore de facto owners. However, the United Steel Workers of America didn't want to provoke a real struggle. Instead they drained the energy and patience of the workers so that it looked like there was no alternative but to give in and surrender a little less than originally demanded by the company. Nevertheless, these concessions constituted a 60% wage cut in the most modern plants in the industry in the name of "improving the company's competitive position."

One of the worst features of the Wheeling-Pittsburgh strike was that the USWA, notwithstanding the key significance of such a highly modernized plant, tried to bottle up the struggle within the confines of these small communities without enlisting the support of the workers and the mass of the population nationwide. It was nothing less than obscene that the union leadership spent many thousands of dollars for advertisements in the *Wall Street Journal* and the financial pages of the *New York Times*, with their limited readership. The union used these advertisements to try and persuade the banking community and industrialists of the justice of the steel workers' case, rather than utilizing its immense resources to appeal to the broad working class public.

Question of legality

Workers' control usually can start by the workers taking possession of their plant and equipment in areas which are characterized by a big industry. Aside from the bosses themselves, the greatest hindrance to any real form of workers' control is the prevailing conception of the union leadership, inculcated systematically by the bourgeoisie, that it is illegal.

The employers' legal conceptions of the relationship between capital and labor are sunk very deep into the consciousness of the workers. Thus, at the beginning it is very necessary to try to formulate ways and means of showing that whatever the workers are doing in the way of taking possession of the plants is in accordance with legal procedures and that the law is on the side of the workers.

Some legal form of approach is very necessary in order to overcome the initial ideological resistance of the workers. Where the strike struggle or the pre-strike situation has aroused the continued interest of the workers in shaping strategy, it is almost always possible to find a legal formula to take possession of the plants.

It is important to formulate the issues in such a way that they are devoid of class collaborationist schemes for co-ownership with the employers, as these ultimately turn out to be nothing more than schemes to transfer authority back to the employers in some indirect way.

Workers' control, once it becomes a reality, has the tendency to provoke a political crisis. Employers may be forced to retreat under the impact of the political consequences of workers' control. In other words, workers' control in and of itself will not solve the basic problem, but it will put the workers into a far more favorable position where they are able to determine for a period of time their own conditions within the framework of the bourgeois system of production.

Even if it remains merely a threat of overcoming the bourgeois system by breaking up the capital-labor relationship, a protracted occupation will nevertheless put the workers on higher economic ground than prior to taking possession of the plants.

Workers' control needs considerable planning. It needs a certain amount of cooperation with the technical, supervisory and engineering personnel of the company or even the industry. It initially needs a certain understanding of the relation between the suppliers and producers in the industries and of market conditions. Workers in a general way understand this much more than they are given credit for by the bosses. Under certain conditions where their interest has been awakened, they can show tremendous skill not merely in operating the equipment but in plotting the course of production.

One merely has to examine situations in which society is temporarily thrown into disorder as a result of a natural catastrophe and see how spontaneously workers make plans and in fact carry out miracles in restoring the productive apparatus of the area. Once the creative initiative of the workers is unloosed, their capabilities are absolutely stupendous.

This is precisely why the employers seek to create an unbridgeable chasm between the production plans and the workers. Of course, the planning of the employers is strictly for profit, which is the fundamental reason why it is necessary for them to keep the workers out of it. But once it is conceived as part and parcel of the useful aspect of production, then the picture changes immediately.

Of course, it would be utterly illusory to feel that workers' control could become a stable, general economic phenomenon in the capitalist system without a profound change in the political consciousness of the workers. The two must go together. Workers' control can exist for only a brief period unless it is a move in anticipation of a general upsurge of the working class.

One of the basic reasons why workers would be opposed to workers' control, as we said, is the prevailing conception of bourgeois legality. Labor leaders are forever trying to exclusively confine their strategies to the accepted legal norms for conducting the struggle. Their bent is always in the direction of maintaining the same framework, which in effect means maintaining the capital-labor relationship, a relation of exploiter to exploited.

While it is absolutely necessary to construct some legal basis for a working class strategy, it is very important on the other hand to be on guard against creating illusions with respect to bourgeois legality, since the courts are traditionally the most conservative, reactionary elements in the capitalist government.

Struggle engenders new laws

Law is merely an adaptation to conditions. Progressive laws almost always merely ratify what has already been accomplished on the picketline or in other struggles. Once a forward strategy, a great leap forward to match the quantum leap in the technological revolution, has taken hold in the labor movement, laws will ratify the struggle.

The movement cannot remain in a sterile, static condition but needs a dynamic, affirmative offensive. Daring, boldness and determination must be put on labor's agenda.

Unions must learn how to utilize the so-called "custom and practice" legal theory of Anglo-Saxon jurisprudence on which the common law of the U.S. and Britain is based. Custom and practice is recognized by all U.S. courts as the equivalent of law where one can show custom and practice exists. This is as applicable to the struggle of the workers as to any struggle in the business community, such as the continuing internecine struggles over commercial, maritime or corporation law.

The right to a job is a property right. The right to seize and occupy the plants is an accompanying right.

Doing it will make it lawful if carried out in earnest and on a mass scale. The great need is for a positive program. The labor movement cannot be confined to a one-dimensional strategy. It needs flexibility. The formulation of a no-concessions program must be linked to the primary struggle to reverse the anti-labor offensive of the bosses. Every worker will ask, as they did in Wheeling-Pitt, "If you're against concessions to the company, what do you propose?"

Of course, the trade union movement has to be selective in deciding where and when such a strategy is applicable, just as we know where and when to strike.

The Saturn plant agreement between the United Auto Workers and General Motors shows how perilously close to abandoning the basic elements of unionism the leaders have come. The technological revolution is taking its toll. Owen Bieber of the UAW said about the Saturn plant: "We hope this thing will work out, that all the pieces of the jigsaw will fall together. But it may not. The worst thing in the world we could do is to try to make it fit in traditional operations."

He recognizes that it is upsetting the traditional relations, but his answer is to go backwards. His conclusion is to abandon some of the essential elements of collective bargaining rather than find a new strategy to fight the deleterious effects of the scientific-technological revolution!

The brazenness of the bosses must be met with a new confidence and militancy arising out of a new program. It must be shown that plant seizures and occupations are a logical and inevitable outcome in the evolution of the workers' movement, which has gone from the old Luddite strategy of sporadic struggles to mass organization and strike struggles, and now must move further ahead with a new form of struggle in order to meet the danger.

In labor relations we must reverse the biblical adage, "In the beginning was the word," to read, "In the beginning was the deed"—mass action, a new revolutionary strategy. The legislative word will follow; it will be ratified.

Note

1. Marx, *Capital*, pp. 170-171.

Chapter 10

A Mixed Bag of Other Tactics

The Youngstown case: what went wrong

While it is important to attempt to widen support for the workers in plant closings or plant takeovers, care has to be taken not to rely on public officials, the government and courts as the fundamental lever in the struggle against the huge multinationals and conglomerates.

The classic example of this is the case of the Campbell Works of the Youngstown Sheet & Tube Company, which was shut down in September 1977 by the predatory, New Orleans-based conglomerate, Lykes Corporation. The subsequent passage of years should not dim the significance of the crisis it caused and the overwhelming suffering inflicted on the workers and their communities.

A group of clergymen together with trade unionists from the area, Mahoning Valley in Ohio, formed a coalition to fight the shutdown. It was called the Ecumenical Coalition to Save Mahoning Valley.

The overall objective was correct: a community takeover of the plant, to be operated by the workers. But it was based on pledging their own savings to purchase stock in such an enterprise. They also felt it necessary to convince the U.S. Department of Housing and Urban Development to grant them $300,000 to finance a detailed feasibility study.

Under pressure of the times and the then-existing mood of militancy, the pressure exerted was sufficient to get the grant of $300,000. The contract, however, was given to the National Center for Economic Alternatives (NCEA). After more than a year of study and research the NCEA, led by economists Gar Alperovitz and Jeff Faux, concluded that a profitable community takeover could work if the federal government would provide $15 million up front in grants and $394 million in federally guaranteed loans, plus a list of Sheet & Tube's old customers.

It is often thought that the plant-closing era started with the Reagan administration. This is altogether erroneous. The administration in this major case demonstrated no greater regard for the workers.

The Carter administration at first agreed in principle to the plan, but this was in reality a ploy. After a long delay and maneuvering by U.S. Attorney General Griffin Bell and others, and the runaround to the U.S. Economic Development Administration, the loan was turned down. That ended the matter.

The idea of a takeover was correct, and so was putting pressure on the Carter administration. But what was woefully wrong in all this was for the researchers to attempt to prove over an extended period that if the money were granted, it would be a profitable enterprise. That should not be the aim of a takeover at all. It should not be contingent on profitability but on the maintenance and operation of the plant.

The U.S. post office was run by the government for almost two centuries, and profitability was never a criterion. It was deemed necessary to meet the needs of industry and of developing communications and also because of the growing number of communities that needed service. The airlines were all granted monumental sums by the government, and it was not based on any conception that the particular enterprise had to prove its profitability. The expenditures were all seen as necessary for development.

What could be more important than the maintenance of such a key project in the heart of the steel area as Youngstown Sheet & Tube?

The aim of a workers' takeover is to demonstrate the willingness, the determination to take hold of the means of production and to operate them, forcing the government to subsidize the plant as it has done for the infrastructure of all U.S. industry—but this time for the benefit of the workers.

This can only be done by broadening and widening the struggle, not by conducting it on an isolated basis. More than ever the responsibility rests on the top trade union leaders who have the allegiance of millions of workers. These apparently local struggles have national significance for all the workers and all the oppressed. To leave the communities to deal with them on their own is not only gross neglect but downright malfeasance in office.

Another attempt by the workers to keep the plants open took place at U.S. Steel in Youngstown. The case went before Judge Thomas Lambros, who had this to say: "The court has spent many hours searching for a way to cut to the heart of the economic reality that obsolescence and market forces demand the closing of the Mahoning Valley plant and yet the lives of 3,500 workers and their families and the supporting Youngstown community cannot be dismissed as inconsequential. U.S. Steel should not be permitted to leave the

Youngstown area devastated after drawing from the lifeblood of the community for so many years."[1]

So far, so good. Then comes the punch line. "Unfortunately, the mechanism to reach this ideal settlement, to recognize this new property right, is not in existence in the code of laws of our nation."

But it is! It's enshrined in the 14th Amendment to the Constitution, which states that no person shall be deprived of their property without due process of law. The Youngstown workers over these many, many years, like all other workers, have a property right in their jobs.

It would be as easy as pie to see this as not only just but perfectly logical if the judge himself were not beholden to other property rights, the rights of the bosses, while sanctimoniously shedding crocodile tears over the workers.

Of course, there should be local legislation to deal with this as well as federal legislation, and that's what prenotification is all about. But local laws are set up merely to implement from a legal point of view what already is and should be considered as the basic, organic law that supposedly rules the country—the Constitution.

Eminent domain

Eminent domain means the right of the government to take private property for public use, indeed, any use that the government sees fit. Every state in the union, including Hawaii and Alaska, has that right enacted into law. It is also sanctioned by the federal government, which has long used eminent domain to acquire land or other forms of private property for public use. Almost all of the states have some provision which gives the various units of the state—county, city or other municipality—the right to use eminent domain.

The method by which this is done is called a condemnation proceeding. It usually calls for a public hearing; after a certain period of time the city, state, county or federal government proceeds to take over the private property.

It's important to remember how the practice of eminent domain started. It began way back when the feudal monarchies were just establishing themselves and when they actually robbed the peasants of the land to establish their domain—the palace grounds and the royal estate. During the period of capitalist development, this power was taken over by the bourgeois state, but many provisions were made to ensure some form of compensation, which was left up to either a jury or the judicial process.

Condemnation proceedings are an everyday occurrence in the U.S. and the law journals carry regular notices of them. The importance of eminent domain to the workers has arisen in the light of the current epidemic of plant closings and threats from the employers which make job insecurity a daily worry. Workers in plants that have already been closed or partially disman-

tled, or are on the verge, have given consideration to the possibility of utilizing the stratagem of eminent domain as a means to take over the plants,
equipment and facilities of the corporations in an effort to stop the barbarous
vandalism these giant multinational corporations and big banks are pursuing.

It should be noted that not only the federal government but the state, city
and municipal governments have a right to delegate their authority for the use
of eminent domain to a nongovernmental body. The government contributes
funds, that is, appropriates money for this authority and gives it the right to
operate, sometimes almost autonomously.

One example is the construction of a bridge to connect two cities divided by
a body of water. The bridge authority, whether instituted by two cities or two
states, is authorized to build the bridge and often to collect the tolls. The same
procedure is used in the building of a tunnel like New York City's Holland and
Lincoln tunnels, both operated by the New York-New Jersey Port Authority.

The most famous example was the Tennessee Valley Authority (TVA), established during the Roosevelt administration. It was subsidized by the federal government and turned out to be a vast boon to the communities it served.

How does this process start? It doesn't usually originate with the government. Most often it's big businessmen, real estate developers and construction
companies who present plans to the government to show how it can be done.
The government then creates an authority, composed mostly of these very
same people, and money is appropriated to run the project. Where there's
a considerable degree of community awareness, which most of the time has
been lacking, or where the labor movement has concerned itself, they have
some input. This happens rarely, however.

Considering the magnitude of the havoc created by plant closures, a group
of community and church leaders and activists from the steel areas met in the
spring of 1985 in Homestead, Pennsylvania, for the purpose of using eminent
domain for a workers' takeover. They took the idea of eminent domain from
the Tri-State Conference on Steel which has been in existence for a number of
years, and announced an effort to establish a Steel Valley Authority.

The city of Pittsburgh is said to have given $50,000 to help in the proj-
ect. A number of officials in the tri-state area have given their approval to it.
It includes mayors from cities in the three states of Pennsylvania, Ohio and
West Virginia and some state representatives from the Pennsylvania legisla-
ture. The question is how to get this off the ground since it has already been in
the discussion stage for a considerable period of time.

There is no question that the idea of a tri-state Steel Valley Authority (SVA)
could take on considerable momentum. It already has a wide variety of community people and steel workers who have shown interest in the project. The
United Steel Workers union (USWA) through some of its local leaders has

shown considerable interest. The international thus far has given it minimal attention, but it could become involved to a much larger extent. The problem really is how to proceed from here. That's what most workers are concerned with—what next?

We have seen how the bosses, real estate developers, construction companies and bankers do it. They approach the government and the government delegates the authority to them and also gives them abundant funds to start whatever project is suggested. By giving a small donation, the city of Pittsburgh has done one thing. It has validated the legal existence of the SVA. This could be important depending on what is done next.

If it remains a study group or, worse yet, a means of diverting the interests of the workers in the area, which is apparently what the capitalist politicians and bosses in the tri-state area hope, then of course it's an exercise in futility, just as in the Youngstown case.

But there's a very important opportunity if the SVA begins to act in earnest. First, it must demand a considerable sum of money from the tri-state legislatures. Second, it can subpoena the books and records of the banks and companies and then project mass actions on the basis of the tri-state authority, supported by the unions—which must be the integral part, the most important component in the SVA.

Truly mass actions have to be planned with a view toward occupying the most sensitive facilities connected with the tri-state area, which has all these years lived on the sweat and blood of the workers and is now contemptuously disregarding their plight. This involves not merely the occupation of the idle plants threatened with foreclosure but also the banks, particularly the Mellon bank and its various instrumentalities.

In an earlier period the groups involved carried out sporadic activities, demonstrations and self-sacrifice, including imprisonment. The problem was that all this had not yet attained mass proportions. This time around, from a strictly objective point of view, it is possible to renew the process on a larger mass scale and to claim full legality.

The very existence of the SVA and the fact that a central city, the city of Pittsburgh, recognized its existence, provides a significant legal means to perfect the whole process of eminent domain. From here on the actual utilizing of eminent domain depends on mobilizing the broader sections of the steel workers and their communities for the purposes of a takeover of not only the idled plants but of such facilities as banking, insurance companies and their satellite corporate entities.

Another conference is definitely needed, but this time an attempt must be made to broaden it into a rank-and-file movement of workers in the tri-state area. This conference should detail the next concrete steps to be taken, which involve the mass of the workers and all segments of the communities in the affected area. The masses must be made confident that this time around they have a legal right to do what needs to be done to perfect the right of eminent domain.

Actually doing it lays the basis for legal ratification in custom and practice, as we said earlier. All this could be used as a stimulus to arouse the mass movement to take the necessary measures. If bankers, real estate developers and construction companies can draw up their own plans for their projects, come to the city or state and get it to ratify their plan by creating an authority, why can't the workers in the distressed communities get the same treatment?

Surely if the bankers, real estate developers and construction companies felt it was feasible to construct a new bullet rail line such as the ones now in vogue in Japan and Europe, the governments would jump at the opportunity.

Well, the workers have their own plan to reopen the plants and do whatever else is necessary for the survival of the tri-state steel communities. This requires funds of a massive character, which must not be held up by delaying tactics requiring that the plan be submitted for study to demonstrate its feasibility and profitability. No, what mass struggle can do is show that the plans are not only feasible and practical but are based on urgent necessity.

ESOPs

What are ESOPs? ESOPs—Employee Stock Ownership Plans—are a form of veiled ownership by management where nominal ownership is by the workers. A study by *Business Week*[2] showed that in early 1985 there were already 7,000 companies which had enrolled nearly 10 million workers into ESOPs. In the 1970s, there were fewer than half a million workers in ESOPs. There is no breakdown available on the percentage of union as against non-union workers. Most are in unorganized plants, but a considerable number are covered by union contracts.

ESOPs pose a problem of considerable importance to the trade union movement. Not only are they one of the crudest forms of class collaboration, but they also have a tendency to eventually swallow up the trade unions and deprive them of their independence.

The idea of employee stock ownership is not a new one. It began to flourish in the late 1920s and was fueled by the wild stock market speculation of that period. The idea at that time was for large corporations to put on promotion schemes for workers to buy company stock. However, what was considered a strong current for workers to become part "owners" of management came to an abrupt end with the great stock market crash of October 1929. The embryo ESOP movement collapsed, as did thousands of corporations, in the wake of the great capitalist crisis. It didn't get revived until the early 1970s.

During the great CIO upsurge of the labor movement in the 1930s such stock schemes were almost always disregarded and scorned by the trade unions. But, as can be seen, the capitalist crisis which began in 1979 and has continued for many industries up until this writing has revived them to an alarming extent.

The problem for the union is a two-fold one. First, how does the union devise ways and means to resist them where possible in the face of what is sometimes great eagerness on the part of the workers, who hope to save their jobs? The other problem is how to protect the workers' investment in the many plants and industries where ESOPs have already been established for some period of time and see to it that management does not plunder and pillage the savings of the workers by various stock schemes which dilute the workers' share in the company.

The purpose of any and all stockholding schemes is to tie the workers down to management's fundamental interests, to win loyalty to the company as against their own interests. In this connection it should be remembered that stock manipulation fraud is a long-time characteristic of big business and especially the huge multinational corporations. No corporation, however big, is free from stock fluctuations and deliberate attempts to water down classes of stock in order to liquidate the interests of the stockholders.

The usual scheme by which an ESOP is put across is very much aided and assisted by a series of laws enacted by Congress beginning as long ago as 1974. Sixteen laws in all were passed, mostly the result of big business lobbying. The most important one, passed in 1984, gives the banks some very luscious tax incentives pushed through by the Reagan administration along with other tax breaks for big business and the banks.

The way these things work is as follows: A company suddenly demands huge concessions from the workers, claiming bad business conditions. Layoffs are threatened and finally management seemingly throws up its hands and says the company is on the brink of failure. It suggests that the workers should now become the owners of the plant as a result of accepting an Employee Stock Ownership Plan.

Usually the plan does not give the workers the right to vote their stock but, depending upon the situation, does give them a director or two or, as in the case of Hyatt-Clark Industries, where the workers are represented by the UAW, three directors. The plan is worked out by expert ESOP consultants who have long worked on these things, especially the company headed by Louis O. Kelso, a San Francisco investment banking firm.

What happens then? The company often claims that it's got a cash-flow crisis and proceeds to get a bank loan. Banks, which are usually reluctant to advance money to companies in danger, are eager in the case of ESOPs. That's because they get special privileges and can write off as much as 50% of the interest as well as the loan, and other complicated privileges. The bank passes the money to ESOP. Then ESOP passes the loan to the company.

The company in return issues the stock to ESOP and it is then held in trust for the workers, but is not given to them directly. It is held in their account.

As we said earlier, corporate manipulation and fraud is a long-time practice of big business to which the Securities and Exchange Commission, especially under the Reaganites (assuming that the company is one obligated to register with the SEC), frequently "closes its eyes."

How have things worked out thus far? There are two principal examples which should be borne in mind. Hyatt-Clark Industries, previously mentioned, and the Dan River textile plant in Danville, Va. Before any ESOP plan, Dan River had 12,000 workers. Over a period of time this has now been reduced to about 8,000. The workers as a result of a campaign of fear and the constant propaganda about imports were persuaded not only to make considerable wage concessions but also to trade in their pension plan rights in favor of the ESOP.

The company thereafter sold its three Greenville plants and the workers had to learn about it from the newspapers. In addition the company closed another plant under an ESOP plan and buried the money from the workers' earnings in an account operated by trustees, who are usually appointed by management. (In this case, the trustee is the United Virginia Bank.) And the trustees of these ESOP accounts usually vote with management on the board of directors.

In the case of the Hyatt-Clark Industries UAW local, the union had three representatives on the board of directors, which included former UAW President Douglas Fraser. After considerable wage and benefit concessions made by the union, the company did show a profit. The company then decided that the $600,000 profit should go to purchase new machinery for modernization. The workers wanted it to be added to their wages. The company directors outvoted the union 9-to-1, which outraged the workers. After a series of occasional slowdowns the union agreed to cutbacks and layoffs instead. The overall result was concessions by the union which strengthened the hold of management.

As of this writing, the Hyatt company has been sold off to an Oklahoma company and Owen Bieber, the president of the UAW, has assured the new owners that the union will make further concessions.

There are cases where, as a result of threats of shutdown and bankruptcy, union or non-union workers have accepted very far-reaching concessions resulting in steep cuts in wages and benefits in exchange for two or three directors. This happened in the airline industry at Eastern and TWA, which used the strikebreaking pushed through by Continental Airlines as a weapon of intimidation. A study remains to be made on how many other workers have been pushed back in this way.

The entire experience of ESOPs, and there are a great many varieties of them, is that they not only leave the workers with a lowered income but are attempts to tie the workers securely to the chariot wheels of class collaboration. With some of the large oil and other multinationals intent on making steep cuts in the workforce and depriving the workers of benefits, they deliberately instigate a campaign of fear that the companies will be taken over by "raiders," such men as Carl Icahn, T. Boone Pickens and others. These are cases where ESOPs have been in progress for a period of time, such as at Phillips Petroleum, National Can Corporation and others.

In Weirton Steel, an old union-busting company which formed a so-called independent company union many years ago, many concessions have been made and the company has eked out an existence only because of the steep concessions made by the workers, who have no real rights over management of the company.

In the Phillips Petroleum case, the management had promoted one of the most sophisticated fear campaigns among the workers about a piratical takeover by outside interests. It virtually mobilized the employees in entire towns where the company had locations behind its defensive strategy to ward off a takeover, which would have allegedly lost many jobs for the workers.

In the end, however, the management made a secret deal with Icahn; then the company proceeded with the layoffs and cutbacks, including of salaried staff people as well. This also happened in National Can. And at Dan River, the company also put up Icahn as the great danger who was threatening a takeover. It then of course made a deal which resulted in more concessions.

The same thing happened with CBS and Ted Turner. CBS launched a campaign to line up the workers on its side against this extreme rightwinger who threatened free speech, but once the takeover threat from Turner was over, it proceeded to lay off hundreds of workers.

What workers can do about existing ESOPs

In industries and plants where ESOPs already prevail, the union's position should be first, that on the expiration of the contract, ESOP accounts should be converted into cash to be distributed to the workers in the form of wage increases. Where this proves impossible, the union should demand that there be open board meetings, and that the ESOP trust account be run by union-appointed administrators. If the union has a vote on the board, there should be prior consultation with the union and membership, and where decisions are made they should be ratified by the union membership. Local unions should have their constitutions amended in such a way as to make the ESOPs and ESOP management subject to union control.

As against ESOPs, where the workers feel that a strike may be ineffective because of the deterioration of the industry as a whole, they should fight for workers' control. Workers' control is not a permanent or stable form of struggle, given the nature of the capitalist system. However, it is superior to the ESOPs as a transitional form in the overall class struggle against the bosses. In the first place, it makes all decisions regarding operations and control only in consultation with and by consent of the workers. Unlike ESOPs, it does not put financial control in the hands of a bogus group of management-appointed or bank-controlled supervisors who in effect make decisions without any vote of the workers.

Workers' control was instituted in some of the European countries in the period immediately after the Second World War and made significant gains in West Germany, some areas of Belgium, France and other countries. But in the absence of the perspective of a socialist transformation they gradually gave way to greater and greater management control. However, as in the case of Sweden, they are still far superior to anything that the ESOPs have accomplished in the U.S. In Europe, to the extent that workers' control was instituted, it was a means of elevating the workers' interests within the framework of the capitalist system. The ESOPs here have been mostly a form of attacking the workers' interests.

ESOPs and the Great Crash

There are any number of bourgeois economists who have drawn parallels between the present speculative surge in the stock market and the one which touched off the great economic collapse of October 1929. Financial news writers in particular have drawn attention to the fact that the widely heralded period of capitalist prosperity in the late 1920s was characterized by a growing agricultural crisis which sent grain and other agricultural commodities slumping to lower and lower levels. At the same time the apologists from bourgeois academia were still singing praises to the wonders of the free enterprise system and how well it was performing.

What is of particular interest now is that an anti-labor offensive was also in progress during that period. It was little noticed in the merry celebrations of the capitalist class over their growing prosperity.

An element of exceptional importance in relation to the present situation was the big drive to get the workers to purchase corporate stock and also increasing pressure on the workers to get into various employee stock ownership plans. Among those pushing hardest from bourgeois academia during the booming 1920s was Thomas Nixon Carver, a professor of political economy at Harvard. He wrote a widely publicized book at the time with the attractive title of *The Present Economic Revolution in the United States.*

Carver was lyrical about the developing period and vigorously pushed the stock ownership idea. Louis Kelso and his collaborators of today are really a sort of 1980 version of Carver, who at that time wrote, "The only economic revolution now under way is going on in the United States. It is a revolution that is to wipe out the distinction between laborers and capitalists by making laborers their own capitalists and by compelling the capitalists to become laborers of one kind or another.

"There are at least three kinds of evidence that indicate roughly the extent to which laborers are becoming capitalists. First the rapid growth of savings deposits; second the investment by laborers in the shares of corporations; third the growth of labor banks. The saving power of American working men is so great that if they would save and carefully invest their savings, in 10 years they would be one of the dominating financial powers of the world."[3]

As everyone now knows, the Great Crash which followed wiped out many of the stock flotations held by workers and even more by middle class elements. It brought on not 10 years of dominating financial power by the workers but a 10-year worldwide capitalist recession which was only diverted by the gathering momentum of the Second World War.

There were also attempts during the 1920s to draw elements of the trade union movement into the organization of labor banks. The economic collapse virtually wiped them all out. Some, such as the Brotherhood Holding Company of the Brotherhood of Locomotive Engineers, had made huge investments and collapsed even before the capitalist economic crisis got underway.

It is well to bear all this in mind at a time when millions of workers have part of their wages in stock ownership, a variety of private pension funds and other methods of deferred wages. While a good many of these are supposed to be guaranteed by the government, pension funds and all kinds of life insurance plans by municipalities and states and even the federal government have yet to be tested in the event of an economic collapse.

Once a worker's paycheck is deposited in the bank, it enters into the mainstream of the flow of capital formation. It is true that the capitalist class as a whole controls it, but on the other hand it is the blind forces of the capitalist market which motivate the capitalists in their insatiable drive for profits.

Every effort has to be made by the trade unions, indeed by all progressive organizations, to preserve and secure the savings of the workers. These are prey to being pillaged, plundered or defrauded by an endless variety of schemes concocted by the growing multitude of labor consultants hired by the bosses whose aim is to tie the independent class interests of the workers to that of the avaricious and predatory interests of the giant corporations and banks. The only certain power of the working class and particularly of the trade union movement lies not in collaboration with the bosses but in independent organization and class struggle against the bosses.

Vigilance committees

In the wee hours of December 11, 1985, the General Electric Company (GE) acquired the Radio Corporation of America (RCA), owner of the NBC television network. It is said to be the biggest non-oil merger or acquisition in history, worth $6.28 billion.

The merger was carried out in secret by a meeting of the board of directors for both companies. There are many facets to this giant merger of two multinational defense contractors, but what ought to interest most of the workers at these two companies is that none of the several strong unions which represent them were in any way consulted or even notified. It should also be noted that the stockholders were not informed either, except those big ones who were on the inside track and close to the banks which engineered the deal. This merger or acquisition, whichever you call it, involved no less than 300,000 workers at GE and 106,000 at RCA.[4] This deal concerned them.

These more than 400,000 workers created the wealth of these two industrial giants, counted in the billions. Yet the joint statement issued by the two companies announced that they now had "an excellent strategic opportunity for both companies that will help their competitiveness in world markets" and that they would "successfully compete now with anyone, anywhere, in every market we serve."

This meant first embarking on a program to cut down on duplication and reduce costs, which in the final analysis means cutting labor time and eliminating thousands of jobs. Both these companies have been doing it with a vengeance since 1978.

There have been no big mergers in the recent wave of mergers and acquisitions which did not end up with vast cutbacks and layoffs. That's their whole purpose. When a giant merger like this takes place it means that these corporate monsters have targeted the workers for job elimination. None of this, by the way, was mentioned in the announcement by GE and RCA. But the layoffs will follow as night follows day.

Both of these companies also have had experience in spinoffs or breakups. The two seem to be contradictory but are not. For instance, when RCA sold off Hertz Rent-A-Car and the CIT financial corporation, layoffs in the sold-off divisions followed. When GE sold off Utah International, the same thing happened. The purpose of mergers as well as spinoffs and breakups is job elimination. That's where the savings for the bosses come in. For them, raising productivity means cutting down on labor time.

This is what all the predatory struggles among the giant corporations are all about. They concern how to get rid of as many workers as possible from the payrolls in order to line the pockets of the top corporate bureaucracy and the bankers.

Most of these mergers and acquisitions are carried out in secrecy. While one of the purposes of secrecy is to guard against competitors as well as stockholders, the other is to keep the workers in the dark. When a rumor starts regarding a merger or acquisition, workers become more and more worried about their jobs, especially since they receive no information about what will happen to them once these industrial combinations or divisions take effect.

What must be done in this connection? Vigilance committees have to be established among the workers to monitor the situation long before these acquisitions, mergers and resulting plant shut-downs begin. These vigilance committees should act as intelligence groupings for the security of the jobs of all workers. Of course, where possible these committees need to be established not only by local union committees but by international unions on an industry-wide basis. Most people would be surprised how easy it is for workers to get the necessary information. Some information can be obtained from the press, where it is usually hidden in the financial pages. But there are other ways.

Working cooperatively, the unions and production workers have access to clerical help and maintenance workers in the executive offices of the corporation, even in the board rooms where the corporate officers meet. It is well known that these giant corporations have a network of spies of their own who eavesdrop on workers, even in the restrooms. Is that not so?

Well, workers have the right to do the same thing. It is one thing when a union is large and strong enough to be able to get expert financial advice, analyze the annual reports of the corporations and follow the stock of the individual corporation on the stock exchange. That shifts the task away from the workers to more specialized people. But workers have a way of finding the information through workers.

Remember the secret internal memo in which General Motors' plans for cutting back the workforce were spelled out in some detail? Well, it was obtained because a clerical worker brought it to the attention of the union. Telephone conversations and internal memos can and often do get into the hands of the union leadership. These are sometimes derelict in making them immediately available to the union membership or the appropriate committee, which in this case should be the vigilance committee. (Barry Bluestone and Bennett Harrison in their book[5] refer to reconnaissance committees, whose purpose is limited to research, while we are suggesting worker intelligence committees to counteract management's spy network.)

What is needed is to apply the same strategy unions use at the beginning of every strike when the possibility of scabbing exists. The company has its informers and the strike committee knows some unfortunate workers may be susceptible to scabbing. Immediately upon calling the strike, a vigilance committee aware of this potential establishes a telephone tree where contact is immediately made with those susceptible to boss psychology.

Also, before a strike takes place, the vigilance committee finds out the list of suppliers, customers, banking connections, everything. Its function is to watch out for all developments and present reports to the union and the public. All this should be in addition to what the union regularly does by way of getting the public literature of the company and analyzing it.

All these measures have become more and more vital as the predatory corporations and their lust for super-profits relentlessly drive the workers and even themselves into a blind alley.

Hormel strike and the AFL-CIO leadership

Beginning on August 17, 1985, the 1,500 members of United Food and Commercial Workers Local P-9 at the Hormel company in Austin, Minnesota, went on strike against drastic wage cuts and for improved medical benefits, compensation for on-the-job injuries, seniority and grievance and arbitration procedures. In October 1984, the company had unilaterally reduced wages from $10.69 an hour to $8.25, although through arbitration this was raised to $9.25 by the time the strike was forced on the union.

Despite the fact that the international union sanctioned the strike, the local union was subjected to considerable attack by the international and the top officialdom of the AFL-CIO. William H. Wynn, president of the United Food and Commercial Workers, attacked the local for its "suicidal strategy," and issued a seven-page statement smearing the strike to the AFL-CIO Executive Board meeting in Bal Harbour, Florida, on February 17, 1986. Lane Kirkland, the president of the AFL-CIO, gave his full endorsement to this statement.

At the same time, the local was continuing its strike under the guns of the National Guard, which had been called out by Democratic Governor Rudy Perpich. By the middle of February the company was claiming it had resumed production with scabs brought in by the force of the National Guard and the courts, and was having strike leaders arrested for picketing the plant.

There may be dozens of other strikes that are similarly bitter and protracted but are not publicized. It's not easy to tabulate them since the Reagan administration has ceased taking note of such events. The Bureau of Labor Statistics no longer counts strikes which involve less than a thousand workers.

The bitterness and duration of the Hormel strike, important as they are, don't account for its special significance. The fundamental reason why this strike attained special importance and drew the attention and support of so many rank-and-file workers from coast to coast is that it became the symbol of resistance to the steady, undeviating line of concessions to the bosses by most of the AFL-CIO trade union hierarchy.

Enormous sympathy was accumulated by the local leadership precisely because it had taken on a task which millions of workers felt was necessary and indispensable for their future welfare. The strike became a veritable struggle between capital and labor, a test of strength between the working class and the capitalist class, which was still going on as of this writing.

However, there has been no real test of strength between the organized working class with all its millions of followers and the capitalist class. The potentialities of the struggle of the two class camps have not been brought forward.

Hormel is at best a medium-sized company among the giant corporations of the U.S. Whatever its financial connections may be, as an economic and industrial unit it can count its assets in the millions, or at the most a couple of billion. However, it is by no means of the stature of General Motors, Ford, or U.S. Steel, which count their assets in the tens and hundreds of billions.

The organized labor movement as a whole is the product of struggles which have successfully taken on all of these major corporations and accumulated vast experience, resources and a following of millions upon millions of workers, both organized and unorganized. While the capitalist press and media as usual may have been solidly lined up on the side of the company, in the eventuality of a real test between labor and capital, between the workers and the bosses, it remains to be seen whether the ruling class would go even a short distance to support such a middle-sized minion of high finance and big industry.

The ruling class is monolithic in its general advocacy of the anti-labor offensive. It would be another matter if, in an actual struggle, the labor movement dared to make a test case. The most advanced and militant sections of the trade union movement generously supported the strike, but mainly with moral support plus limited financial resources. In addition, many hundreds demonstrated militant solidarity by traveling many miles to help picket in sub-zero weather.

Important and invaluable as this support was, it did not constitute a test of strength as against big capital. Instead of roundly denouncing the strike, what the AFL-CIO should have done was to show that they regarded the Hormel strike as a test of their collective strength and of their willingness and readiness to engage the company in a genuine contest. That would have turned around the whole situation in no time.

The ruling class in the U.S. would be terrified at the prospect of a breakup of class peace between the workers and the bosses at a time it is faced with unprecedented revolutionary struggles around the world.

The only thing the U.S. ruling class has going for it, in light of the international situation, is that at home it has been able to maintain class peace, the submission of the working class to the extortionate demands of the bosses at a crucial time in its history.

The AFL-CIO labor bureaucracy, in its aversion to any test of strength, reflects the fear and apprehensions not of the workers but of the ruling class. It lacks a true measure of the potential political and social strength of the working class in the crucible of struggle.

This is the crudest and narrowest form of what Lenin called economism—conducting a trade union struggle or any kind of localized struggle on the basis of narrow economic conceptions when the battle is in reality of a profoundly political character. The Hormel company, like dozens of others throughout the land, giant corporations as well as smallfry, joined the pack and demanded onerous concessions precisely because the labor hierarchy was more responsive to the demands and fears of the ruling class than to the class interests of the workers.

Of course, in the initial stages of every capitalist recession the objective situation is unfavorable for the workers. They have to take a defensive posture while the capitalist class has the initiative and can take the offensive. But the whole historical experience of the working class shows that every prolonged anti-labor offensive was eventually followed by a labor upsurge. The time came when the workers did say, "Enough!" Such a time is now long overdue.

The head of the UAW, Owen Bieber, speaking at a legislative conference of the UAW in Washington, D.C., on January 16, 1986, characterized the situation prevailing in the country and the labor movement as "the strongest conservative reaction in our lifetime." While this may be true, it is a general political trend generated by the ruling class. Bieber and others who politically lean in a social-democratic direction are using this as a rationalization for a policy of concessions to the bosses and swimming with the tide, rather than bucking it or finding ways and means to respond to the anti-labor offensive. That's the only way to overcome the political reaction.

It's appropriate to recall an historic example of a test of strength between both classes that the workers won without firing a shot. After the 1937 victory of the General Motors workers as a result of the sit-down strike and the occupation of the plants by the workers, there was an unprecedented outcry from the capitalist press condemning Michigan Governor Frank Murphy, who had been the mediator between the UAW committee and the company's representative. They screamed about anarchy, chaos and the threatened revolution and warned John L. Lewis and all other labor leaders of what would befall them if such a struggle continued.

At that time the Steel Workers Organizing Committee (SWOC) headed by

High Tech, Low Pay

Philip Murray, John Brophy, Van A. Bittner, Bill Mitch and David McDonald, all working under the direction of John L. Lewis, were preparing for a test of strength in the most difficult and at that time strongest anti-labor and unorganized fortress of the capitalist class. The steel strike of 1919 had been crushed with many beatings, arrests, many families ruined and their homes lost.

Even in the ranks of labor, many felt that U.S. Steel was mobilizing not only the capitalist media but the courts and the state's repressive forces to do it again if the SWOC leaders were to seriously embark on an effort to organize and win. There were many forebodings and fears, even in the ranks of militant workers, but at the same time they felt confident, not only because of the victory over General Motors but because they knew SWOC leaders could draw on the strength of labor in the event of a test between the seemingly omnipotent U.S. Steel Corporation and the organizing committee.

It would have been a real test of strength, because the leaders were ready to do what was necessary in order to win. But the test was never carried to its ultimate conclusion. Why?

Because this all-powerful, omnipotent corporation, supported by the biggest banks, capitulated without a struggle. "(T)he largest steel company in the world surrendered. The foe that the CIO had thought would be the toughest succumbed without a struggle. By a mere show of strength the SWOC had won a 10% wage increase, a 40-hour week and union recognition for thousands of steel workers employed by United States Steel. It would be difficult to say who was most surprised at U.S. Steel's capitulation, the workers or the tycoons. . . ."[6]

It is precisely such preparation for a test of strength that is lacking in the labor movement today. The AFL-CIO let the struggle be carried on the shoulders of one local, with the widespread moral support of many other workers. It may have feared a generalized struggle between capital and labor, but the capitalist class itself is not ready or willing to undergo such a test. The most valuable asset it has at the moment, class peace in the midst of a revolutionary international situation, it would not surrender in the interests of just one of a multitude of huge companies.

If U.S. Steel, backed by the mightiest bankers of the time, J.P. Morgan & Company, could calculate that in its own interests it was the better part of wisdom to sign up with the SWOC, there's no valid reason why a similar evaluation would not be made this time as well. At any rate, should the ruling class, not just Hormel, alone decide to challenge the organized labor movement in a general contest between capital and labor, it would be a thousand times preferable to go through the experience of a great enriching struggle than to endure an abject, divisive, humiliating policy of surrender which history will not forget and a resurgent working class will condemn and pillory.

Inner struggles in the ruling class

Everywhere and in almost any period there are contradictory interests not only among the various capitalist states but among the various capitalist industries, as well as conflicts within each industry. Capitalist contradictions tear apart even the most giant corporations. Indeed, there is scarcely a huge conglomerate or multinational corporation that is not characterized by the sharpest antagonisms in the struggle for profit.

Take, for instance, some of the terminology that is utilized in the inner struggles for control of their corporations. The last decade has brought forth such terms as "poison pill," which applies when one group of capitalists tries to ward off a takeover by another. The idea behind this is that the group making the offer for the takeover looks very attractive, but in reality is poison and full of booby-traps. It may intervene to ruin a takeover attempt by hostile forces, but that does not necessarily make it friendly, meaning that it would offer more profitable terms to reorganize or merge.

Or take their attitude to bankers, who are frequently referred to not in hallowed terms like "advisers," but as "undertakers." Those who come out on top in any of these struggles are said to have engineered a "killing."

Thus their relationships are anything but cooperative and harmonious. They may demand harmony and cooperation from the workers, but among themselves they are torn by the most destructive forms of inner struggle. All this is due to the driving force of capitalist competition, which in turn of course is based on the chase for super-profits.

Taking advantage of the inner struggles inside management or among different cliques in the corporation or ruling class is of course very important. Vital as it is, however, to take cognizance of the antagonisms between various cliques and in management, especially among the giant corporations, it is utterly false to paint them as good guys and bad guys and try to construct a labor relations policy based on these inner struggles.

The main and fundamental lever of the struggle at all times is the unity and solidarity of the workers. The inner antagonisms of the ruling class of even a small plant or corporation can be utilized as an auxiliary weapon but that should not interfere with organizing and mobilizing the workers for struggle.

Notes

1. Quoted in Bluestone and Harrison, *The Deindustrialization of America*, p. 254.
2. *Business Week,* April 15, 1985
3. Quoted in Foster, William Z., *American Trade Unionism: Principles, Organization, Strategy*, International Publishers (New York, 1974).
4. *Wall Street Journal*, Dec. 12, 1985.
5. Bluestone and Harrison, *op. cit.*
6. Boyer, Richard. O. and Herbert M. Morais, *Labor's Untold Story*, United Electrical, Radio & Machine Workers of America (UE) (New York, 1955).

Chapter 11

Conclusion

Two bourgeois theories
on the scientific-technological revolution

What, then, is the ultimate destiny of the scientific-technological revolution?

The bourgeois economists tend to fall into two not very distinct but none-theless discernible schools of thought on this subject. One of them points to the past two centuries, which have seen a great many technological revolu-tions, beginning with the spinning wheel, the steam engine, the railroads, and so on. They argue that insofar as the functioning of the capitalist social system is concerned, the scientific-technological revolution does not really change much—no more, they say, than did the introduction of the automobile as a form of transportation, superseding the horse and buggy days.

While it is true that the functioning of the capitalist system, meaning thereby the exploitation of wage labor by capital, has not been fundamen-tally altered, the recent changes, however, do introduce a new social develop-ment. The older revolutions in technology can be compared to the scientif-ic-technological revolution as an arithmetical progression is compared to a geometric one. This new revolution of course doesn't change the character of exploitation, but it multiplies its intensity, as the data we have presented discloses, and this becomes cumulative with each passing day as more and more statistical data is available.

The other school of thought, somewhat older and more craven in its apolo-gies for the system, deals with the scientific-technological revolution from another angle. Its view, which has been extensively covered ever since Daniel Bell relieved himself of his thesis of the post-industrial society, is that the new stage of capitalism tends to disintegrate the proletariat as it has been presented ever since the days of Karl Marx. This thesis says that the old working class is vanishing and is being replaced by middle class elements, and that the old polarization between the capitalist class and the proletariat is softening and the antagonisms are diminishing. These new broad middle layers are said to be taking on more numerical strength and to be leaving behind the old class antagonisms. It's a familiar enough theme.

We have demonstrated earlier how high technology results in low-paid jobs. But the thesis of these Post-Industrial Revolution apologists is that a tremendous increase in white-collar workers, professionals, middle managers, administrative assistants, secretaries and so on—a huge group often referred to as the "Yuppies"—effectively neutralizes the potential for class struggle of the type of the great working class struggles of the 1930s. In their view the shrinking number of steel, auto and electrical blue-collar workers enhances the growth of the so-called middle class.

Among other things, they close their eyes to the most recent data. For instance, an article in the *New York Times* in October 1985 dealing with recent layoffs at the Ford Motor Company threw light on white-collar layoffs at the giant U.S. corporations.[1] It showed that there had developed a virtual campaign against office workers, similar to the anti-labor campaigns against blue-collar workers, but this time in the name of fighting "corpocracy."

The article dealt with layoffs at not only Ford but American Telephone & Telegraph, Union Carbide, General Motors, Bethlehem Steel and CBS. Now we can add ABC, GE and RCA to this list. You can really count in all the Fortune 500, as a matter of fact, for all are now engaged in what the *New York Times* article called trimming the "corpocracy." It is a wide-ranging and ever-deepening attack which may not have quite the same measure or intensity as the anti-labor campaign but nevertheless is just as painful and drastic for the much-touted "middle class" elements.

At the earliest stage of the anti-labor offensive, some misguided officials of unions, in an effort to ward off layoffs, cutbacks and plant closings, demanded similar layoffs of management. They got more than they wanted.

The post-industrial school of bourgeois economics has closed its eyes to the fact that the middle class itself is being polarized into two camps, one of which is steadily falling below its previous status while a smaller fraction whose earnings are supplemented by stock and bond ownership tends more in the direction of higher management.

We discount here petty proprietors, the traditional middle class between the capitalists and the workers. Rather, we are dealing with the so-called new middle class, which bourgeois statisticians lump all together in the service sector. Now, banking is a service industry. So under this reasoning, Walter Wriston, the former head of Citicorp, the world's largest banking corporation, and all the bank's maintenance workers, all the window washers and cleaning people, are lumped together as service employees! But even this most powerful bank recently took its credit card division out of the city of New York and relocated it in the Middle West, thereby shrinking the white-collar staff, especially the so-called middle layer.

What also gets overlooked completely is the assembly line character of the new so-called white collar workers. In fact, they are the clerical proletariat. Most are women, and many are Black, Latin and Asian. These jobs more and more tend to require less skill and give less pay.

All these layoffs of the so-called middle management "corpocracy" are taking place in a period that has supposedly passed out of the recession of 1979 and is now enjoying capitalist prosperity. Again, if this is what happens in a period of prosperity, what will conditions be like in this solid mainstay of the capitalist system once the anticipated collapse is felt?

All truly service-oriented industry is industry which supports manufacturing, which is essential to the distribution of the products of industry. The service sector is not an autonomous, independent factor immune to the laws of capitalist crisis. It is wholly dependent on capitalist industry as a whole. Economic crisis, once it hits, may reach it later, but it inevitably arrives. Even Paul Volcker, the conservative chairman of the Federal Reserve Board, has continually called attention to the relationship between the industrial and service sectors and how dependent the latter is on the former.

Capitalist concentration and the middle class

The bourgeois reactionary utopia of a middle class solidly in line with the ruling class is based on a false economic foundation. Its attempt to lump together the millions of low-paid workers with upper-level corporate executives from banking, insurance, and stock brokerage houses is a fraud. Yet even among the very top, the fear of economic crisis, which impels them to push the drive for mergers and acquisitions to the limit in a frenzy of speculative schemes, has produced the so-called golden parachute stratagem. It's a means whereby top executives, in fear of the ultimate consequences of mergers, acquisitions and buyouts, are trying to make sure that they have a bailout for themselves.

In 1981, a Senate committee staff released a computer-aided study of data on corporate ownership compiled in 1980 by the Securities and Exchange Commission. According to the *New York Times*, the study showed "a high degree of concentration rooted in overlapping institutional stockholdings and interlocking directorates. The study found that the top levels of ownership in almost all major corporations are held or controlled by as few as 15 financial institutions, including major banks and insurance companies."[2] The conclusions of the study merely confirmed a trend that has been noted in similar studies made over the past 35 years.

The study covered 100 of the country's largest companies in 17 areas of finance and industry, including banking, insurance, automotive, steel, energy, transportation, and retail.

J.P. Morgan & Co. through holdings it manages for others is effectively the first or second largest stockholder in 25 other companies studied in the report. They include IBM, Bank of America, Eastern Airlines, Citicorp, Sears, Mobil, General Motors, and General Electric. "The aggregate holdings of pension funds in large financial institutions like Morgan 'place them in a special position to exert control or influence over the management of their portfolio companies,' the Senate study concludes. Citicorp was found to have the most interlocking directorates—49 direct interlocks with the other companies and 887 indirect interlocks. A direct interlock occurs when two corporations have a common director, while an indirect interlock takes place when directors of two corporations meet as directors of a third corporation. Interlocking directorates among direct competitors are forbidden by federal law."

The recent wave of mergers, acquisitions and buyouts, the biggest ever to take place in this country, has undoubtedly accentuated this trend. In almost every case, the new corporate entities have effected not only layoffs and plant closings, but also cutbacks in the professional and managerial staffs. The fear which has gripped the managerial staffs, especially the lower levels, in this new wave of the concentration of capital in fewer and fewer hands has filled the financial pages of the capitalist press. How could this be overlooked?

Rather than presenting a false homogeneous picture of what is passed off as the middle class, attention should be drawn to the polarization within it. The concentration of capital continually lops off large segments of the former elite groupings in the managerial staffs and throws them onto the market to compete for lower-paying jobs (if they are still of an age to do so). This is the grim reality, not the self-serving portrait of the middle class which tries to obscure the class contradictions between monopoly as a whole and the various middle layers.

In areas such as airlines, electronics and other high-tech industries, the Reaganite deregulation drive is affecting the so-called middle management layers, especially in the huge corporations, to the extent that it is showing up in the shrinking of mass markets designed to appeal to the middle class.

A summary of a *Fortune* magazine article, "The Mass Market Is Splitting Apart," explained: "Most businessmen don't realize it yet but the middle class, the principal market for much of what they make, is gradually being pulled apart. Economic forces are propelling one family after another toward the low or high end of the income spectrum. For many marketers, particularly those positions that sell to the well-to-do, this presages good times. For those used to selling **millions** of units of their product to middle-income folks, the prospects are altogether darker."[3] (Our emphasis—S.M.) This illustrates the polarization we referred to, rather than the growing homogeneity and so-called upward mobility about which the second school of bourgeois economists preaches.

This polarization is not only the result of the recent economic crisis. The "number of families with low incomes has climbed" for a longer time, said Fortune. "But the decline of the middle really began during the long expansion of the late 1970s when the families began to find the economic ground under them shifting." An accompanying chart showed the dwindling of the middle class. Below it, Fortune said: "The percentage of families in the 'middle class,' here defined as having an annual income of $15,000 to $35,000 in constant 1982 dollars, dropped sharply over the past ten years. Families at the extremes increased as a proportion of the total, particularly from 1978 on."

This illustrates the divisiveness inherent in the nature of the capitalist economy in general and what the blessings of the scientific-technological revolution in particular bring on. It devastates not only the working class but also the middle sections.

How they go from higher-paying to low-paying jobs was well illustrated in the late 1985 California supermarket strike conducted by the United Food and Commercial Workers union and the International Brotherhood of Teamsters. The management of the supermarkets proposed creating a new job classification, meat clerk, with an hourly wage of $7.25, for meatcutters who performed essentially the same job but who at the time earned $13.48 per hour. A company official insisted, predictably enough, that changes in technology and services offered by supermarkets had eliminated many tasks previously performed by meatcutters. Where meatcutters used to handle many whole sides of beef or pork, the company said, a great deal of meat now arrived at stores boxed in smaller portions. Therefore, they insisted on this new classification. Under these circumstances, they insisted that the employees, whom they now called meat clerks, should be paid the $7.25 rate. This is really using a meat axe to cut wages!

"Just because they are getting the boxed beef, that doesn't give them the right to put a seven-dollar an hour employee in the place of an eleven-dollar an hour one," said the UCFW. "These cutters," said union officials, "have been apprentices for four or five years, have been journeymen for seven or ten years. We can't agree to this at all."

This struggle illustrates both the significance of the scientific-technological revolution as a source for super-profits for the bosses and the iron necessity of the unions to resist with vigor and determination.

A *Washington Post* article entitled "Middle Managers Under Siege, No Longer Immune from Layoffs," stated: "Middle managers, the staff people long thought essential to a smooth-running corporation, are becoming increasingly expendable because of the rapid rise of office automation."[4]

The pressure to reduce the middle element has been especially strong in GM, which has acquired the Hughes Corporation and earlier the Electronic

Data Systems Corporation. Investment bankers and their analysts who act as advisers to these giant corporations are speed-up artists in Brooks Brothers clothing who often find bulges in the waistlines of corporations like GM and the others. According to the *Washington Post* article, they found that GM had a "bloat" of white-collar workers. "It's temporary, say GM officials, and the pressure is on to reduce it."

"'Most of the white collar reductions will come out of the ranks of middle management and out of the clerical staffs,' said one of those automotive industry consulting firms, Peter C. Van Hull, director of Arthur Andersen and Company. 'Many times the middle management and clerical groups are involved in work that doesn't add value to the product.'" How quick they are to use Marxist terminology whenever it comes to increasing super-profits for the big bosses in the ruling class! " 'They tend,' continued Hull, 'to become self-perpetuating bureaucracies. . . . Jobs that don't add value to the product are not needed.'"

Petty bourgeois theoreticians have time and again attempted to draw a false analogy between a bureaucracy and a ruling class, insisting that both serve an identical function and therefore there's no real difference between them. This should be an eye opener to them. Bureaucracies in ancient slavery and in feudal times, from ancient Rome to ancient China, have always served as mere instruments of the ruling property-owning classes. These in their own way have sought to either augment or diminish the size, power and influence of the bureaucracy, but it has always served a different function than that of the ruling class.

The ruling class under capitalism has historically served as the organizer of production, but the development of the productive forces, particularly the momentous dimension of the scientific-technological revolution, makes them superfluous. Centralized, collective, socialized production, which is what we have now, makes the ruling class wholly unnecessary. The process of production is now ready made for the working class. It only needs to overcome the gap between its objective position and the consciousness which is indispensable to harmonizing collective, centralized production with collective, centralized ownership by the workers.

Notes

1. *New York Times*, Oct. 13, 1985.

2. *New York Times*, Feb. 5, 1981.

3. "The Mass Market Is Splitting Apart," *Fortune*, Nov. 28, 1983.

4. "Middle Managers Under Siege," *Washington Post*, Sept. 1, 1985.

Appendix A

In 1984 the U.S. census issued a report on Sun Belt-Frost Belt which illustrates the point that no economic trend under capitalism is ever fully followed through to the very end. It shows that there has been a reversal in the consistent trend of heavy migration from the North and Middle Atlantic states to the South that had been especially prominent in the 1970s, but began two or three decades earlier. (See Table 6 in Appendix B.)

These new findings were summarized in the *New York Times* of April 7, 1985, as follows: "(T)he migratory streams from the Northeast to the South and West are markedly shallower and narrower than they were five years ago, and the flow in the other direction is a bit wider and deeper."

The oil boom of the 1970s significantly accelerated the rate of migration from the so-called Frost Belt to the Sun Belt. The artificial oil shortage created a period of high employment in the South as well as the West. Texas, Oklahoma, California and Florida in particular gained considerably from that trend. But the upswing soon turned into a vast speculative phase in the development of the capitalist economic cycle. Then came the failure of the Penn Square bank of Oklahoma in 1982 and the Continental-Illinois bank in 1984, and the economic upswing turned into a virtual collapse. Capitalist overproduction in oil produced an unprecedented glut which continues to this day; drilling was halted in many areas and bankruptcies followed.

This was as true of Tulsa as of Houston, Dallas and part of the California area. The halt of drilling and marketing of oil resulted in the loss of jobs in many of the satellite industries that had developed as a result of the oil boom and now began to sink. What seemed to have been a huge labor shortage turned into a vast pool of unemployed, although it didn't reach the high level of unemployment in Detroit, New York, Pittsburgh, Chicago or Youngstown, Ohio.

The result was a significant decline in the mass migration toward the Sun Belt. Of course, the population of the Sun Belt has continued to increase, but not necessarily because of migrations from the Midwest, Middle Atlantic states and Northeast. For one thing, the region has a higher birth rate, but also and much more important is the increase in undocumented workers, notwithstanding severe government repression. As we indicated in Chapter 2, the agricultural workers—Latin and Black, sharecroppers and farm laborers—are generally the backbone of the food industry in this country and the basis for the tremendous agricultural capacity of the U.S.

Some of the bosses' reasons for migration to the Sun Belt were the right-to-work laws and a variety of other anti-union advantages to the industrialists, as well as lucrative racist practices in the South. This trend was facilitated over many decades by the increasing speed of transportation seen in the development of the automobile, the railroads and the airplane. The reversed trend in population shift cannot be fully accounted for by the collapse of the oil boom in the Sun Belt. The current reversal can only be more fully explained in terms of the continuing, relentless shift of capital to wherever even the momentary rate of profit is highest.

The earlier flow of high technology to California and to some enclaves in the Southern states has now given way to a flow of capital back to the Northeast and some of the Mid-Atlantic states for the same reason which prompted it to flow into the Sun Belt in the first place: a significantly higher rate of profit.

This recent trend in the population shift from the South to the North, as indicated by the charts and graphically shown by the 1984 Census Bureau statistics, is the result of one of those great "cooperative projects" between bankers, city governments, state legislatures and the industrialists to lure high tech. All too frequently this is done in the name of "getting jobs," but in reality it is an attempt by finance capital to once again flow into selected areas in the North and Mid-Atlantic states where the rate of profit has again become higher.

It is common knowledge that New Jersey, New York, Connecticut, Michigan and some of the Mid-Atlantic states and the area around Boston's Route 128 have been offering tremendous concessions in taxes and creating special conditions for high-tech industries, which live on low wages notwithstanding all the glow and glitter about spawning multi-millionaires. In the New York-New Jersey area especially, "enterprise zones" have been established which are calculated to lure industry away from other states by offering lower wage levels free from many restrictions. Long Island in particular has become notorious because the limited economic upturn there is based mostly on pirating industry from other states.

States and cities now continually engage in a frantic bidding contest for industrial sites, all in the name of luring high technology. The setting up of "industrial parks" for a while creates excitement and an aura of coming prosperity, but ends up providing very low-paying jobs. It becomes a contest over which states and cities will offer the most anti-labor, pro-big business environment, in which prospective employers can expect to find docile, unorganized workers.

The population shift as evidenced by the 1984 census projections is of a tentative character as yet. It has to be monitored by the trade union movement as well as by Black, Latin and women's organizations from the point of view of being an attempt to lower the wage patterns. These studies should not be left to bourgeois sociologists or to demographers appointed by the various arms of the capitalist government that are working hand-in-glove with big business in flagrant and utter disregard of what it does to the living standards of the masses.

Population shifts also have to be viewed from the viewpoint of environmental impact, including the health and safety of the workers. It takes a heavy toll on men and women when in order to get work they must move to areas where housing, schools and recreation facilities are poor and/or inadequate.

What the reversed trend from the Sun Belt to the Frost Belt confirms is that shifts in the population are determined by the general economic laws governing capitalist society. It is not demography alone which explains this shift in the population. That is a surface manifestation. Of course, some geographical areas are more hospitable than others, but that has prevailed since the formation of the planet. In analyzing population trends under the capitalist system, it is the economic laws of capitalist development that have to be taken into account first of all.

Appendix B

Table 1
Farmworkers as percentage of total civilian employed, 1964-1984

Year	Total employed (in thousands)	Farm Workers (in thousands)	Farm Workers as a percentage of total employed
1964	69,305	4,212	6.1%
1969	77,902	3,292	4.2%
1974	86,794	3,064	3.5%
1979	98,824	2,737	2.8%
1980	99,303	2,741	2.8%
1981	100,397	2,749	2.7%
1982	99,525	2,723	2.7%
1983	100,834	N.A.	N.A.
1984	105,005	N.A.	N.A.

Source: Bureau of Labor Statistics

Table 2

Comparison of Weekly earnings in manufacturing and retail trade, 1962 to September 1985

	Manufacturing (A)	Retail Trade (B)
Actual Weekly Wages		
1962	$ 96.56	$ 60.96
1972	154.71	91.85
1982	330.65	163.55
September 1985	389.23	177.90
Gap between A and B		
1962	$ 30.60	
1972	62.86	
1982	167.10	
September 1985	211.33	
Percentage of B to A		
1962	63.1%	
1972	59.4	
1982	49.5	
September 1985	45.7	
Percentage of Total Employed		
1962	30.3%	15.1%
1972	26.0	16.1
1982	21.0	16.9
September 1985	19.6	17.9

Source: Bureau of Labor Statistics

Table 3

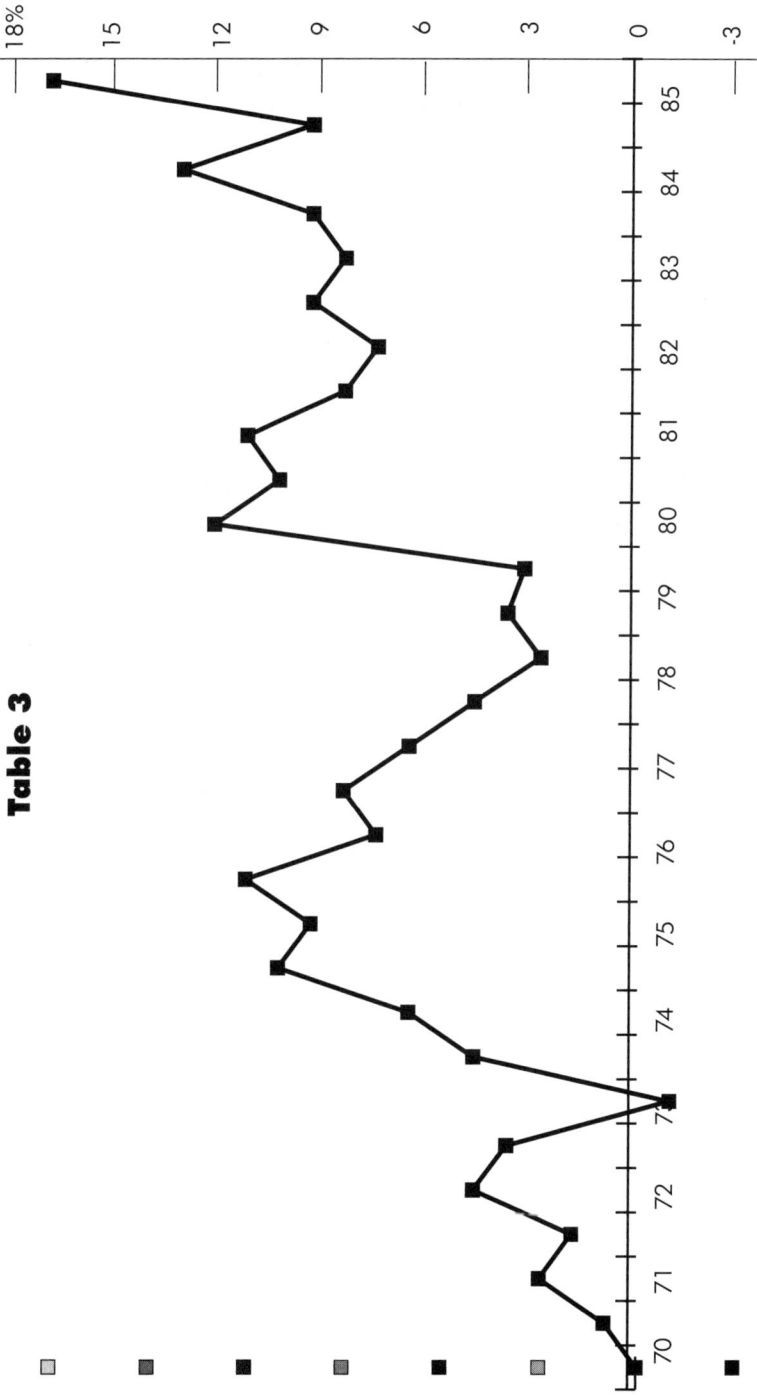

Source: Bureau of Labor Statistics

Appendix B

143

Table 4
Characteristics of people
below the poverty level.

	1975	1983
Person below the poverty level	25,877,000	35,266,000
Per cent of all persons	12.3%	15.2%
Males below the poverty level	10,908,000	15,182,000
Per cent of all males	10.7%	13.5%
Females below the poverty level	14,970,000	20,084,000
Per cent of all females	13.8%	16.8%
Children under 18 below the poverty level	11,104,000	13,807,000
Per cent of children under 18	17.1%	22.2%
Working women over 15 who are below poverty level	3,220,000*	4,580,000
Per cent of working women over 15 below poverty level	30.0%*	32.3%

* Data are for persons 14 years old and over

Source: U.S. Department of Commerce, Bureau of Census

Table 5

Ten industries with the largest number
of employment losses from
March 1979 to March 1985

Blast furnaces and basic steel products 245,000

Construction and related machinery 145,000

Women's and misses' outerwear 50,000

Plastic materials and synthetics 43,000

Footwear (except rubber).......................................42,000

Weaving mills, cotton 41,000

Glass and glasswear..38,000

Yarn and thread mills..32,000

Knitting mills...31,000

Tires and inner tubes...30,000

Total job loss 697,00

Source: Bureau of Labor Statistics

Table 6

The slowdown in population shifts from the Northeast to South and West.

Population of the Northeast

1940	35,977,000
1950	39,478,000
1960	44,678,000
1970	49,061,000
1980	49,135,000
1984	49,728,000

Fewer are leaving for the South and West

Net population loss, in thousands, by the Northeast to the South and West. (Data for '77-'78 and '79-'80 were not available)

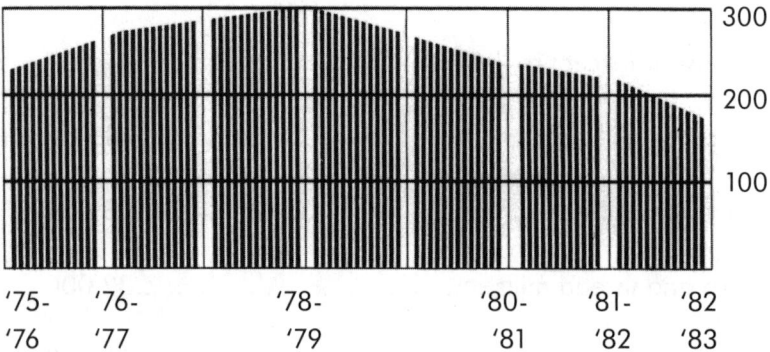

'75-'76   '76-'77   '78-'79   '80-'81   '81-'82   '82-'83

A breakdown

Percentage increases in population fron 1980 to 1984 for each state

Connecticut	1.5%
Maine	2.8
Massachusetts	1.1
New Hampshire	6.1
New Jersey	2.0
New York	1.0
Pennsylvania	0.3
Rhode Island	1.6
Vermont	3.6

Source: Census Bureau

Bibliography

BOOKS

Aptheker, Herbert, *American Negro Slave Revolts*, International Publishers (New York, 1974)

Beard, Mary, *A Short History of American Labor*, Arno Press (New York, 1969), pp. 80-81.

Bluestone, Barry and Bennet Harrison, *The Deindustrialization of America*, Basic Books (New York, 1982).

Boyer, Richard. O. and Herbert M. Morais, *Labor's Untold Story*, United Electrical, Radio & Machine Workers of America (UE) (New York, 1955).

Carroll, Joseph C., *Slave Insurrections in the United States, 1800-1860*, Chapman & Grimes (Boston, 1938), reprinted by New American Library (New York, 1969).

Engels, Frederick, *The Origin of the Family, Private Property and the State*, in *Marx/Engels Selected Works*, Progress Publishers (Moscow, 1970), Vol. 3.

Engels, Frederick, *Socialism, Utopian and Scientific*, in *Marx/Engels Selected Works*, Progress Publishers (Moscow, 1970), Vol. 3.

Foner, Philip, *History of the Labor Movement in the United States*, International Publishers (New York, 1980).

Foner, Philip, *Organized Labor and the Black Worker, 1619-1981*, International Publishers (New York, 1982).

Foster, William Z., *American Trade Unionism: Principles, Organization, Strategy*, International Publishers (New York, 1974).

Goldstein, Fred, *Low-Wage Capitalism—Colossus with Feet of Clay: What the new globalized, high-tech imperialism means for the class struggle in the U.S.*, World View Forum (New York, 2008).

Haber, Louis, *Black Pioneers of Science and Invention*, Harcourt Brace Jovanovich (New York, 1970).

Hilferding, Rudolf, *Finance Capital*, Routledge & Kegan Paul [London & Boston, 1981 (1910)]

Hightower, Jim, *Hard Tomatoes, Hard Times*, Schenkman Publishing Co. (Cambridge, 1973).

Hill, Helen D., *George Mason, Constitutionalist*, as quoted by William Z. Foster in *The Negro People in American History*, International Publishers (New York, 1954).

Hogben, Lancelot, *Science for the Citizen*, Allen & Unwin (London, 1956), p. 620.

Ki-Zerbo, Joseph, *Histoire de l'Afrique Noire, d'Hier a Demain*, Librairie A. Hatier (Paris, 1978).

Lenin, V.I., "Data on the development of capitalism in agriculture," *Collected Works*, Progress Publishers (Moscow, 1964), Vol. 22.

Lenin, V.I., "Imperialism, the Highest Stage of Capitalism," *Collected Works*, Progress Publishers (Moscow, 1964), Vol. 22.

Lenin, V.I., "Marx on the American 'General Redistribution,'" *Collected Works*, Foreign Languages Publishing House (Moscow, 1962), Vol. 8.

Marx, Karl, *A Contribution to the Critique of Political Economy*, in *Marx, Engels, Lenin on Historical Materialism*, Progress Publishers (Moscow, 1972).

Marx, Karl, *Capital*, Progress Publishers (Moscow, 1984).

Marx, Karl, *Grundrisse*, Penguin Books (London, 1973).

Marx, Karl and Frederick Engels, "Manifesto of the Communist Party," *Marx and Engels Collected Works*, International Publishers (New York, 1976), Vol. 6.

Marx, Karl, "The Poverty of Philosophy," *Marx and Engels Collected Works*, International Publishers (New York, 1976), Vol. 6.

Marx, Karl, *Wage Labor and Capital*, Progress Publishers (Moscow, 1976).

Melman, Seymour, *Profits Without Production*, Alfred A. Knopf, Inc. (New York, 1983).

Michel, Lawrence, Jared Bernstein and Sylvia Allegretto, *State of Working America 2006/2007*, Cornell University Press (Ithaca, New York, 2007).

Struik, Dirk, *The Origins of American Science*, Cameron Associates, Inc. (New York, 1957).

Articles and Reports

"The Changing Situation of Workers and Their Unions," a Report by the AFL-CIO Committee on the Evolution of Work, February 1985.

Henderson, Lenneal J. and Charles Murphy, "Perils of Black Postal Workers in a Technological Age: Some Strategies for Survival," *Urban League Review*, Summer 1983, Vol. 7, No. 2.

History of the U.S. Postal Service, 1775-1984, published by the U.S. Postal Service.

Marcy, Sam, "Capitalist Economic Stagnation and the Revolutionary Perspective," *Workers World* (New York), Aug. 8, 1975.

Marcy, Sam, "The Changed Character of the Working Class," *Workers World* (New York), Oct. 25, 1984.

Morehouse, Ward and David Dembo, "The Underbelly of the U.S. Economy: Joblessness and Pauperization of Work in America," a series of special reports prepared by the Council on International and Public Affairs (New York, 1984-85).

Index

A

ABC, 132
Africa, colonization of, xiv
Agricultural workers, 31, 71, 138
Agriculture and
    crisis in, 29-34
    collectivization of, 33
    sharecropping, xxvi, 32, 138
    socialization of, 33
    wage labor, 31
Airline industry, 120; and PATCO, 36, 50, 76
Albizu Campos, Don Pedro, 81
American Revolution, 62
Amtrak, 4
Angola, xiv, 63
Arabs, 59; and compass, 55
Asiento, 57
American Telephone & Telegraph (AT&T), vii, 4, 14-6, 26, 69, 77, 79, 132; and Star Wars, 26
Atlanta, 71
Auto industry, ix-x, xxvi, 12-3, 22-3, 26, 43, 70, 133
Automation, 16, 26, 27, 45, 49, 55, 76, 78, 135

B

Bail Reform Act of 1984, 85
Bailouts, xxviii, 24, 133
Bank of America, 58, 134
Banks, ii, viii, x, xv, xxiii, xxviii, 8, 16, 33, 57-8, 66, 86, 106, 116-7, 119, 123-4, 129, 133
Bankruptcy, vi, ix-x, xxi, 101, 106-9, 120
Banneker, Benjamin, 66-68; letter to Thomas Jefferson, 68
Bardeen, John, 68
Beard, Mary, xxxviii-ix
Bell, Daniel, 131
Bell Laboratories, 26, 84
Bernanke, Benjamin, xv-vi, xxxii
Bernstein, Jared, xxxii
Bethlehem Steel, 132
Bieber, Owen, 112, 120, 128
Birmingham, 71
Bittner, Van A., 129
Black Jacobins, 62
Black migration to North, 70-1
Black rebellions, 62, 72
Black scientists, 64-6, 68

Black struggle, 52, 55-79, 82; and slavery, 62, 71, 82
Blast furnaces, vii, 146
Boeing, xiii, 25, 29, 75
Brain drain, 69
Brattain, Walter H., 69
Brophy, John, 129
Brown & Sharpe, 100, 103, 106, 108
Bureaucracy, 40, 73, 125, 128, 136

C

Capital,
    accumulation of, xx, xxii, xxviii-ix, 28, 33, 37, 56, 64
    and falling rate of profit, xii, 48
    and surplus value, xii-iii, xxvii, 28, 48-9, 64
    flight of, 14, 17, 49
    flows to where profits are highest, 17, 57
    variable (wages), xii-iii, xxviii, 48
Capitalism and
    agricultural crisis, 29-34
    agricultural workers, 31, 71, 138
    bourgeois theories of, 175
    chattel slavery, 57, 63
    child labor, 46
    class peace, 128
    class struggle, vi, xiv-v, xx, xxxii, 4, 7, 11, 43, 49, 73, 90, 97-8, 105, 122, 124, 132
    corporate bureaucracy, 136
    deregulation, xviii, 33, 75, 134
    development of productive forces, xxiv-v, xxix, xxxv-vi, 15, 78, 86, 136
    division of labor, xv, xxiv, 4-6, 21-2, 60, 88
    economic crisis, vii-x, xiii-iv, xvii-ix, xxi-iii, xxv-xxxi, xxxv-viii, 13, 16, 18, 28-9, 35-8, 41, 45, 49-50, 86, 92, 100-2, 118-9, 123, 133, 135
    feminization of labor, 45-6
    inflation, 1, 36, 144
    inner struggles in ruling class, 130
    land ownership, 33
    mergers, viii, 17-8, 22-4, 45, 124-5, 133-4
    monopoly, xiv v, xxxvii-ix, 8, 14-5, 26, 33-4, 56, 69, 82, 84, 86, 92, 134
    multinational corporations, 8, 12, 21, 33, 76, 89, 116, 119, 124, 130
    nationalization, 33
    overproduction, xiii, xxiii, xxvi, xxviii, xxx, 34, 36, 65, 100-1, 137

outsourcing, xxii, 16
pauperization of workers, v, xiii, xxix-xxx,
  xxxiii, xxxvi, xxxix, 44, 46-7
planned obsolescence, 12-3, 40, 114
plant closings, v, viii, 12-3, 38-40, 113, 115,
  132, 134; and Pentagon, 39-40
service industries, 87, 101
the state, xxxi, 26, 28-9, 33, 37-8, 78, 102, 130
strikes, v, x, xxxviii, 100-1, 103-4, 126
wage competition, xiii, xvi-vii, xix, xxii
wage slavery, xii, 55, 59, 63-4
Caribbean, 32, 62, 82, 86
Carney, Dennis, 109
Carter administration, vi, xxxvii, 1, 73, 76, 114
Carver, George Washington, 65
Carver, Thomas Nixon, 122-3
Castro, Fidel, 81
Catastrophes, natural and workers, 111
Caterpillar Tractor, 16
CBS, 121, 132
Central America, 32, 82
Central Asia, 92
Chase Manhattan Bank, 58
Chemical Bank, 58
Cherokee, see Native nations
China, xv-xvii, xxvi-vii, 28, 33, 55, 59, 63, 87, 136
Chinese Revolution, xiv, xxxii, 63
Chrysler, ix, 33, 72
CIT financial, 124
Citicorp, 132, 134
Civil rights movement, 52, 78
Civil War, xxvi, 61-2, 77, 93
Communications industry, 13, 78
Communications satellites, vii
Communist Manifesto, vi, 63, 91
Compass, xii, 5, 55-6, 58
Conglomerates, 15, 113
Congressional Office of Technology
  Assessment, xxxiii, xxxv, xxxix
Conrail, 4
Construction industry, 13, 16, 116-8, 146
Containerization, 78
Continental Airlines, 121
Continental Illinois Bank, 33, 137
Cotton industry, xii, xii, 4, 58-61, 63-6, 87-8, 146
Creek, see Native nations
Crocker National Bank, 58
Cuba, xiv, xxvi, 41, 63
Cuban Revolution, 41, 62, 81

D

Dan River textile plant, 120-1
Debs, Eugene V., 91
Debt crisis, xxviii
DeKruif, Paul D., 68
Del Monte, 30
Dembo, David, xxxiii-iv, xxxix, 46-7
Denmark, and slave trade, 56
Deregulation, xviii, 15, 33, 75, 134
Dineh, see Native nations
Dow Chemical, 29
Down-sizing, vii-ix, 16
Drew, Charles R., 66
Drug trade, 57-8
Duvalier regime, xxxvii, 61

E

Eastern Airlines, 120, 134
Eastern Europe, xiv, xix, xxvii
Edison, Thomas 68
Egypt, xiv, 59; and pyramids, 22
El Salvador, xiv
Electronic Data Systems, xxxv
Electronic mail systems, 74, 76-7
Electronics industry, xiii, 13-4, 23, 134
Eminent domain, vi, x, 115-8
Engels, Frederick, xx-xxiii, xxxii, 79, 90-1, 93
England, 60, 62; and slave trade, 56
English Revolution, 63
Enterprise zones, 138
Environment, xxiv, 39, 139
Ethiopia, xiv
Europe and unemployment, xxv, xxxi, 74
European migration, 70-1

F

Farm foreclosures, 39
Federal Reserve System, xv, xxii, 30, 133
First Boston Corporation, 58
Foner, Philip, 79, 93
Ford, Gerald, 76
Ford, Henry, 6, 21, 87
Ford Foundation, 69
Ford Motor, 20-23, 38, 45, 70, 127, 132; and
  mass production, xiii, 6, 20-2, 87
Fortune magazine, 132, 134-6
Foster, William Z., 79, 93, 130
Fourier, François, 90
France, xxxv, 33, 37, 62, 67, 83, 122; and French
  Revolution, 62-3; and slave trade, 56-7

Fraser, Douglas 120

G

Gabriel's Rebellion, 62

Gay men, xxxiv, 51-2, 73

General Electric (GE), vii-viii, xvii, 17-8, 79, 84, 124, 132, 134

General Motors (GM), vii, ix, xiii, xvii, xxxv, 19, 22-5, 45, 83-4, 98-9, 104, 112, 125, 127-9, 132, 134-6; and Hughes merger, 22-4

Globalization, xv-vii, xxxi-ii

Goldberg, Jerry, 19

Goldstein, Fred, xxxii

Great Crash of 1929, xxvi, 118, 122-3

Great Depression of 1930s, vii, xxv-vii, xxix, xxxi, 75

Grenada, xxxvii

Greyhound, 29

Grundrisse, xxxii

Guevara, Che, 41

Guinea-Bissau, xiv

Gunpowder, 5, 87

H

Haber, Louis, 65, 68, 79

Haiti, xxxvii, 61-2

Haitian Revolution, ii, 61-2

Hall, Lloyd A., 66

Harrison, Bennett 34, 125, 130

Hawaii, xxvi, 92, 115

Health care, xvii, 101

Hightower, Jim, 29, 34

Hilferding, Rudolf, 100, 102

Hitler, Adolf, 28

Holland, 56-7

Homestead Act, 32

Hopi, *see* Native nations

Hughes Aircraft, 23-5, 135

Hyatt-Clark Industries, 119-20

I

Icahn, Carl, 121

Immigration from Mexico to U.S., 32, 86

Imperialism, xv, xxv, xxvii-viii, xxx, xxxii, xxxvii-viii, 70, 81-4, 86, 89, 92
   and oppressed countries, 33, 58, 69, 84
   and super-profits, xxviii, 24, 39, 84, 86, 126, 130, 135-6

Imperialist war, xxv, xxviii, 23, 71, 88

India, xv-xvi, 59

Indigenous nations, xxvi, 90-2, *also see* Native nations

Indonesia, 86

Industrial Revolution, viii, xiii, xvii, 2-3, 5, 13, 60

Inflation, 1, 36

Interlocking directorates, 133-4

International Business Machines (IBM), xiii, xvii, 16, 84, 134

International Women's Day, 46

Iran, xiv, xxxvii

Iraq, xiv, xxviii

Iroquois, *see* Native nations

Irving Trust Company, 58

Italy, 59, 65

ITT, 29

J

Jackson, Andrew, 68, 89

Jacobins, 62

Japan, vii, xiv, xvi, xxxvi, 4, 11, 22, 27-8, 64, 116; and World War II, 11-2; high-tech industries in, 4, 11-3, 19-20, 22, 83, 118

Jefferson, Thomas, 67-8, 89

Julian, Percy L., 66

Just, Ernest E., 66

K

Kelly, Pete, 20

Kelso, Louis O., 119, 123

King, Dr. Martin Luther Jr., assassination, 73

Kirkland, Lane, 126

Knight, Gowin, 56

Kochan, Thomas, 2

Korea, Democratic People's Republic of, xiv; south Korea, xxxvii, 22

Korean War, xxvii, 28, 40, 71

Kriege, Hermann, 90-1

L

L'Ouverture, Toussaint, 61

Labor Party governments, 33

Latimer, Lewis H., 66

Latin America, xii, xxvi, 62, 81-6

League of Revolutionary Black Workers, 72

Lebron, Lolita, 81

Lenin, V. I., xxv, xxxii, 31-4, 84, 86, 90, 92-3, 128

Lesbians, xxxiv, 51, 73

Lewis, John L., 128
Liberalism, 12
Luddites, 4
Lykes Corporation, 113

M

Mahoning Valley, 113-4
Malaysia, xvi
Mandela, Nelson, 81
Manufacturers Hanover Trust, 58
Manufacturing, xi, xiii, xvi, xxviii, xxxiii-v, 4-6,
    12, 14, 16, 23-5, 27, 36-7, 44-6, 84, 99, 133, 143
Manufacturing Technology Advisory Group, 27
Marx, Karl, v, xii, xv, xx-xxii, xxiv-v, xxix, xxxii,
    3-5, 9, 33, 37, 42, 48, 56-8, 60, 63, 79, 90-3,
    107, 112, 131
Marxism, v, xii-iii, xvii, xxiii, xxv-vi, xxx-xxxii,
    15, 37, 48, 91, 136; revisionism in 19th
    century, 37
Mason, George, 61, 79
Mass production, xiii, xxvi, 6, 20-1, 70, 87-8
Matzeliger, Jan, 66
May Day, xxxviii
McCoy, Elijah, 66
McDonald, David 129
McGovern, George, 92
Mellon Bank, 117
Melman, Seymour, 24-5, 34, 39-40
Mergers, viii, 17-8, 22-4, 45, 124-5, 133-4
Mexico, xvi-vii, xxvi, xxxv, 32, 82-3, 85-6
Middle class, 44, 123, 131-5
Migration, 11, 69-71, 86, 90-1, 137-8
Military-industrial complex, xxvii, xxxv, 12,
    23-4, 26, 88
Mitch, Bill, 129
Mobil Oil, 134
More, Thomas, 90
Morgan, Garrett A., 66
Morgan, JP & Company, 129, 134
Morgan, Lewis Henry, 91-2
Morgan Stanley, xx
Mozambique, xiv
Murphy, Frank, 104, 128
Murray, Philip, 129
Mussolini, Benito, 28

N

Namibia, xiv
National Can Corporation, 121
National Guard, vi, 126

National Labor Relations Act (NLRA), 104
National Labor Relations Board (NLRB), vi
Nationalization, 33
Native nations, iii, 73, 87-92
    Cherokee, 89
    Hopi, 89
    Iroquois, 92
    Navajo, 89
    Seminoles, 89
Navajo, *see* Native nations
Nayan, Chandra, xxxii
New York-New Jersey Port Authority, 116
Nicaragua, xiv, 62
Nixon administration, 1, 75-6;
    strike breaking, 77

O

Oil industry, 16, 85-6, 101, 121, 137-8
Organization of Petroleum Exporting
    Countries (OPEC), 15
Owen, Robert, 90

P

Palestine, xiv
Paine, Thomas, 62
Paulson, Allen, 109
Peltier, Leonard, 89
Penn Square Bank, 137
Pension funds, xvii, 120, 123, 134
Pentagon and industry, vi, 8, 14, 23-8, 39-40;
    and scientists, 68
Perkins, Frances, 104
Perpich, Rudy, 126
Peru, 59
Phelps Dodge, 100, 103, 106, 108
Philippines, xiv, xvi-vii, xxvi, xxxvii
Phillips Petroleum, 121
Pickens, T. Boone, 121
Portugal, 56
Poverty level, xvii, xxviii, 44, 47, 145
Prussia, and slave trade, 56
Puerto Rican political prisoners, 81
Puerto Rico, xxvi, 81, 83-5

R

Radio Corporation of America (RCA),
    vii-viii, 17-8, 79, 84, 124, 132
Ralston Purina, 30
Reagan administration, v-vi, viii, xxvii, xxxvi-
    vii, 1, 17, 23, 33, 37, 49-50, 73-4, 7
    6, 100, 114, 119-20, 126, 134;
    and deregulation, 134

Rilleux, Norbert, 65
Robotics, 16
Robotization, xiii, 6
Rockefellers, 69
Roach, Stephen, xx
Roosevelt, Franklin D., vi, 65, 89, 116
Rust Belt, 15

S

Safeway, 30
Saint-Simon, Henri de, 90
Samoa, xxvi
Saturn auto assembly plant, 6-7, 19-22, 26,
    83-4, 112
Saturnization, 6, 19, 26, 83
Schlesinger, Arthur, 89
Sears Roebuck, 134
Self-determination, xxxii, 92
Semiconductor manufacturing, xxxv, 15
Seminoles, *see* Native nations
Service industry, 74, 132
Singer Sewing Machine, xxxv
Slater, Samuel, 11, 67
Slave trade, xii, 55-8, 60-1, 91
Slave insurrections, 62-3, 79
Slavery, chattel, xii, xxxvii-viii, 55, 57-68, 82,
    88, 136
Socialism, xiii-iv, xxi, xxxi, 18, 34, 52, 86,
    90-2, 97, 105, 108, 122
Socialist countries, xiv-vi, xix-xx, xxvii, xxxii,
    xxxv, xxxvii, 18, 23, 26, 33
Socialist International, 46
Socialist Party governments, 33, 37
South Africa, xxxvii, 63, 82
Soviet Union (USSR), xiv-v, xix, xxvii, xxx,
    xxxii, 23, 28, 33, 92
Spain, 33, 37, 56-7, 59
Star Wars (Strategic Defense Initiative), 23-4, 26
Steel industry, vii, xxxiii, 7-8, 13, 15, 18, 43, 49,
    51, 70, 74, 98, 100-1, 108, 114, 116-8, 127-9,
    132-3, 146
Steel Valley Authority, 116
Stock market crash of 1929, *see* Great Crash
Subprime mortgages, xviii, xxiii
Sugar industry, transformation of, 64-5
Sun Belt, 17, 137-9
Supreme Court, U.S., 46
Sweden, xxxv, 33, 56, 122

T

Telecommunications industry, 58, 77-9
Tennessee Valley Authority (TVA), 116
Thailand, xvi
Trans World Airlines (TWA), 120
Transistor, invention of, 68
Treaty of Utrecht, 57
Tri-State Conference on Steel, 116
Triangle Shirtwaist Company fire, 46
Tulip trade, 57
Turner, Nat, 62
Turner, Ted, 121

U

Underdevelopment, xvi, 81-5
Unemployment, x, xvii, xix, xxvi-xxxi, xxxix,
    1, 7, 15, 40, 42, 44, 48, 55, 59, 71, 74, 82, 89,
    105, 137
Union Carbide, 132
Unions
    American Federation of Labor (AFL), 70
    AFL-CIO, 1, 6, 8-9, 26, 49, 51, 103, 126-9
    American Postal Workers Union (APWU), 75
    Committee for Industrial Organization
        (CIO), x, 1, 119, 129
    Farm Labor Organizing Committee
        (FLOC), 31
    International Association of Machinists
        (IAM), 40, 51
    International Ladies Garment Workers
        Union (ILGWU), 51
    International Typographical Union (ITU), 51
    National Alliance of Postal and Federal
        Employees, 78
    National Association of Letter Carriers
        (NALC), 75
    Professional Air Traffic Controllers
        Organization (PATCO), 36, 50, 76
    Service Employees International Union
        (SEIU), 51
    Steel Workers Organizing Committee, 129
    United Auto Workers (UAW), ix, xxxiii,
        xxxv-vi, xxxix, 19-20, 22, 38, 51, 72, 83,
        99, 112, 119-20, 128
    United Electrical Workers (UE), 130
    United Farm Workers (UFW), 31
    United Food and Commercial Workers
        (UFCW), 126, 135
    United Mine Workers (UMW), 108
    United Steel Workers (USWA), 51, 106,
        109-10, 116-7

Unions and
  child labor, struggle to end, 46
  collective bargaining, vi, 19, 50-1, 99, 104, 112
  comparable worth, struggle for, 47-8
  contracts, 98-100, 109
  eight-hour day, struggle for, xxxviii
  ESOPs, 118-22
  jobs as a property right, vi, ix, 104, 109, 112, 115
  labor relations, vi, 36, 50, 52, 103, 112, 130;
    "new type," 6-8, 19, 21
  layoffs, vii-ix, xvii, xxviii, 15-7, 20, 24, 36, 40,
    69, 78, 119-21, 124, 132-5
  militancy, xxxviii, 40, 97, 112-3
  occupation of the plants, 106
  Pentagon, vi, 8, 40
  prenotification, 38, 115
  strike strategy, iii, v, x, xxi, 37, 100-3
  strikes: Browne & Sharpe, 100, 103-4; Ford
    Mahwah walkout, 72-3; GM sit-down,
    104; Hormel, 126-9; PATCO, vi, 36, 50, 76;
    Phelps Dodge, 106; postal, 77; steel strike
    of 1919, 129; supermarket, 135; Wheeling-
    Pittsburgh, 110
  vigilance committees, iv, 17, 124-6
  wages, v-vi, xi, xix, xxxviii, 36, 48-50, 79, 97-9,
    107, 120, 126, 135; two-tier, 75-6
  workers' control, iii, ix, 18, 103, 105-6, 108,
    110-1, 122
  workers' party, 97
United Black Brothers, 72
United Virginia Bank, 120
Urban League, National, 70
U.S. Steel, 114, 127, 129
Utopian socialists, 90-1, 93

V
Van Hull, Peter C., 136
Venezuela, 86
Vesey, Denmark, 62
Viet Nam, xiv, xxvii, xxxvii, 19, 28, 40, 63, 71
Viet Nam War and employment, 71
Volcker, Paul, 133

W
Wage and price controls, 1
Wagner Act, 104
Weirton Steel, 121
Weiss, Bernard, Air Force general, 27
Wheeling-Pittsburgh Steel, 36, 100, 103, 108,
  110
Whitney, Eli, 59, 66, 87-8, 93
Wickwire Steel, 38

Williams, Daniel Hale, 66
Working class
  Arab workers in U.S., 51, 69, 74
  Asian workers in U.S., v, xi, xvii, 42, 51, 69,
    70, 73-4, 81, 133
  auto workers, ix, xxxiii, xxxv, 24, 51, 83, 98,
    104, 112; at Ford, 45, 70, 72
  Black workers, xxxiii-iv, 32, 42, 51, 55, 70-9,
    82, 133, 138; and postal service, 74-79
  Chicano-Mexicano workers in U.S., 82
  clerical workers, 44, 125, 133, 136
  coal miners, 108
  computer programmers, xvi
  copper miners, vi
  disabled workers, 51
  farm workers, 31-2, 141
  hospital workers, 43
  Latina/o workers in U.S., 51-2, 73, 81-2, 106
  maintenance workers, 48, 125, 132
  migrant workers, xvii, 31-2
  Native workers in U.S., xviii, 51, 74
  postal workers, ii, 74-9
  rubber workers, vi, 51
  secretaries, xvi, 48, 132
  service workers, vii, xvi, 44
  social composition of, xxxiii-xxxiv, 42-3, 45,
    51-2, 70
  standard of living, xi, xxii, 35-6
  steel workers, 51, 106-110, 116-7, 128-9
  undocumented workers, xi, 42, 51-2, 69, 137
  underemployed workers, xxxvi
  white-collar workers, 132, 136
  women workers, v, xi, xxxiii-iv, xxxix, 42, 45-
    9, 51-2, 69, 73-4, 76-8, 133, 139, 145; and
    daycare centers, 46
Work-flow software, xv
Workers World newspaper, xxxiii, xxxix, 19-20,
  34, 40
World War I, xiv, xxv-vi, 45, 70
World War II, vi, xxvi-vii, xxxv-vii, 6, 12, 26,
  37, 40, 69, 71, 100, 122-3; post-war era, xviii,
  xxi, xxx
World Wide Web, xv
Wounded Knee, 89
Wright, Louis T., 66
Wriston, Walter, 132
Wynn, William H., 126

Y
Youngstown Sheet & Tube, 113-4

Z
Zimbabwe, xiv

Low-Wage Capitalism

Fred Goldstein

Colossus with feet of clay:
What the new globalized high-tech imperialism means for the class struggle in the U.S.

Low-Wage Capitalism provides an easy-to-read analysis of the roots of the current global economic crisis, its implications for workers and oppressed peoples, and the strategy needed for future struggle.

World View Forum paperback, 336 pages, $19.95.
The author is available for lectures & interviews.

• • •

"This book helps us to understand the root of the present neoliberal globalization– a new stage of the international capitalist crisis– which was imposed by U.S. imperialism and which devastated Latin American economies. ..."

Ignacio Meneses,
Co-chair, U.S.-Cuba Labor Exchange

"In this period of economic uncertainty, Fred Goldstein's 'Low-Wage Capitalism' could not be better timed. Beautifully written, deeply considered and backed by impressive research, this is essential reading for anyone wishing to understand the true nature of the world we live in and the factors that have led to so much turmoil. ... Urgently recommended."

Gregory Elich,
Author of **Strange Liberators**

"We need to get this book into the hands of every worker. It clearly explains the capitalist economic threat to our jobs, our pensions and our homes. But, even more importantly, it shows us how we can fight back and win!"

David Sole, President, UAW
Local 2334, Detroit, Michigan

"*Low-Wage Capitalism* by Fred Goldstein is a most timely work, as the working class prepares for a fightback during the greatest crisis of capitalism since the Great Depression."

Clarence Thomas, ILWU Local 10 and Co-chair Million Worker March Movement

"*Low-Wage Capitalism* is truly outstanding, Hits us like a body punch, and provides the perfect context for what we all need to know about the evolving conditions of workers and their struggles. ... Deserves the widest readership."

Bertell Ollman, author and Professor of Political Theory, NYU

"Patriarchal prejudice serves capitalism in two ways: it keeps the whole working class divided, and it holds down wages for women and for lesbian, gay, bisexual, and transgendered workers. *Low-Wage Capitalism* shows the necessity and the great potential for solidarity among all the low-wage workers of the world."

Martha Grevatt, Nat'l Executive Officer Pride At Work, AFL-CIO, UAW Local 122

"Lucid, deeply accurate and informative, as relevant and useful as a book can be, Goldstein offers a compelling analysis of the exploitative world of global corporate capitalism. ... "

Michael Parenti,
author of **Contrary Notions**

"160 years after the publication of the **Communist Manifesto**, Fred Goldstein takes on the challenge of applying Marxist political economy to the burgeoning crisis of capitalist globalization in the 21st century. ... "

Abayomi Azikiwe, Editor,
Pan-African News Wire

"From the point of view of Filipino workers in the U.S. the largest exploited and abused Filipino workforce outside the Philippines ... we are pleased with the exposé of imperialist globalization as the main culprit of global forced migration. ... "

Berna Ellorin,
Secretary-General, BAYAN USA

Review online at **LowWageCapitalism.com**
Available at bookstores nationally, or order from **Leftbooks.com**

MARXISM, REPARATIONS
& the Black Freedom Struggle

An anthology of writings from Workers World newspaper.
Edited by Monica Moorehead. Includes:
- Racism, national oppression and self-determination
- Black labor from chattel slavery to wage slavery
- Black youth: repression & resistance
- Black & Brown unity:
  A pillar of struggle for human rights & global justice!
- Are conditions ripe again today? 40th anniversary
  of the 1965 Watts Rebellion
- Racism and poverty in the Delta
- The struggle for Socialism is key
- Domestic Workers United demand passage of a bill of rights
- Reparations for Africa & Caribbean

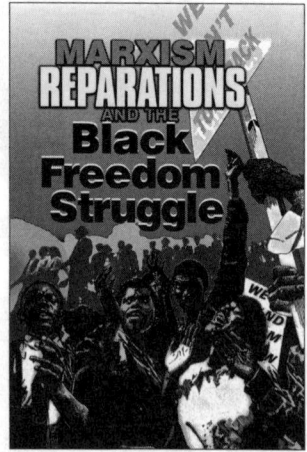

Rainbow Solidarity
In Defense of CUBA

This new book is a compilation of 25 articles by Leslie Feinberg about how the Cuban Revolution has worked to overturn prejudice against same-sex love from the colonial and imperial eras. The articles are part of the Lavender & Red series from Workers World weekly newspaper.

The never-before-compiled information offers a factual vista on the trajectory of progress of the Cuban Revolution. It's a must-read to understand the revolutionary process required to uproot prejudice.

A Voice from Harper's Ferry, 1859
By Osborne P. Anderson, *a Black freedom fighter*

Prefaces by Mumia Abu-Jamal, Monica Moorehead and Vince Copeland on the 'Unfinished Revolution.'

A unique book from the raid on Harper's Ferry. Few history books give Osborne P. Anderson the recognition he deserves. Anderson was the only Black combatant to survive the raid and to write about it. His account of this turning point in the struggle against slavery—an armed attack by Black and white volunteers on a citadel of the South—refutes those who try to minimize the role of African American people in fighting for their freedom.

Available at bookstores or order from Leftbooks.com.